Crimson Roses

&

Purple Irises

JONATHAN IAN ELLIOTT

ISBN: 978-1-960146-47-2 (hard cover)
      978-1-960146-48-9 (soft cover)

Edited by: Amy Ashby

Warren publishing

Published by Warren Publishing
Charlotte, NC
www.warrenpublishing.net
Printed in the United States

I dedicate this memoir to Tony S. Abbott, the man who made it possible. During the three years or more when I took noncredit poetry classes under Tony, every year he said, "Jonathan, you really need to write that memoir." My poetry was often autobiographical.

When I completed my first draft in May 2020, I sent Tony an email to let him know it was finally done. He sent back, "I'm so pleased. I'm going to be inducted into the North Carolina Literary Hall of Fame," he said, "but I doubt that I will make it there physically for the induction." The induction was in November. He passed away from cancer on October 3, 2020.

I miss him terribly.

"Those who danced were thought to be quite insane by those who could not hear the music."

—Friedrich Nietzsche

Preface

After I had taken my fourth noncredit class with him, former Davidson College professor Tony Abbott pulled me aside. Tony had been up for a Pulitzer Prize earlier in his career and was now about to be inducted into the North Carolina Literary Hall of Fame. He had less than a year to live.

"Jonathan, you need to write that memoir." This was at least the third time he had advised me to write it. "There are people who have gone through what you have gone through who need to hear it!"

Although he was only twelve years my elder, he was like the father I never had. Many of his elderly students in his classes would have said the same.

I had reasons for not writing it. Foremost, why would someone want to read what a no-name had to say? I thought most people wanted to read about the success and failures of famous people, rich people, or movie stars. Also, I loved my parents. Writing about those early years would be extremely painful.

Two events turned me around.

One was that the man, my mentor, whom I loved so much was dying, and the other was that *Hillbilly Elegy: A Memoir of a Family and Culture in Crisis* came out in paperback and later became a Netflix movie. I suspect J.D. Vance, the author of the book, may have also been a no-name prior to his memoir's publication. After watching the movie, my wife of thirty-five years said, "That's your family!" Yes, there were quite a few similarities—and quite a few differences.

This is the story of a boy who had no apparent future. This is the story of a boy who grew up with two violent parents, each subject to his and her own brand of absurdity at times. This is the story of a boy raised in poverty who suffered from physical and mental ailments almost from the time of birth into his early thirties. This is the story of a boy who would eventually become a senior advisor and chief financial analyst to the US Treasury Department and who advised presidential staffs.

I had made several feeble attempts to start the memoir when Tony first asked me to write it in 2017 but wasn't sure I wanted to expose our family, including many of my life events, publicly. When I found out Tony was in late stages of cancer, I knew it was time to get serious. I spent hours late into the night writing my first draft.

In May of 2020, I emailed Tony to let him know that I had completed my first draft of the memoir. He seemed pleased. Then he told me, "I recently heard I'm going to be inducted in the North Carolina Literary Hall of Fame, but I doubt that I will make it there physically for the induction." He was right. He died just months before his official induction. In some ways, at that moment, the memoir seemed inconsequential, and in some ways, it seemed as though it was as important as anything I had left to finish in life.

Prologue

In December 1989, at age forty-one, I applied for a job in the US Defense Department. I had filled out a questionnaire, and in the interview, the human resources director questioned me. "Can this be true? You lived in more than thirty residences by the time you were eighteen?"

Embarrassed, head down, I answered, "Yes. I'm not sure I remember all of them."

"Can you tell me a little bit about that?" she asked.

What followed was a very short version of the story that later became this memoir. And at the end of our conversation, she simply said, "Thank you for coming in. We'll be in touch."

I had completed my master's degree six months earlier in finance and economics and had been searching for a job ever since. I completed the master's degree six months after the stock market crash of 1987. There were a lot of Wall Street analysts out of work who had significantly more experience than a former English major and former truck company salesman and general manager. I had come to know what "We'll be in touch." meant. However, several weeks later, I received a call from her. She asked me to come into her office.

Without saying a word initially, she simply pushed her report across the table toward me. At the bottom of the report, where she had crossed out *Rejected* instead displayed *Accepted*.

"Congratulations," she said simply.

I had wondered why she rejected me initially. Did she see me as someone who was unstable, even though those years had long since past? Or was it, more likely, the ten years of therapy I had admitted to as a requirement of the security investigation? I never knew. I only knew it was time to look forward and learn from my past.

Author's Note:

Most of the early chapters regarding years before my birth until my first cognizant moments of my story are based on stories my mother told or journal entries from my paternal grandmother.

Crimson Roses and Purple Irises

I am the son
    of a sixteen-year-old girl who married to escape
  what seemed like poverty to her then,

only to discover
    her poverty was a name her married man used
  to break her down,

again, and again. He came from good folks, he said.
    I was the outsider at home to him, save
  my skin most seasoned to a belt buckle slash.

"If you fall or whine, we will start again," this man
    called father said. "Never tell anyone what goes
on in this house!" my mother once screamed.

As I grow older, the memory
of those words is as powerful as
  the belt slashes themselves.

I call the blood on my legs back then my crimson roses,
    and the purple and yellow bruises my irises—
  my mother's favorite flower.

And as I've made peace with all this, I called it poetry.

Chapter 1

IT WAS ONLY A NOVEL: 1982

"Why are you leaving?" Mom asked.

She sat on the edge of my bed while I packed my clothes.

"I've been accepted to the University of Oregon for a writing program."

It was the summer of 1982.

I had wanted to attend U of O for several reasons; one was that Ken Kesey of *One Flew Over the Cuckoo's Nest* fame lived in Eugene, where the school was located, and *Cuckoo* was one of my favorite novels.

"Do you have to go clear across the country to write a book?" she asked, picking up my manuscript off the bed. "What's this?"

"That's what helped me get accepted to the program."

The Little Bit Berserk Blues. I had sent in the first two chapters for hopeful admission. Later, the department secretary, who seemed to have a crush on me, asked if I would like to read what the submissions readers had said about me, all glowing remarks except for one—a second-year student in the MFA program who may have seen me as competition. His thumbs-down had been overruled by the other four readers.

Mom read the first few pages and then threw them across the bed.

"This is about me, isn't it?"

It was technically a novel.

"Damn you! This isn't me! This isn't me!"

"It's fiction, Mom. It's just a book." But we both knew it *was* about her, Dad, and even my own insanity that had reigned over me for nearly a decade from my early twenties until just recently in my early thirties.

"I know what a book is! Why do you hate me?"

"I don't hate you, Mom. I love you …." I tried to wrap my arms around her, but she pulled away and looked out the window. "But I do wonder why you stayed with him all those years."

"You think I wanted to? Do you really think I wanted to? I was sixteen when I married him. He was going to show me the world. He showed me the world all right. I would have killed him if I could. So you take your stinkin', filthy book, and you go to that school, but you'll never be my son again."

It wasn't the first time she had made that threat, and likely not the last. In the past, she would call or write to say she really didn't mean it. This time took longer.

I stopped over at Mom's house before taking off for Oregon. I thought if I stayed overnight before leaving, she would change her mind about our relationship.

"Why are you here?" she asked.

"Mom, I really don't want to leave with things between us like this."

"You go on, Mr. Big Pants. Go out there and tell those people how crazy your mother is."

As one last attempt, I stayed over in the spare bedroom, hoping that by morning she would change her mind. Usually, she asked me what I wanted for breakfast. Not this time.

As I came out of the bedroom that morning, she just waved me toward the door.

"Go now. You just tell 'em how crazy I can be."

My old Audi Fox sat in the driveway. One door wouldn't lock, and when I stepped inside, I noticed the new stereo system I bought to keep me company on my way there had been cut from the dashboard. So often I had been told by friends that I made the best of bad situations. Most of them didn't know about what I had been through as a child— the many moves, the changes required of me at any given moment. I sang old songs at the top of my lungs all the way out to Eugene, Oregon. "Take Me Home, Country Roads" by John Denver. "You Can't Roller Skate in a Buffalo Herd" by Roger Miller.

I hadn't given a second thought that my old car wouldn't make it. I had a mechanic friend, Bill Bezick, who had always found a way to keep it running. I was no more than a hundred miles away in Frederick, Maryland, when the water light flashed on. Steam came from the hood. I had no plan B if the car stopped running, but I wasn't worried. If the car didn't make it, I'd have dumped it by the side of the road and just hitchhiked like I had dozens of times before. The thoughts of hitchhiking actually gave me a buzz. I loved being on the road. The only question was how would I carry my manuscripts? That brought me back to reality. I had to make it work. I had to somehow find a way to *fix* my car.

I pulled into a truck stop where there was a hose not far from the gas pumps. After giving the engine time to cool down, I flushed the radiator until water spouted over the sides of the car.

Any sane person would have thought, *That's it. Game over. No way this car is going to go another twenty-nine hundred miles.* That was, indeed, what a sane person would have thought, but within the hour, I was back on the road.

The trip to Eugene should have given me reasons to pause. I didn't feel sleepy or tired at all for most of the trip, which was strange. I hadn't had a manic attack for the better part of three years, but I was beginning to wonder if my newfound energy was evidence that one was on the horizon. I stopped off at rest areas from time to time to attempt to sleep an hour or two. Nothing. I didn't sleep for the better part of three days. Still, I didn't pause. I pushed the twelve-year-old Audi as far and fast as I thought I could go.

I had been on the road less than twenty hours—fourteen hundred miles—when I stopped at a diner to grab a quick meal. A Nebraska state trooper pulled in behind me and then took a seat two stools away.

The speed limit was seventy-five. I had been doing well above that—ninety at times when I thought the engine could take it—as I passed by the hundreds of miles of corn that bordered Interstate 80.

"You know, we take people in for speeding around here," the trooper said. He turned to his coffee and said nothing more.

I nodded. Maybe he had noticed my overalls and figured I wouldn't be able to pay for a fine anyway. It wasn't true, though. I had often worked fourteen-hour days as a general manager in the trucking industry. As a result, I bought three houses for rent by the time I was twenty-nine and rented all the spare bedrooms in my main residence.

One of the renters in my main residence was a Vietnamese woman who had started her own restaurant business. She often brought leftovers from the restaurant.

"You must eat," she said often. "You don't eat enough."

Eventually, our relationship became something other than late-night meals, though she seemed much more interested in me than I was in her. I had been in an on-again, off-again relationship with a married woman I met in AA, which made this woman jealous. And as much as I liked this renter, my life had been filled with people who had depended on me, and I could be overly dependable at times; I helped folks to my detriment. However, I could also be undependable when those around me least expected it.

When I put the houses up for sale, she said, "I have no place to go." I didn't say anything. It seemed like a guilt trip for getting back together with the married woman. And besides, she was part of a big Vietnamese community in the area; I rationalized that she would find another place to stay in short order. I often thought about her when I entered a restaurant—where she had gone, whether or not her restaurant had made it during this time of high interest rates.

Now my mind wandered back to my novel. Sometimes I stayed up all night working on *Berserk*, writing chapter after chapter into the night, only to start over again the next night. It had taken ten years to complete, thousands of pages to arrive at a 230-page novel.

Berserk was to be a tell-all fictionalized story of my family's collective life, but much of the dialogue had come straight from the horses' mouths. It was bibliotherapy for me as much as writing for publication, attempting to make sense of a kaleidoscopic life as colorful as it had been chaotic.

I hadn't written it for entry into an MFA program; that came later as the trucking industry began to collapse under the weight of strict Interstate Commerce Commission regulations that made it difficult for trucking companies to make a profit. One company after another had gone out of business.

Counters at diners were good places to contemplate what had past and what was yet to come: the grief I had caused my mother and what might be in store when I arrived at the U of O. It was also a time when I reflected on my relationship, or lack thereof, with my father. We hadn't spoken to each other in several years. The diner's comfort food—a burger, fries, and milkshake—lessened some of the downheartedness.

The trooper pulled out of the diner parking lot as I was leaving. He trailed me for some fifty miles, then finally sped by me. In my heightened frenzied state, I nearly passed him down the road but broke just in time prior to his pulling off the highway.

As I drove, my mother weighed on my mind. She'd had a hysterectomy years earlier, and her moments of rage had been heightened by the surgery and activated what my sister and I liked to call her toggle switch. She could tell us how much she loved us one moment, and the next moment, she'd be screaming at us, face contorted. It was questionable how much of her outbursts was due to the hysterectomy and how much was due to the abuse she had received from Dad from the time she was sixteen.

I felt guilty for having left her in her current state. She had always been great at making my sister and me feel guilty when she felt most victimized by what life "had done to [her]."

My mother's dementia late in life and her continued rage even then from time to time was something that kept my sister, my half brother, and me walking on eggshells. Sometimes it might require ducking a shoe thrown directly at our heads, or her little fists pounding our chests, or words that hurt like the cut of a scalpel without anesthesia.

Several years before, in one of those rare moments when it had appeared my father and I might be making some progress in our relationship, Mom told me out of the blue that she'd had an abortion.

We were living in a basement apartment in Landover, Maryland. Dad was at his most unstable; he stayed away for long periods. One night he showed up drunk and angry. We ran upstairs into the main house where our landlord lived. She closed and locked the door to the basement, and he began knocking on it with the butt of a shotgun. He vowed to kill, and Mom vowed to—and almost did—kill him.

I was twelve then.

When she found out she was pregnant soon thereafter, she aborted the fetus herself with a coat hanger.

"I wasn't going to bring another child into this world—not like this," she told me years later, "not while married to that man. I had enough trouble feeding you and Debbie."

Those earliest memories of rage would continue to play over and over. The fears and memories of a twelve-year-old spun through my mind—a vivid kaleidoscope that sometimes went dark. I put it all in my novel.

From the time I was born, Mom had been my protector. Nearly a third of the thirty moves I had reported by the time I was eighteen when applying for a job with the federal government had been Mom's and my exoduses to West Virginia to keep me out of harm's way from Dad.

My sister, Debbie, was born in April of 1956, so was only exposed to little of those most heightened times of rage. She remembered little of the times when the potential for a fatal outcome—Mom, Dad, or Debbie and me—seemed possible, if not probable. There were times I protected Debbie from Mom. Debbie was four in 1960 at the height of my mother's rage against my father. Less than a year later, Mom's anger turned against Debbie and me for what became the last days of our parents' marriage. Debbie came to know more about Mom's outbursts later in life than those of Dad's.

My parents' marriage had been on the rocks for as long as I could remember, but during those days in the basement in Landover, their troubles were at their most heightened state. The violence between them, the mistrust, was like a West Virginia cock fight that went on much longer than it should have. It had started before I was born.

When I discovered recently through my paternal grandmother's journal entries what my mother had been through prior to my birth and the years prior to my knowledge of those times, I was saddened for my mother, who had lived through such trauma. Those journal entries were a road map to how a naïve young girl grew to foster her own brand of violence.

My tears in the diner came from a new awakening, as happened often when writing—some for grief, others for regret. If *Berserk* were a story of picking up the pieces of our brokenness, each in his or her own way, maybe the story was also about how Mom had kept us alive in those early days and how the tables turned when I had to protect Debbie and me from her. And the story would be revealing to me. Some of the pieces of my life I had either forgotten or had been unwilling to face previously became evident, at times so evident I wondered if I should have written the book at all. But I had written it. I was on the highway to reveal myself and my family to a group of students and faculty. I was well beyond the stage of my mother's warning, "Don't you ever tell anyone what goes on in this house."

Chapter 2
STORIES TOLD: 1945-1949

My mother, born Nancy Rae Tucker, repeated parts of her story frequently. But it was only when Shirley, my cousin on my father's side, sent a copy of five years of our paternal grandmother's journal entries that I understood the story as much as anyone who wasn't there could.

Prior to her marriage, Mom lived in an unincorporated coal town—Dry Creek, West Virginia, population four hundred—in the late 1940s. The village where she lived, Dry Creek's Friendly View, housed about fifty coal miners and their families. Dry Creek's population later dried up to less than a hundred folks, as mining disappeared.

"She was an impish girl," her sister Mary Ann once said of my mother. She wore her beauty simplistically. She had brown hair and green eyes and was petite at five-four, weighing slightly more than a hundred pounds. But she was full of life and always laughing. Aunt Mary Ann explained how they could hardly bring any boys home. My mother liked to play tricks on everyone.

And she hated Friendly View.

The farthest away she had ever been from the miner's village was to visit her sister in Beckley, West Virginia, nearly thirty miles from Friendly View, on rare occasions when her brother Billy drove her there.

Later, Billy was my dad's naval shipmate during the war, and they became the best of friends. Unfortunately, their friendship would be cut short by Billy's remorse for ever having introduced Dad to Mom.

Mom at sixteen, prior to her first marriage to my father

No Guardians for the Half Broken

Most of what I know about Dad's life before I was born comes from conversations with Billy and photos Mom had taken of Dad. Dad was a handsome six-three, no more than one hundred eighty pounds, with dark brown hair and green eyes.

After the war, Dad was assigned to a land base. While the navy still saw him as an enlisted man, he believed his service to his country had ended with the end of the war. So he treated the remainder of his time in the navy as though he were a civilian, often taking off from the barracks whenever he wished to without giving his commander any idea where he was going or when he would return. This became a theme in my father's life.

He rarely spoke of his time at war except once to say proudly that his destroyer had served in both the Pacific and Atlantic campaigns and that he would never buy anything Japanese because "I fought those bastards during the war."

He had been a signalman. Signalmen were responsible for transmitting, receiving, encoding, decoding, and distributing messages obtained via the visual transmission systems and advanced lookout skills. Missing or misinterpreting messages could mean the end of the ship's existence and the men who were on it.

The USNS *McDougal* was an elite ship that had escorted Winston Churchill back to England from a meeting when air traffic was too risky for a world leader's travel. The destroyer was designed for cat-and-mouse actions with enemy submarines.

At war's end, there were no guardians for the half broken. Dad's mother, my Grandma Maude, often documented his troubles in her journals, unraveling what had been expected of him on board ship and what civilian life seemed to impose. He relied heavily on his mother for forgiveness for his often poor behavior or when he needed to sort out his priorities, especially when it came to asking for money. She continued to care for, if not enable, him until her death in 1955. Most of what I know about their relationship and about Grandma Maude comes from those journals.

For the remainder of his life, Dad developed hand tremors, perhaps from the PTSD he experienced as a result of his stress. He never spoke much of the war, and the two of us barely spoke to each other for nearly twenty-five years, so I can't be completely certain what caused the feelings of sadness, worry, anger, and emotional numbness he faced until his midthirties. Prior to my father's death, it never occurred to me that much of his earlier erratic behavior may have been caused by the war. Was it just bad behavior or a geographical cure attempting to escape a war that refused to be forgotten?

On numerous occasions, he left for Florida, California, and to Friendly View, West Virginia, to visit his old shipmate, Billy, where he also met a fifteen-year-old girl—my mother-to-be. He was twenty-three.

While Billy's tour of duty in the navy had already ended, my dad's had not. He would frequently go absent without leave (AWOL), including immediately after disembarking from the ship for the last time.

On several occasions, the shore patrol or police found him at Billy's house. Dad made no pretense that he was *hiding* there, as the shore patrol liked to say. Sometimes he got caught, other times he turned himself in when he'd had enough visiting. "Your dad was no stranger to the brig," Uncle Billy said. "Often, he was arrested by the shore patrol even when we were on leave, and he didn't seem to care. Man, did he love to fight. He got us kicked out of a lot of bars."

Early on in his life, Dad had always been in debt to his mother. He traveled on her money. Occasionally, he paid back his debt, only to borrow from Grandma Maude again soon after—in one case, just a day later. She seemed eternally hopeful that Dad was going to change.

Dad used some of that borrowed money to marry Mom on January 3, 1947.

Grandma Maude recorded in her journal, *Tommy married Nancy Tucker. It rained and was getting cold.*

The weather was a foreboding of our future.

Dad was released from the navy three weeks later, barely escaping a bad conduct discharge, Uncle Billy said.

★★★

The summer of 1947, before I was born, marked Dad's first violent act toward Mom. She was bleeding when Dad's sister Alice arrived to help her out. Mom and Dad had been married for less than eight months, and Mom was seventeen. A week later, Grandma Maude wrote, *Tommy was drinking last night and said he was going to die. The Lord was not going to let him live any longer.*

He lived for another fifty-five years.

Later in life, he became a lay minister, searching for forgiveness, searching to save souls for a God who had little tolerance for those who didn't believe the way Dad believed. In our visits near the end of his life, he never spoke of God again. Did he feel, as Jesus had, that God had forsaken him?

"You Better Have a Boy"

I was born December 28, 1947, and was named after my paternal grandfather—John Elliott Pitts, a name I would change years later. My mother told me the story of my father's joy just afterward.

"He told me, 'You better have a boy,'" she said. "When I had you, he was so proud. He carried you around in your blanket and would pull it down to show you were a boy. I would tell him, 'Tommy, pull up that blanket! He'll catch his death of cold!' He didn't listen. He never listened. And then, there were those times early on when he just never came home."

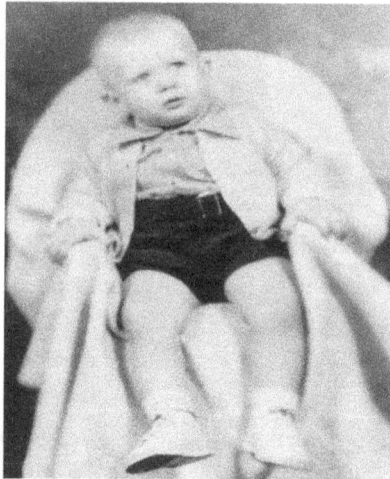

Me at about six months.

After I was born, my mother, father, and I lived in a farmhouse on the outskirts of Richmond, Virginia, owned by Grandma Maude. "It was really out in the country," my mother said. Dad rarely stayed there, leaving my mother to tend to a large garden where he planted vegetables to sell. One time Mom found me in the garden, pulling up carrots and eating them dirt and all. We rarely had much food.

Another time, she heard the chickens squawking, and when she came outside, I was going into the chicken coop where there was a black snake. My mother had lived around snakes all her life in West Virginia, so I'm quite sure she must have killed it to save the chickens and eggs.

One night when Dad had left us for some time, an intruder tried coming through the window. I was asleep in my crib when my mother fired a shotgun at him just before he made it in. "I don't know if I hit him," she said matter-of-factly, "but he never came back." That was the first instance of her protecting us both from what was to come. She had never fired a shotgun before but would soon learn to weaponize whatever was on hand.

Still a teenager, Mom needed financial help while Dad made his excursions throughout the US. As a result, my mother started her exodus back to a place she'd wanted so desperately to leave just a year before. She now found it to be her cocoon, temporary as it was. At one point early in my life, I reminded Mom of our treks back to Friendly View. "We went back at least three times, right?" I suggested.

"Oh honey," she laughed. "I took you back to Mom's a dozen times, if not more. You were too young to remember a lot of our visits. I wanted to leave for good so many times but always went back." Mom had completed only two weeks of the eighth grade; had she left, she wouldn't have had a place to go.

Richmond, Virginia, Dad's home, never became Mom's home. It only reminded her of what she had done in marrying my father and who she was becoming by staying married to him. She was no longer the impish girl from Friendly View. Instead, she retreated, like any good soldier who had been overwhelmed by the enemy. Friendly View became a place to plan her next move, to learn defense and what it took to survive, and learn that the best defense was a good offense.

In 1948, just over a year after they married and about a month and half after I was born, Dad once again struck Mom. He'd often go out to bars and come home blind drunk with lipstick on his shirt. So again she fled home to West Virginia. During her stay, Mom considered divorcing Dad and marrying a man named Donald. All there was to know about Donald was that she didn't like his attitude toward her young son. She liked him, but she couldn't stay with Donald either if it meant he wasn't going to treat me well. Donald was interested in Mom, but definitely not interested in her having a child. She was eighteen then, and her antenna for knowing what she wanted and didn't want in a relationship was beginning to take shape. Once that antenna went up, she learned to make rapid decisions for the rest of her life.

Finally, she returned to Dad.

It never took long for him to forget what had led Mom to leave in the first place.

During his rages, Dad was prone to accidents. When he drank, he'd often gun the gas pedal of his old Ford, tires taking to the air where the roads undulated, the chassis pounding the stubborn asphalt as it landed. Cars, over the years, became his rage-mobiles, his flesh and blood sometimes comingling with windshields and dashboards when he crashed.

He couldn't have cared less what those actions led to—accidents, totaled cars, hospital stays, short jail times—they were all the same to him. But his rage had the effect of a forest fire. It burned all that was around him and ravaged those less prepared for its onslaught.

During Dad's worst moments, Grandma Maude would support Mom, buying us clothes, groceries, and providing us with small amounts of money to get by, sometimes enough to journey back to West Virginia.

Other times, when Dad attacked her, Mom would leave after he passed out, often before dawn. She'd scoot out of bed and silently take us by cab to a bus or the train station—after frisking Dad's pockets for cash. And Mom wasn't concerned whether the money came from Grandma Maude or one of Dad's jobs. It was money she needed to get away. Even when we stayed at home, she often picked his pockets to buy groceries or pay the bills. He rarely noticed, but when asked, she'd always deny her pilfering.

★★★

No matter what Dad had done, Grandma Maude enabled him—helped him buy a used car in one instance so he could get to work. He went to work for the Independent Cab company. I recall seeing his yellow cab when I was five on one of our trips back to Richmond. But I think he only drove cabs when he was unable to find other jobs. Whether driving a cab, driving a bread truck, or selling Fuller Brush products door-to-door, Dad worked jobs where he collected cash. This allowed him to stop off at bars after work and, without giving it much thought, spend his commissions for the day, as well as some cash that was meant for companies he worked for prior to checking in. From the time I was seven to twelve, before he left, he only took jobs with companies that would allow him to come up short after a night of drinking and spending company money.

But no job was so important that Dad couldn't go on another exodus—one time to Newark, New Jersey. There is no indication why Dad went to Newark, but his mother's journals and Mom's suspicions pointed that many of his wanderings were to go see women.

His wandering was a time for us to fear that he *would* come home.

Red Wagons

One of the two times I ever saw my father cry was when he spoke of one Christmas. His family had been relatively well-to-do prior to the Depression, a time when his father was laid up in bed with rheumatoid arthritis. Doctors used to think that the best cure for arthritis was to remain in bed, whereas now we know the opposite to be true.

Dad never received Christmas gifts, though he often watched other children tout theirs. Emotionally, he must have felt abandoned by his father, who spent his last few years in bed with rheumatoid arthritis. From what I could gather, my dad had no relationship with his father during those years.

But on one particular Christmas when he was a little boy, a woman down the street bought him a red wagon. "I didn't even know her," he told me. "I loved that red wagon."

When he told me that story, it altered my terrible memories of Christmases past, though I still feel some anxiety during the Christmas season until it passes. Somehow his sharing the story of the red wagon, while making Christmas no more enjoyable, helped bring me to a greater peace for who he was and who he later became.

Ironically, similar to Dad's story, one of my earliest memories is a Christmas when one of the many times Mom left Dad, she sent Uncle Billy money to West Virginia from Chicago to buy me a red wagon. I was five. Mom was in Chicago where she had moved with her sisters to work the assembly line at a ball bearing company. She left me with my grandma on many occasions. But on this occasion, when I was five until I was seven, I wouldn't hear from her for months, though she and Grandma Tucker exchanged letters from time to time.

Often, I pulled that red wagon across the rutty dirt road up to the blacktopped Route 3, which zigzagged like a snake. A hundred yards or so away, I could see cars occasionally come round the bend. I waited there for the magic of Mom to come from Chicago and take me away with her. I waited incessantly to go home with her, wherever home would be. Those days of waiting by the tar-covered road were filled with hope one moment and disappointment in the other. Those years were the most trying for me, the longest period I was away from Mom. Those were the first days of my vivid memories of my time in Friendly View, well after the worst recession and snowstorm that Dry Creek and Friendly View had ever witnessed. I was old enough to know very distinctly what abandonment felt like.

Photo of me in Dry Creek, age five, in a red wagon.

Chapter 3

WHERE *HOME* WAS: 1949

Financial Hard Times

The Recession of 1949 was a downturn in the United States that lasted for eleven months. The recession began in November 1948 and lasted until October 1949, making it the worst recession in most Virginians' and West Virginians' lifetimes.

The year 1949 was a particularly challenging year for our family financially. Mom and I spent considerable time that year in Friendly View. But when we were back in Richmond, Grandma Maude often took out loans for Dad. She provided him with only enough to help us get by and consistently gave Mom one dollar at a time.

It was evident that enabling Dad was beginning to take its toll on her financially. She borrowed money against her various properties to help Mom and Dad. In early 1949, she borrowed $300 from the bank as collateral against her farm and took out a bank note for Dad shortly thereafter. She borrowed another $1,000 from the bank by providing the "house on hill" as collateral for a sixty-day loan.

Some of the money would go to pay for my hospital stay.

My illnesses required several major hospital stays from a year-and-a-half old until I was twelve, only to resurface in my early twenties until now. I had a hernia plus urological issues from birth that required restructuring of my plumbing and ureters.

Dad never came to the hospital during any of those occurrences. Each time, as the hospital bills mounted, he ignored them.

A month after my hernia operation at one and a half, Mom received a card from him. He was in Florida. For the fourth time that year, Mom considered going back to West Virginia. Grandma Maude gave her money to buy a ticket, but I don't think she used it. She had a baby to attend to.

Just as he had done while he was in the navy, Dad would return year in and year out to wherever we lived at the time. Our home was his temporary base. It's difficult to say whether Dad ever thought of any place as *home* during those years. Every place we lived was a stopover until it was time for him, or us, to get up and go again.

★★★

Even during this very difficult time, Grandma Maude saw hope that my father's situation would improve. Oddly enough, despite the severe recession, Dad had decided to take up farming. He and his brother Chester both loved to raise tomatoes and often bragged about whose tomatoes were the best.

In early May of 1949, according to her journals, Grandma Maude paid $90 for hogs and paid off a total of $115 of the $460 that remained for the note she had taken out for him. Dad bought a mule against the remaining funds she had taken out for the note. He used part of the loan that Grandma Maude had taken out for him to sell cantaloupes. This must have given her hope that, as a farmer, Dad was ready to settle down once and for all. Her hopes were that things would "return to normal." She wrote how she dreamed of "lots of water and fat hogs."

However, during a drinking bout that year, Dad wrecked the pickup truck she had paid for that he used to sell his cantaloupes. Settling down was not to be. Shortly after, she gave him another $150. Some of that money went to refund the navy thirty-seven dollars for an undisclosed reason. With the rest, he left the farm unattended and headed to West Virginia to visit his old navy buddy—and Mom's brother—Billy. There is no indication that Mom accompanied him on that trip.

On August 19, Grandma Maude noted: *Tommy's birthday 27 yrs.*

To help out with our financials, Mom started working on the assembly line in a candy factory, where she worked on and off for years to help pay the bills between her trips to West Virginia. She never made enough to pay them all. Instead, part of that money went to pay for Dad's occasional bail, downtime for his accidents, and to fund his "excursions." So Grandma Maude paid our utility bills. Heat and lighting were small comforts for the violence that would follow.

When Bad Wasn't Bad Enough: 1950

While Grandma Maude's entries for 1948 and 1949 illustrated a stressful relationship between Mom and Dad, 1950 proved to be an even worse year for all of us. As usual, Mom went to West Virginia several times, and Dad, as he had become accustomed to, went to Florida for a time. In Grandma Maude's later journal entries, it became evident that Dad had, as with other trips, gone there to visit a woman.

Dad's misconduct only exacerbated the burden on his mother. Grandma Maude had longed for stability that continued to escape her year after year. Her husband, my grandfather, had passed away fifteen years earlier from the effects of the rheumatoid arthritis that had long ailed him, so Dad and several siblings had had to find work to help pay the bills at home. Dad was fourteen when his father died, and he became the primary provider for his family. He and Chester worked twelve-hour shifts on the railroad in Norfolk, Virginia. Chester talked about how Dad would often go off on binges, leaving Chester to cover his shifts and work twenty-four hours at a time. So even at fourteen, my father was a wanderer.

At eighteen, he joined the navy for six years and then married my mother at the end of his tour.

Now as Dad added to his mother's burdens, it was also becoming apparent what it was doing to my mom. The mental and physical strain of carrying an infant and wondering how she was going to get by financially was too much of a burden to carry on her own. During one of Dad's excursions to Florida, Mom spent two months with Grandma Tucker. But it became clear that her comings and goings to her mother's house and the costs to her mother for having to support her daughter and son were significant. Mom could not leave her infant to her mother's care while finding work. That was too much to ask. So again she returned to Dad.

Yet later, Mom left for West Virginia once more—this time to drop me off at her mother's house before going to Chicago to work the assembly line at the ball bearing company for one dollar an hour. I came to call my mother's mother Mom Tucker over the years because she came to be known as my *other* mother.

Mom Tucker's rental only had two bedrooms. When Mom wasn't there, Cousin Joe and I slept together on a bed that was about three-quarters the size of a double bed. What we called a bedroom may have at one time been a closet, its walls now removed. It was just off to the left of the front door. When anyone entered in the winter, the cold wind blew over us.

While Mom Tucker came to feel like a surrogate mother to me, her house never felt like home. Joe's mother, Bobbie, had left him with Mom Tucker at birth, and he had come to call her Mom because she was the only mother he had ever known. Our grandmother said Bobbie "liked to party," and she was rarely around.

So from the start, our grandmother treated me very differently from Joe; she gave me the bulk of chores. I helped her take vegetables from the garden—snapping peas, cutting up carrots—and I stoked up the coal burner stove in the mornings. Joe had no chores and even determined what I could eat or not eat for breakfast.

Joe hated my being there to take our grandmother's attention away from him. So when he refused to share breakfast, that seemed to be his way of saying, "I don't want you here, and I'm going to keep you hungry."

Later, from our twenties to our sixties, Joe and I would come to refer to each other more as brothers than cousins. We rarely saw each other in those later years. Joe died when he was seventy-two, having returned to the drinking issues that had plagued him in his twenties and thirties.

He was one of the most personable men when he was around most people, but I sensed some anger that most wouldn't have been privy to. I always believed that was because his mother had abandoned him. Even after his mother picked him up at age nine to come and live with her and her second husband, Uncle John, Joe still called his mother "Bobbie" and Mom Tucker "Mom."

He became a really successful business man. He owned two used-car dealerships, a mechanical shop, and during the recession of 2008–2009, he bought fourteen rental properties. He also owned seven acres of land next to the largest mall in Northern Virginia. When he died, his house was worth well over a million dollars. He always called me "the smartest guy I've ever known." I always countered with, "Then why am I not as wealthy as you?" We had a great deal of admiration for each other.

★★★

Mom, Dad, and I shared one important aversion in life: no place we resided in those early days ever felt like home. For Mom, that feeling would last until she remarried in the early 1960s; for Dad, it would last until he found peace with Jesus on Lookout Mountain in Georgia in the 1970s. And for me? I have yet to find home—even today at seventy-four.

Chapter 4

1951: THE CAGED BIRD RETURNS

"The caged bird sings
with a fearful trill
of things unknown
but longed for still ..."
—MAYA ANGELOU, "CAGED BIRD"

Grandma Maude's entries in her journal for 1951 give evidence of what appeared early on as a most volatile love-hate relationship between my parents. But as time moved on, the entries showed more of the frenetic life of a young woman who appeared to be losing her affection for her husband.

Mom wrote to Grandma Maude on several occasions in January and February. Grandma Maude responded twice in March. She seemed well aware that something was different from all the comings and goings between Mom and Dad. In February, Grandma Maude recorded her own awakening from a dream, crying that Dad had come home.

During that time, she had been paying interest on notes that she had taken out for Dad, as well as paying our electric bill. Suspecting the worst, at the end of May, Grandma Maude wrote to Mom Tucker, with whom Mom was staying at the time.

Grandma Maude had received a letter from Police Chief J.R. Reichert asking her to post bail and, shortly after that, received a letter from "Tommy and Mrs. F.O. Carlson" in St. Petersburg, Florida. Grandma Maude then wrote to "Mrs. Tucker." I suspect that this was to tell her that Dad was going to stay with the woman—Mrs. F.O. Carlson—who had co-authored the letter.

Concurrently, Mom wrote a letter to Dad's older sister Turman. Of the siblings, Turman was the alpha of the siblings, the one the others turned to when there was trouble or decisions to be made. Mom was well aware of that and wrote to Turman that she had divorced Dad.

The Florida relationship didn't last.

Dad returned, and eight days after the divorce, he and Mom remarried.

Mom had certainly felt the agony of wavering between creating a further burden on her mother or returning to an unfaithful husband. Grandma Maude recorded the weather that day was "cloudy, sleet, and cold," just like it had been the first time my parents married.

Less than two weeks later, we moved to the tar-shingle house that Grandma Maude owned on Blueridge Avenue in Richmond, the same home where my father planted a vegetable garden.

On December 31, Grandma Maude recorded in her journal, Tommy owes me ...." She outlined a series of charges totaling $423.71. One of the most significant years of Mom's, Dad's, and my life ended with Grandma Maude recording a debt, as any creditor might.

What Christmas Came to Mean to Me

The house on Blueridge Ave. was one of three houses Grandma Maude had purchased after years of saving money as a practical nurse. Grandma Maude took care of an old gentleman for years. We moved there just three months before Christmas and less than two weeks after Mom and Dad had remarried.

One evening just prior to Christmas 1951, Mom put on her red lipstick and curled her brunette hair, then waited on the sofa in the living room. Dad had promised to take her to a party that night. It was going to be a night to make up with Mom for his unfaithfulness.

I had been listening to my records, "I Saw Mommy Kissing Santa Claus" by Jimmy Boyd and Gene Autry's "Rudolf the Red-Nosed Reindeer," when Dad came through the door.

What I feared most in life was Dad's bourbon breath. I had few, if any, hopes and dreams then. I was days away from turning four. But my fears had already turned viral and would continue to escalate until my midthirties.

When my father came home that night, he smelled of perfume, and there was lipstick on his shirt. My mother was the first to speak. Maybe she asked him where he had been or if he had been out with other women. I don't remember the exact question; I recall the response.

When angered, my father's price for perceived provocation, humiliation, was vengeance. He grabbed Mom's curls as someone might struggle with a fish trying its best to break free. He ran her head into a wall, then beat her with his fists.

I ran to Mrs. Smith's house next door. Mrs. Smith would often watch me while Mom worked on the assembly line at the candy factory. I pounded on her front door.

"Mrs. Smith! Mrs. Smith!" I screamed.

Soon, the lights went out. I was left in darkness to mull over my father's anger.

I hurried back to our front door near where Mom lay. Foam dribbled from the side of her mouth. She was unconscious.

My father screamed, "Get up! Get up!"

His fury was as time-limited as it was volcanic.

I backed off, and on the side of our house, I pressed my arms against the tar shingles. I was in a place so distant, the feeling was of a different universe. I rested my head on those shingles, scraping my arms and head against them, maybe as a punishment for my helplessness, and wept—a soft, silent weeping.

The tears always came silently.

Even then, if Mrs. Smith wasn't going to open up her door, I wanted no one else in the neighborhood to hear me. I wanted no one else to know the sound of a physically beaten mother and an emotionally beaten boy. I wanted no one to know what went on in our house. That was one of the earliest lessons my mother taught me, a vow greater than putting one's hand on the Bible.

My father came out, lifted me on his shoulder, and took me to a large tree just beyond his vegetable garden where he often "worked off" a hangover.

"Your daddy is going to go away for a while," he said.

He was used to Mom calling the police after his abuse, and after Mom came to, the red spinning lights soon showed up near where we stood. Dad placed me gently on the ground as someone might place a fragile heirloom. His demeanor was one of submission as he placed his hands obediently behind his back without the officers asking. He was familiar with the culture of seizure and arrest. And after he'd sobered up the next morning, the police would release him.

★★★

Dad wasn't working much in those days. His cab remained dormant in the driveway during the day, and he'd use it mainly to go out at night. Maybe it was days, even a week after the most recent beating, when a neighbor complained that I had chased his son with my belt. The boy had shot a rubber arrow at me, probably as a sign that he wanted to play. Most of the time, I was a really meek little kid who kept to himself, but I had a temperament that was just starting to bubble.

My father was tending to his garden after a drinking bout. He only nodded to the neighbor as if to say, *I'll take care of this.*

He grabbed my hand and took me into the house. My mother was at work. His face distorted, he took off his belt. "If you fall down or cry, we start again," he said.

Beating me was not a step over the line; it was a leap over it. Yet even then, I wanted to love my father, maybe even more than previously. Maybe it was just me or what I had done, but I didn't cry. I didn't even whimper. I did what he asked of me. The state I fell into from a combination of dull pain from the buckle and the stinging that I felt intermittently became one of the first instances of mindless detachment I had experienced. I would later call it Zen.

When my mother came home, she saw the blood marks and bruises on my legs from my father's lashings.

"You will NEVER touch that boy again!" she said.

★★★

Youngsters who are abused often recall their surroundings in detail, one of my therapists told me years later. Even though I was not quite four when we moved there, I can remember that house so vividly. I can recall where every piece of furniture was positioned, the texture and color of each. The tar-shingle house had several steps, a walk-up to a small concrete slab—possibly about four feet by four feet—to face the front door just to the right. Inside, there was a cranberry-color sofa off to the left in the living room and a navy-blue chair across the room from it, both with a bristly material, uncomfortable to the touch, especially to my young legs.

Just past the sofa, within several feet, was the kitchen, with a metal-legged table and four chairs. Just beyond the kitchen table was the screen door that led out to my father's garden, maybe twenty feet away. The garden was his harbor where he spent most of his time nursing hangovers when the seas of his life turned tumultuous.

Inside the kitchen, beside the screen door, was my mother's wringer washer, the kind you see nowadays in museums. Outside, she hung up her clothes on thin-roped clotheslines. Beside the wringer washer was a small enclave that was my makeshift bedroom. And just before the enclave were stairs that led up to the attic where Grandma Maude sometimes stayed, though I never saw her much at all. I never knew for certain where she stayed otherwise—possibly at the home of the old man she cared for, possibly in one of her other homes—and I never went up to her attic-room.

Grandma Maude's attic was a place of retreat from her nursing duties when she wasn't taking care of her elderly patient. It was the only time that I can recall when she stayed in the same house with us. All of the houses we lived in during my early youth were houses she owned.

She was an avid reader of the scriptures—a Seventh-day Adventist. But my mother told me later that Grandma Maude never threw away a newspaper. She loved the written word and evidently did not feel it should be destroyed.

While I never saw her in her own house, the few times I remember seeing Grandma Maude were during the year I returned from West Virginia at age seven. What I recall most about her then was that she always insisted on giving me a spoonful of castor oil. That would be the year she died in her sleep of a heart attack.

House of Violence: the tar-shingle house.

The Eyes of a Drowsy Owl,
The Gray Sway of Sycamore Shadows

For a moment, the eyes
of a drowsy owl nearly
    camouflaged on a poplar tree

eased the recall, the sting of flesh,
    the quick white crack of a backhand.

There were no Jesuses to protect
    a boy from this, only a run to the woods
where the bloom of hope rose

from the sun on the river, the gray sway
    of sycamore shadows and boughs of pines
displaying what godliness was.

The air drenched in solitude, the rush of a frenetic
    heart submerged into the slow calm
away from the ungodly.

The threads of pain and beauty wove into
    a boy becoming who he was.

A boy becomes a man so quickly; it is only
    near the end he understands.

A man called father left the earth with
    his sorrows, regrets.

"I can't sleep at night, thinking
    what I did to you back then," the man
called father once said.

"It's okay," the boy turned man said.

There is forgiveness in recalling the drowsy eyes
        of an owl, the bloom of hope that rose
    from the sun on the river,

the gray sway of sycamore shadows and
boughs of pines displaying what godliness is.

For all that, it's what makes
        up the sweet nature of poetry
    in pain, in beauty.

Chapter 5

1951-1955: REMEMBRANCES:
MY LAST YEARS LIVING IN THE MOUNTAINS

Only on the rarest occasions did Dad attempt to stop drinking, usually lasting only for days. Even when he wasn't drinking, Dad was unapproachable in the mornings. For most of my childhood while he and Mom were still married, as much as I wanted to be near him, I learned to keep my distance, to stay in my bedroom until he left for work.

He typically fixed himself what he called batter bread—a concoction of flour, butter, and a fair amount of salt and pepper—and/or scrambled eggs for breakfasts he only made for himself. He'd read the newspaper, cover to cover, and was not to be interrupted. When he died of lung and brain cancer in 2002, his second wife of nearly forty years called to let my wife Kate and me know he was dying. She knew he was dying, she said, because he no longer had an interest in reading the newspaper.

On those mornings, he was like a cold kettle that built to a slow boil during the day. By the time he came home, the steam from that kettle had to go somewhere. Someone had to pay, and more often than not it was Mom, when he came home at all. Her exhortation that he was never to touch me again seemed to resonate with him, at least when it came to violence. He never touched me after that, other than an occasional slap. But we had little defense from his hurting Mom other than to find shelter elsewhere.

He paid a price of his own mental and physical pain: the scuffs and bruises he suffered from barroom fights, the blackouts that often landed him in unknown places, the unexpected paybacks from Mom that increased over time.

Any moments of happiness back then were stolen by those thieves—loneliness and rage—and the distance that had developed between my parents. Mom had become as hardhearted in the mornings as Dad had. It wasn't always because of his physical abuse; sometimes she felt she just couldn't take all the screaming back and forth.

Typically, when Mom and I would escape, we'd do so when he was gone, leaving him to come back to an empty apartment. Over the years, our trips back to Friendly View became fewer but with longer stays. The six-hour drives to West Virginia from 1951 to 1955 became as casual as taking a Sunday drive in the country. Either Uncle Frank or Uncle Billy would pick us up. They'd drive thirty-five miles an hour where speed limits were fifty-five on Virginia highways, and they'd drive thirty-five miles an hour around twenty-five mile an hour curves in the mountains. I came to think of those trips as adventures. When Mom's brothers were unavailable, we took the train or occasionally a Greyhound bus.

I loved to ride on the train. To watch the small towns sail by, to wave back to the people waving to me outside, to take in forests and swamps that changed every season. I have always been enamored with forests and nature. I didn't yet know what Zen was, but in nature I could escape to a place of mindlessness where I no longer felt emotional pain. And I came to love swamps—the eeriness, the darkness that matched how I felt inside. These vernal areas were what led me to love those train rides and what made Friendly View tolerable. When someone is abandoned, self-sufficiency becomes a must. But the healing also comes from becoming a part of the nature around them.

Even today, I feel a lot of discomfort being around concrete.

The adventure always ended when we arrived in Friendly View. I knew the drill by this time: Mom would leave me with Mom Tucker. My grandmother's village, Dry Creek, was a quick stopover for her to drop me off before heading out to find work in various cities from the East Coast to the Midwest, often with one or more of her siblings. Wherever she ended up, it was always assembly line work. She said later, with her education, it was all the work she could find.

Once when Mom and I were watching the episode of *I Love Lucy* where Lucy is working on a candy factory assembly line and the line is moving faster than Lucy can keep up, Mom chortled, "That's the way it was! That's really the way it was!"

★★★

As the months grew into a year, and then another, I worried she would never come back for me when she left me in Friendly View to work in Chicago or places I was never privy to. I waited for the mail each day to see if she had written my grandmother and had mentioned me. Mom had previously only left me there for weeks or months, and each trip from the age of four until I was seven seemed to be longer than the previous one.

Dry Creek was also becoming more of a culture for me than Richmond ever had been. Richmond represented anger, hurt, and chaos. Dry Creek represented feelings of abandonment and isolation but also the physical and mental healing that came from the mountains, the river, and the beginnings of self-sufficiency.

But I don't remember crying then. I was too numb to cry, and I had been trained not to. By the time I was an adult, I'd learned never to cry, not even at funerals. I fostered inward compartments to counterbalance the emotions of others around me.

The Culture of Friendly View:
What is Best Forgotten and Unforgettable

Though I felt isolated in Friendly View, I came to understand later in life what a part Mom's own feelings of isolation must have played in marrying Dad. In her later years, Mom only mentioned West Virginia when I brought up the subject, sometimes to fill in the gaps for chapters of my novel.

In those times, nothing seemed to erase her earlier memories better than taking family photographs. It was as though taking each of those thousands of pictures would wipe away the beatings, the lipstick, the perfume. During family get-togethers, she would catch us in the moment, camera ready, and say, "Smile." Then she would laugh, as though she'd gotten away with something. Maybe it was even a little bit of returning to that impish girl, a cleansing of all that had happened in between. Later in her life, Mom only seemed happy when she was with her children and extended family. She wanted to capture those moments forever on film. But I felt like a player on the stage as one of those many participants.

As seldom as it occurred, I loved my mother's laugh. It came from the gut, honest and, at times, so unrelenting it brought tears to her eyes. It seemed to be her way of saying, screw all that had gone on in her life over those years of marriage to Dad, a combat veteran, as she heroically snubbed her nose at the war she had engaged in.

Looking back, no song describes my mother's mental state better than Janis Ian's "Between the Lines." The song tells of how broken dreams can slip away between books and pages of magazines, and Mom lived the last years of her life through the stories of *People* magazine. Like so many people who have had tragic lives, she lived her life through movie stars. Janis Ian also sings about how between lines of photographs, one can see how the past isn't always pleasing. When Mom passed away, thousands of family photos were found tucked away, filling dressers and chests of drawers, boxes under beds … anywhere there was a space to fill like the void of her unfulfilled dreams. The amount of money she spent on frames that decorated every wall or tabletop must have taken nearly a year of her social security checks.

And of the thousands of photos, there was not one photo of Dad.

While none of the photos revealed the violence Mom, my sister, and I had gone through, we were a family borne from our mother's past. Her sadness and anger still flared up from time to time. Every visit—be it her visits to Friendly View or our visits to Mom later in her life—required a bit of temperature-taking of the air around us.

And, over time, Mom's laughter became an even rarer occurrence.

Weeping for My Mother

Remembrances of those childhood days on my way to Oregon for the writing program—Mom's rare laughter, her love of her extended family in photos—came with a price. I began to wonder why I had written *Berserk* at all. It was not a story about my mother's laughter or better days. What did it say about me that I wanted to write a story about family dysfunction, when I was just as dysfunctional? Hadn't we all survived the worst of it? Become better folks?

I stopped off at McKenzie Pass to give the old Audi a rest. It was starting to show signs of rebellion, and there was still Three Sisters mountains to scale. McKenzie Pass was the most beautiful sight I had ever seen.

I sat by a creek where it appeared that hundreds of trilobites from eons ago were embedded in a calcification in the clearest stream I had ever witnessed. After sitting there for some time, I walked to the car and pulled out *Berserk* from the back seat. Now less than a hundred miles from Eugene, I was focused even more on what I had written about our family and Mom's vehement disapproval of what she had read. Hadn't it really been about all of us?

I read from chapter 5 of my novel:

> *The man called father recoils. The salvo of mouth's blood will stop soon.*
>
> *Everything will be alright soon, the boy is schooled to believe. It is a mother's wish for her son. It is a taste of make believe. It is a rewind of the reel.*
>
> *"You will never touch that boy again!" the mother says.*
>
> *The force that pulses through the flesh awaits solitude. It is what makes the unfaithful faithful knowing the pain will end. To survive*

*means the slightest kind of triumph. The bandage is silence. Quiet.
Peace.*

*In the absence of perfection, beyond the right hand of hatred, beauty
endures nonetheless.*

I closed the text. I wept, if not for the years my mother had
attempted to protect me, then for the most beautiful creation I had
ever witnessed while sitting on the banks of the river at McKenzie
Pass—or most likely for both.

After several hours, it appeared the old Audi was ready for the
challenge of ascending a mile-high series of mountains, Three Sisters
mountains, higher than those I had witnessed as a child, where the
Scots-Irish had found solace in Appalachia's sanctuary two hundred
years earlier, where Mom and I had retreated thirty years earlier.

I had come to believe in the spiritual connectivity between the
mountains and all they meant to me and the Scots-Irish blood that
beckoned me to that upcoming mountain climb. I hadn't felt that alive
in years. Maybe, just maybe, I was coming to understand, if only for
a few brief hours, what home was.

The Scots-Irish Heritage

Mom Tucker spoke the language of the Scots-Irish. When she called
for a poke of blow-gum, I found out years later that *poke* as she used the
word came from fourteenth century Scotland and meant a bag. Like
the earlier Scots-Irish, she showed a sense of rugged independence,
and she was more of a discipliner than one who displayed love. I never
heard her mention the words *love* or *family*. Yet both were critically
important to her.

As was Mom Tucker, Friendly View was steeped in Scots-Irish
heritage; it was a village for only the heartiest of souls. The punishing
winters, the need for neighbors to care for one another in the worst
of times (and there were many rough times), or the isolation that led
so many to turn inward to fend for themselves made this a peculiar

culture for those outside its boundaries. Their historic culture spoke to who they had been for centuries.

Stubborn, proud, independent, rugged, individualistic are all terms used to describe the people known as Scots-Irish. Strong spiritual and family beliefs were instilled in their mindsets, which naturally have been passed down and are still present in the lives of their descendants today.

Numerous books and articles have been written about the Scots-Irish existence and their settling in the mountains similar to their homeland. They lived in small isolated communities, where it was important to them to preserve their cultural ties. What made them noteworthy were the crops they grew similar to those of their homeland, along with their foot-stomping music and instruments from Scotland and Northern Ireland. They were storytellers and makers of crafts that came to be known as distinctive Southern Appalachian creations.

When the Coal Ran Out

That Scots-Irish ruggedness was tested in the Great Appalachian Storm of 1950.

One article claimed as much as fifty-seven inches of snow fell on the Appalachians. The winds were as damaging as they were costly, making the Great Appalachian Storm of 1950 the worst storm ever recorded up until that time.

The end of 1950 into the beginning of 1951 was one of the scariest periods of the lives of those in Friendly View. The coal trucks had no passage to the village. The coal ran low, and folks in Friendly View did their best to cut a path to Mom Tucker's house to provide us with rationings of food. The roads were impassible to get to the general store, the only source of store-bought food.

The storm was the talk of the miners and their families for years. While that period is beyond memory, I do recall the snowdrifts year to year that rose as high as my head on the hill I had to climb to get to the bus pickup point nearly two years later when I started first grade.

But the end of 1951 through 1953 when Mom left me with my grandmother, those were the worst of my West Virginia days. Even with all that had happened in those early years, it became even more evident that I was living with a grandmother who obviously didn't want me there and a cousin full of spite who saw me as competition.

Mom Tucker expected Joe and me to brush the snow aside as best we could and be there when the bus finally made its way to the top of the hill. If the school buses never ran during the ice storms, they wound their way to us after normal snowstorms, snaking around one corner, then another, to Friendly View.

These were the days and years before coal miners knew they were in a dying trade. Currently, the rutty roads only lead back to a village where miners and their families used to live. Only squatters remain, as well as the unkempt tombstones, the raw brindled clapboard once inhabited by the poor but hardworking folks.

For over a century, Friendly View teemed with life while severing its relationship with most of humanity. If the Scots-Irish were foolish, it was only that they thought they were claiming this land as their own. Yet for millennia it had remained untamed, unseen, unheard of, and likely, in time, would be again.

Gone are the old wives' tales that often worked in this doctorless environment. The time I fell on a broken bottle and the blood dripped from my hand all the way to Mom Tucker's house—tightly, she tied a torn T-shirt around my hand and patted me on the shoulder. "See there—good as new." Or when I was stung on the bottom of my foot by a wasp. I warned Aunt Betty I was allergic to bee stings. She simply said, "Just rub some mud on it," that great elixir that took away much of the pain and swelling.

Occasionally, at seventy-four, I stare at the scar that remains on my hand, and if I were ever stung by a wasp, I wouldn't hesitate to slap a bit of mud on that sting.

Daily Summer Walks to
Carl Jarrell's General Store

Just as the winters were harsh there, the summers were hot and humid, and the sun seemed to bear down as harshly. There were no house numbers or street addresses, only post office boxes at Carl Jarrell's General Store. Over a period of three years, when Dad's behavior led me back to Dry Creek, the store was a significant part of my life.

At five years old, I was tasked every day to walk nearly a mile to Carl Jarrell's to get the mail; buy a few supplies, which always included buying Mom Tucker "a poke of blow gum"; and for me, a small cup of Pet ice cream, which Carl Jarrell rarely charged me for. In fact, most of what we purchased was on credit until one of her children sent her money or the welfare check came in.

In the summer, I walked barefoot on the side of Route 3, which required either walking on hot stones on the side of the road or on the bubbly tar of the road. On my way to the general store, I jumped between the bubbly tar and the hot stones. Neither gave my feet relief.

Sometimes I could turn off my mind to the pain as I had at that tar-shingle house back in Richmond. Looking back, I understand where the phrase *tar heel* comes from. I rarely brought attention to the blisters from the walks to the general store. It was a family trait that we bore our wounds silently.

Most of the chores were my responsibility, and at breakfast, Joe rarely shared the ten biscuits my grandmother made; he claimed them as his. She normally conceded and made me a piece of white bread toast and fatback gravy.

To Joe, who had significant fits of anger about most everything, I was an intruder. He had established himself as boss, and to a large extent, he was.

The Unsightly and the Beautiful

My mother told me later that Mom Tucker said to her just before she died that she wished she hadn't been so hard on me. If I had known, I would have told her Dry Creek was where I grew to know some serenity regardless of what life dished out, then or in the future. It was a reprieve from violence, other than an occasional switching that Mom Tucker meted out—mainly in silence. It was a time of welcome isolation.

I do not regret the time we lived in soot-stained shacks. Back then, the trials of who we were came with the cold wind blowing through broken clapboard slats. The old potbelly stove groaned; it could only do so much. Our clothes, at times, seemed to self-soil as we shook the poker back and forth until the embers were all that survived, requiring our clothes to be scrubbed occasionally against the old washboard in our metal tub.

Those were days when crises just seemed like ordinary events. I did not wonder what town Mom, Dad, and I would live in at any given time. Our world in Friendly View was too small for that. I was just a young boy with bitumen-laden eyes.

The smell of coal always surrounded me, whether it was from the coal bucket that stood by the potbelly stove I stoked regularly or Uncle Billy's clothes when he stopped by most nights for his bath in the metal tub to wash off the day's soot before going home to his wife, Tootsie.

I would find solace, even in what felt like abandonment. Abandonment for a loner was better than other options. I was more at home with the sound and flow of the river than being around people. As Coal River flowed over ancient boulders, moving unhurriedly, I spent endless hours there, staring, only staring.

The rainbow trout released in spring by the game wardens jumped the lengths of their bodies into the air, their red-brown speckled sides a thing to behold. The foot-long hellbender salamanders claimed the rocks in the clearest parts of the stream below as their permanent home. I could always find them there. We called them mud dogs.

Friendly View displayed the high meadows in the blue-green mountains, where the deer grazed. It was a rare occurrence to see a stranger passing through. Most days, I could enjoy the slight echo of a pileated woodpecker in the distance, or marvel at an occasional shy bobcat when I took evening walks in the woods.

No, Mom Tucker had no reason to apologize, this woman who, with a life of heartrending consequences, had survived it all. I was in the "she did the best she could" camp. She would have made the ancient Scots-Irish proud.

Other than Mom Tucker, there were no angry folks in Friendly View. For those who came that way, the beauty of the mountains and the river cleansed them of their contempt.

In late spring, the breeze became a rhythmic broom, undulating to clear itself of parachutes, the floating seeds of dandelions. The solar lamp of sundown softened to dim, leaving the tint of the sky to claim that day as beautiful.

The swing bridge separated the miners' village, where most people lived, from the Jarrells, who had turned large fields into farmland. Jarrell was a common name in Dry Creek, although it's difficult to say which Jarrells, if any, were related. They were all independent of each other in their daily goings-on. Aunt Betty and Uncle Frank Jarrell had built a three-bedroom bungalow on the other side of the swing bridge, with a large wraparound porch that was nearly as big as the house itself. It was a porch where the evening breeze came to live.

Surrounding the house were fruit trees they had planted when they first built their house on seven acres of land shortly after they married.

In Friendly View, hand pumps were replaced by indoor plumbing in the 1950s, save the outhouses that likely still exist today. Even more foul than the smell that emanated from the outhouses, especially in the summer, were their offerings that poured into Coal River.

And yes, old catalogs were used to wipe one's rear. The catalog rested near the neatly tailored hole where a five-year-old became skilled at climbing aboard just long enough to do his business for fear of losing his balance. More than once in awe, I watched the depths to the bottom. It was a place to do one's business and hurriedly retreat as the spiders kept watch from the corners.

The Fall and Rise (Again) of Carl Jarrell's General Store

Both the unsightly and the beautiful waned after the closing of the coal mines. Carl Jarrell's store, the epicenter of commercial activity for the area, closed for years.

Years later, Carl's son-in-law Charles (also a Jarrell) reopened the store, and from the pictures, it looks very much like it did back then, only newer. The entire inside had been refurbished.

An article published in *West Virginia Living* magazine in August 2015, after the store's renovation reads, "For more than 130 years the Charles B. Jarrell General Store, located 13 miles south of Whitesville on West Virginia Route 3, has been the hub of the wheel of life in Dry Creek." A resident quoted in the article says, "People come to get their groceries, their mail, their gas. It's a big part of the community. If it ever shuts down, that'll be the end of Dry Creek."

Since reading that article after it was published, I've wondered, with the mines shutting down, if the store still exists.

My grandmother's house.

Our "toilet." We often used a "slop jar"
at night, which some might call a chamber pot.

Chapter 6

FRIENDLY VIEW: VILLAGE AND CASTE SYSTEM

Prior to the closing of the mines in 2010 for good following an explosion, the later fifties into the early sixties were better times for Dry Creek. Mom Tucker moved from a house on stilts in 1950 to one on flat land in Friendly View, one where she had little fear of snowdrifts blocking the entrance to her back door. She had lived in a number of houses in the "hollers."

Her children were beginning to send her cash, and welfare checks continued to roll in. However, it wasn't enough. She worked cleaning the houses and doing laundry for families where the men were miners and the women had children to raise. In some instances, when the miners' wives didn't really need the help, they provided Mom Tucker with work nonetheless to help her get by.

Only a few families in Friendly View were on welfare. Mom Tucker had gone on welfare shortly after her husband left. In the early days, she and her seven children received CARE packages that contained one pound (450 grams) of beef in broth, one pound (450 grams) of steak and kidneys, eight ounces (230 grams) of liver loaf, eight ounces (230 grams) of corned beef, twelve ounces (340 grams) of luncheon loaf (like Spam), eight ounces (230 grams) of bacon, two pounds (910 grams) of margarine, one pound (450 grams) of lard, one pound (450 grams) of fruit preserves, one pound (450 grams) of honey, one pound (450 grams) of raisins, one pound (450 grams) of chocolate, two pounds (910 grams) of sugar, eight ounces (230 grams) of powdered eggs, two pounds (910 grams) of whole-milk powder, and two pounds (910 grams) of coffee. Additionally, packages were packed with nonfood items as well, including tools, blankets, clothing, school supplies, and medicine. All CARE dresses were a certain color gray.

The packages were initially designed to keep Europeans from starving after World War II and were later expanded into rural areas of America where work was scarce. Even the mining families struggled with the usury charges from the mining companies, requiring miners to buy goods from the company store on credit. It was a time when Tennessee Ernie Ford sang about those who owed their souls to the company store.

There was a caste system trickling down to those on welfare. Mom Tucker usually made enough money to supplement the groceries needed after canning spring and summer vegetables and fruit and to buy coal for the cold weather. Only two of her children finished high school. Most quit in middle school. So most had menial jobs.

My mother quit school in the eighth grade because the other children made fun of her CARE package dress. She "hated that gray," my mother said several times over the years. After she left Friendly View, she never wore anything gray for the rest of her life. She had a closet full of lavender and pink clothes when she died.

★★★

I learned in those days what the strength of women meant. I never knew my grandfathers. My father's father, who I was named after, died before my birth. My mother's father left Mom Tucker with seven kids to feed. She only alluded once to the ghost of a man who left her for his Southern "hussy." That was simply what life was, and that was the end of it. Like me, she kept her pain to herself. He had left her with syphilis, leaving her spine bowed noticeably.

If I had male role models in those days, however, they were my uncles. Uncle Sonny lied to join the Marine Corps when he was fifteen and sent Mom Tucker an allotment from his meager pay. He spent thirty-two years in the corps, retiring at forty-seven. Six of those years he spent in war zones, and to this day, his wife, Tootsie, who was married to Uncle Billy before Billy died, said Sonny occasionally screams out in his sleep.

Sonny once told my mother he had been responsible for the deaths of many of his men in a firefight against the Vietcong in Vietnam. His platoon was nearly wiped out. I joined the Marine Corps rather than any other service because of my admiration for Sonny. Currently, he spends the better part of his life on antidepressants.

Uncle Billy had the greatest sense of humor and the most wonderful smile. He found that humor in all that was going on around him. I like to think I gleaned some of that from him. Like Uncle Frank, he died of black lung in his fifties.

The Family's Teenage Brides

All Mom Tucker's girls had babies by the time they were in their mid to late teens. As they married and left home, her women-children sent cash back to pay for their mother's partial dentures and linen clothes. She drew from her garden the rest of her needs, save the price of coal in freezing seasons. There always seemed to be just enough to pay for a dump truck full, emptied by the side of the house. I never saw these women fear much of anything. They seemed to believe that fear had no regard for whether they acknowledged it or not.

My grandmother about two years before she married, likely twelve here.
Mom told both my sister and me at different times that she married at fourteen.

A photo of my grandmother, likely a year or more after marriage,
which would have made her about fifteen or sixteen.
The child is likely Billy, her oldest.

A photo of my grandmother, likely in Pocahontas County, West Virginia,
in a coal camp, likely in her late teens or early twenties. My mother was the
middle of seven children, so this may have been my mother.

My mother had me four months before her eighteenth birthday. My grandmother married at fourteen. And Mom Tucker became a grandmother in her early thirties when her oldest child Billy had his first child.

Aunt Bobbie, Joe's mother, had been married to Bill Harris, Joe's father, when she was in her mid-teens. He came down with diabetes and lost both his legs. Both Mom and her sister Mary Ann said, "Bobbie liked to dance. Bill couldn't dance anymore." That was the likely reason she divorced him.

My mother (on the left) with Aunt Bobbie and Joe. My mother often said that Bobbie rarely came back to see Joe once she left him with Mom Tucker, our grandmother. If that's true, this would be a rare photograph during one of my mother's many exile trips away from my father.

Bobbie met John, who had been in the army during the war. He was from Beckley, West Virginia, where they met and married shortly thereafter. When they had partied enough, they came to collect Joe.

If Joe met his real father, it was only once. Bill had moved to Florida, but when he passed away, Joe was in his late forties. Bill left him an inheritance of $40,000. Even years later, Joe still called Mom Tucker "Mom" and Aunt Bobbi, "Bobbie."

Joe and the Biscuits: 1952

My wife Kate had trouble believing about Joe's mastery of the Friendly View house and his insistence on eating all ten biscuits, until we met Joe for dinner years later, well into our midforties, at an Italian restaurant. Joe ordered a basket of bread. When the bread came, he wrapped his arm around the basket of bread as if to lay sole claim to it. He wasn't joking. Oh, did I smile inside. *Are you watching, Kate? Please show me you're watching!* I thought. Kate would later tell the story to others, still with an element of disbelief in her voice. She had been watching.

As the surrogate son of Mom Tucker, Joe had very little to call his own early in life. His youth was riddled with loss, poverty, and a lack of possessions. While he had so little then, he developed a determination to protect what was his and later turned that determination into possessions of land, rental properties, and several car dealerships. It short, he became a wealthy man.

It was then he felt obliged to provide for Bobbie, unlike she had done for him. Maintaining a certain distance, he showed little love for her but became obsessed with acting as the patriarch of the rest of his extended family. That extended family became the most important part of his life.

Simply put, Bobbie's abandonment made him the man he became.

Uncle Sonny, in the rear, served two tours in Vietnam and two tours supporting Vietnam from Okinawa; Back row: Cousin Frankie, who died at thirty-four of melanoma, leaving four children behind; Aunt Betty, who died of lung cancer, holding her daughter Cathy; Mom Tucker, who lived to be eighty-one in Baltimore; Uncle Frank, who died of black lung in his early fifties; my mom, who lived to be eighty-nine; Joe, tipping his cap to the camera, died at seventy-two; Sheila, Betty's middle child; and me at five or six.

Joe, Mom, and me, likely taken just before Mom took off for a job in Chicago. I'm not a happy camper.

Me and Cousin Joe, ages four and five, respectively. Joe typically sat above me in photos.

Where We Lived

We called it home, Friendly View, a village near where
Dry Creek mountains grieved for ghosts of family miners
buried there. And the women folk yelled to God to rid

them of their rage for a coal company's indifference.
A few miles away, Mount View Elementary School stood,
hill-bound, overlooking coal camps, rutted roads,

and rotten clapboard habitats where potbelly stoves
spun black coal smoke for heat, and wood burner stoves
cooked Chef Boyardee spaghetti and summer kale.

Ms. Jones, our first grade teacher, as much as
said to parents, *Soiled clothes are the Devil's work;
cleanliness, God's temple.* I wore clean ones,

hand-me-downs from Cousin Joe, a year ahead of me.
Frayed homemade quilts warmed us from the winter
freeze. Lightbulbs, dull yellow, when some popped,

spurred our early exits to bed. We, at the bottom
of a hill in winter, felt the snow drifts' wrath. We cut
a footpath up a steep incline to make it to a bus

that whined but always made it to its destiny.
We had visions that those days would end.
We always wished for things we couldn't have.

Going It Alone

What Joe and I had in common were the times we had to go it alone in life. There was at least one time when I made the train trip solo at age five when my mother did the best she could to get us both out of harm's way. I sensed then that I was different from many of the other passengers.

Train stations in the fifties were places where the homeless found benches and stretched out as though they had first dibs. Then, when at last the train came, steam heaving from its throat, conductors dressed in drab uniforms helped dainty ladies up footsteps to where they moseyed lightly, gently, to their seats.

The train poured its smoke, anxious to carry on through mountain valleys cut from stone, a deed done by conservation men, the Civilian Conservation Core (CCC).

Ticket in hand, Mom told me to behave. Uncle Billy would fetch me at the other end: a coal town where men reeked of black dust and women wore cotton dresses, some medium-gray from their CARE packages, and where homes smelled of fat-belly lard.

"The world is full of trickery," my mother said before I left. Now twenty-three, she said "I'll see you when I can," but *can* only came when more than a year had passed. I recall red lipstick smeared below her lip. She was trying the best she could to buck up.

I sat next to a dainty lady who squirmed at the sight of a young boy in tattered jeans.

"First time on a train?" she asked.

I nodded, in disbelief that she had spoken to me. I was hoping she wouldn't ask me any more questions. She obliged me. That was all she asked or said. I was relieved. Her tone was one of an actress or queen. Mindfully, my mother had warned me of her kind. So I stared at trestles passing by, mesmerized by the train's tempo, its pulse.

It seemed to know where it was taking me, to that West Virginia clan—Jerry Canterbury, our neighbor who would die in Vietnam, and Carl Dilly, May Dilly's son of Friendly View, who would later fall, or perhaps jump, off a bridge in Cleveland. He had epilepsy. The Canterburys kept off to themselves. May Dilly had the only television in Friendly View and invited everyone who wanted to come to sit on the floor and watch the Friday night fights. She always had popcorn waiting for us as we strolled in.

In Beckley, the train would not wait patiently. It would set out as quickly as it could to be rid those of us who had less the upbringing than those ladies who wore silk dresses and men who wore overcoats.

Near Beckley—Dry Creek—I would make baseballs out of pieces of coal, newspaper, and miner's tape. Though I was left-handed, the big boys would insist I bat righty. I learned the dialect and learned to fish where rainbow trout, so splendidly, ran along a mountain stream, far from concrete avenues and trains. Dreams there were more of color than cold steel.

The stilt house on the hill had been torn down. The new rental had an outhouse, whereas the house on the hill had neither an outhouse nor insulation of any type. We went in a "slop bucket" in the winter, and as children, we were on our own outside for the most part during warm weather.

Looking back, I wondered if Mom Tucker had been a trespasser in the old house. There was never a mention of paying or getting behind on the rent, only how she was going to pay for coal during cold weather.

Recently, Uncle Sonny, who eventually went back to live near Friendly View, warned me never to go back, to keep my memories as they were; that Friendly View was now nothing but a bunch of squatters.

There had been no windows in the stilthouse. Folks who thought the mountains were always cooler than the flatlands clearly hadn't lived in Friendly View. Maybe it was because Coal River nearby gave off so much humidity, but the summers were stifling. And the inside of that house was worse than most.

If we lived in poverty, or semipoverty, as is often said of those who live within the confines of the mountains or isolated areas, we hardly knew it. The women whose husbands had died of cancer had little chance of getting married there again. All the eligible men were miners who were already taken. And the single men, often on welfare, were often unmotivated to take on a family.

Food and clothes, an old house without much defense against the elements, some handmade hand-me-downs: "We get what we need," my grandmother said, "not always what we want. Ten thousand things won't make you better than who you are."

There was something about the village mentality—caterpillars that never quite made it into butterflies. We only knew what it was to be a caterpillar.

Some things never changed in my comings and goings between Richmond and Dry Creek. Joe sometimes attacked me for no apparent reason. It was only after one attack when he put his fingers close to my mouth that I bit them as hard as I could. He screamed and never attacked me again.

During my years there, Friendly View was a youthful village of thirty kids or so, the children mainly of middle-aged miners. It was also a village of old retired miners. Of its one hundred or more tenants, some inhabitants "worked the system" for welfare.

From what I could see, Dry Creek was neither dry nor a creek. Discarded bottles lay up and down a dirt road filled with ruts and gullies and rusty nails. Every house was a coal camp house. Some might call them shanties, unlike the row houses of Charleston. The rutted road led to Route 3, a left turn to the mines less than ten miles away.

★★★

A few miles away, on a hill, stood Mount View Elementary School. My memories of my first-grade teacher, Ms. Jones, are more vivid than many of my memories at five years old. Once, I raised my hand and asked if I could go to the bathroom. I didn't realize at the time that I had a congenital urogenital disorder. When she said that I would need to wait for the break, I urinated on my chair, pants, and on the floor. It was quite a pool. Classmates laughed.

One girl at recess teased me about the incident. I threw a brick at her that hurled beside her ear. I remember it was quite close to hitting her. The laughter in the schoolyard stopped. Ms. Jones let Mom Tucker deem the proper penalty as she saw fit. It was the way of the mountain.

My first-grade schoolhouse, later turned into an administration building for lack of students.

Path leading from Mom Tucker's house to the river where I spent many days fishing or just staring at its flow.

While my outward anger was rare, it was not so for Joe. The Canterbury boys, three of them, lived halfway down the hill toward the river from where we lived. They mainly kept to themselves, except when Joe decided he needed to make trouble. Joe often picked fights with the Canterbury boys for no apparent reason. They tried to ignore him. That only agitated Joe more.

There was a culture among the kids at the top of the hill, where we lived, and that of the "river kids," where the Aliff boys dominated the swimming hole and the cliff where kids spun into cannonballs. The Canterbury boys didn't share in the "culture" of either group.

"Come on, we're going to kick some ass," Joe exhorted. Mom Tucker disregarded Joe's vulgarity. And he expected me to join in his battles. It was just another way he expressed his reign over the house.

But when Mrs. Canterbury told Mom Tucker of the fights, his reign temporarily ended. Our grandmother told us to go out and pick a switch from the tree. As she had done with me for the brick in the schoolyard episode, if the switch wasn't to her liking, she told us to get another switch.

I remember the sting of the switch, typically on my arms or on the back part of my shoulders as I turned away. That would be one of many switchings I would get. Detachment once again was my friend. The switch was not a belt buckle, but I soon understood it was the silent weapon of someone else's anger.

There was no rule here regarding crying or falling down. I did neither. I was well beyond that phase. I don't recall how long the switchings lasted, but I had already become accustomed to going into a Zen mode, separating mind and body as though it were someone else taking the beating, someone else I hardly knew or maybe didn't know at all. It was not only the price I paid for my grandmother's anger but also the price I paid for being alone, feeling motherless.

I wondered in those days what was on my Mom Tucker's mind. She typically kept her thoughts to herself, with the exception of an occasional admonishment. I had asked my mother, "Did she switch you too?" She smiled and said, "Oh yeah, I got it too." Mom Tucker was quick with the switch, but when it was over, it was over.

It was then more than ever that I bathed in the mountain silence when I could. Eventually, I would come to know I was only a passing visitor, passing through the turnstile of the mountains, one year after another. Memories deeply rooted, the harsh anger of those in custody of me, allowed me those moments, hours, of witnessing the gentleness of a willow's sway. I came to craft who I was there. I came to believe it was the mountains that allowed me to stay there. They surrounded and protected me.

Later in life, the idea of having been taken to a village called Friendly View for protection was not lost on me. That roundabout, those revolutions between Richmond and Friendly View were, in the best of times for me, a world of dispassionate phases. Those strange interludes of Mom taking me back to live with Dad and his unfulfilled promises were the very source of my returning, time and again, to Friendly View.

Chore Bonding

There were times I truly yearned to be close to Mom Tucker and times she seemed to allow me to come near. The times she seemed most grateful for my being there were when I helped her with the chores.

My job on the winter mornings was to bring in coal in our coal bucket and stoke the fire in our potbelly stove. She would sometimes scream out, "That's enough! Do you want to fry us?" I took the job seriously, maybe too seriously, as I have often wont to do in later life as well.

At times I gathered coal before the next snow came. The bucket's dust covered my hands. I planned to gather more than for a night or two. Who knew when the next snow would end? In the house on stilts, the mountainside hill soon pushed the snow down over the coal bin where it butted against the old screen door, half-hanging from its frame.

"Come in, boy," my grandmother exclaimed. "You'll catch your death of cold out there." As I had times before, I peered inside. My grandmother's hands were often half-fisted against her face. I would hug her gently as though I were the parent. I would learn then what burdens she carried. I was one of them. She ignored my hugs.

Yet when I smiled at her and she smiled back, well, that was the rare reward, even if it were just for that moment. She was as alone as I was, only she had been left to take care of more folks than a body should have to. And like Mom, who did everything she could to protect me, Mom Tucker was left to care for her extended family. I would become better, I thought. I wouldn't need as many switchings if I became a good boy.

I swung the porch swing with my feet. My grandmother sat next to me. "Not too fast," she admonished. "That's too much."

My grandmother always had a garden. Across Coal River, Aunt Betty grew fruit trees from which she canned apples and peaches. She would also can vegetables from her garden and my grandmother's. In the evening, Mom Tucker and I often swung on the porch swing.

The swing, to me, was a thing of joy, as though I could swing to the rafters above. For her, a swing was not for joy but to complete her daily chores.

These were times I loved living with her. If only there'd been more of sitting on the porch snapping peas or cleaning carrots from the garden for a stew.

After My Chores

After my chores and often alone as one of the youngest kids in Friendly View, I sat back on the riverbank, staring aimlessly where rocks slowed the river into a babble. Then in strands, it was on its way again. I watched the way it swayed into a surface like glass, and the sun christened it as something divine, an almost blinding light.

There I ran my fingers through the river's curls, if only for the moment, to feel a part of it, myself christened as well. The river, in its rhythm, gave me hymns that can't be sung. But the serenity, even in my dreams was, and is, forever.

One of the areas where I spent a lot of time just losing myself in the river. Occasionally, I would even see a trout come through.

The diving rock: it seemed so much higher up when I was a child.

The Bryants

Other than where the river curled, I had another spot where I fished. I spent much of my free time under the swing bridge. That's where the biggest fish were.

It was also just across from where the Bryants lived. If I had a saint in Friendly View, it was Dixie Bryant. The swing bridge was also where I crossed the river to get to Aunt Betty's house. So Dixie often saw me there.

From time to time, Dixie said, "I worry about you, Johnny. Are you getting enough to eat?" I had learned early on in Richmond that we didn't talk about what went on in our house. I was almost always hungry. But I answered, "Yes, ma'am." That didn't keep Dixie from saying, "You wait here."

Shortly afterward, she'd bring me waffles with syrup. "Here, you eat this."

She was as stern as she was kind. I dared not disappoint her. Sometimes I took pieces of the waffles with me to the river and used them for bait or just to feed the fish. The fish always snapped them from my hook. I never caught fish with waffles, nor did I ever learn the lesson—waffles don't make good bait.

When I went back years later at thirty-five, just before Aunt Betty died of cancer, Uncle Billy took me to see the Bryants at my request. "Do you know who this is?" he asked.

Dixie Bryant answered immediately. "That's Johnny. I can tell him by his eyes." I hadn't been back for a summer visit since I was twelve. Twenty-three years had passed.

Dalton and his wife, Dixie Bryant, who lived next to the river.

The Bryants' children were significant parts of my life too, especially their son Butch. But I recall, and will always recall, the near end to my virginity at twelve.

When I visited Dry Creek at twelve, their daughter Bunny, who was likely about sixteen, grabbed my hand and took me up to the swing bridge, where she started taking off her clothes and suggested I do the same. I abided.

My trousers unzipped, I heard her mother call to her.

"I have to go," she said. "Mom's got some kind of radar or something."

That was it, one of the greatest nonevents of my life, nothing short of a young boy in heat who would stay that way that summer and for years to come. After that, I would only see her frolicking in the waterhole with the older guys, just below the diving rock where many of them spent hot afternoons that sometimes went into evening, well beyond dark. Occasionally, she smiled at me, only to turn back to the older boys.

Butch was about fifteen when I visited then. He was a bit "tetched," as Friendly View said of unbalanced folks. One day when the river was rising, he pushed me in, only to grab me quickly. He knew I couldn't swim.

"See there," he said. "I saved your life."

Later, my Uncle Billy, still a coal miner when I was in my early twenties, visited us in Northern Virginia. I asked about Butch.

A rare photo of Uncle Billy. He died of a black lung-related illness in his early sixties, several years after this photo was taken.

"Crazy as ever," he said. "He lives on an island in the middle of Coal River, and every time the river rises, I have to go fetch him and his wife. The last time I fetched him, I kept hearing a scream. When I went inside, he was throwing his wife over his shoulder onto a mattress. I asked, 'Butch, what in the hell are you doing?' He said, 'I'm preparing to go to Vietnam.'"

Butch never joined. Likely, he never intended to go; it was more of a pastime. He had numerous pastimes that even those on the fringes would have found over the top. He didn't seem to care what others thought. His unique world kept him entertained.

Butch also helped Dalton part time in the only mechanical garage in the area. He said he knew how to take apart cars. He just didn't know how to put them back together—maybe as much an assessment of his mental state.

Life with Aunt Betty and Uncle Frank

Aunt Betty's house. Some apple trees can be seen in the distance.

When Mom Tucker was in "one of her moods" and Dixie's waffles didn't sustain me enough, I stayed with Aunt Betty on and off. She was mild mannered and had the greatest from-the-gut laugh. Most of all, she thought I was funny. I could be more myself with her than I could ever be with Mom Tucker, or Dad for that matter.

She often asked me to go down in the cellar when she was canning to bring up Mason and Ball jars. The cellar was made of dirt/mud, and there were often rats, and how an occasional black snake got in, I'll never know. Her home was also the first place I watched someone, Aunt Betty, chop off the head of a chicken and see it flutter around in the yard, blood going everywhere. Maybe it's the reason I still don't like chicken, even to this day.

Sometimes in the evening she fixed me a Chef Boyardee ready-to-make cheese pizza, my favorite meal.

Their land lay next to Coal River in an area that was more primitive than the other side of the swinging bridge, where most people lived. While I found the river on the other side of the swing bridge to be a serene getaway for me, Aunt Betty and Uncle Frank's side of Coal River was even more so.

I never heard her complain about her life. In fact, I believe she and Uncle Frank enjoyed each other's company immensely. Uncle Frank was also very funny. It was as though he liked to hear himself laugh after a day in the mines. When he laughed, he usually started out a sentence with, Hell's Far! (*Fire?*) That was a sign of one of his jokes to come.

If Aunt Betty complained at all, it was always when she thought I was hardly within hearing distance. "Frank, I don't know how we're going to get out of debt with the company." It became obvious as I grew older that the wringer washer that she used to wash clothes, and many of the appliances she used in her kitchen, had all been purchased on usury credit from the mining company.

The Collapse and Explosion of the Whitesville Mine

There was no such thing as miners' rights until the unions came in the 1950s. However, even then the unions had little power to overcome the favor of politicians toward the mining companies that provided large donations to candidates who were easily swayed by corporate bosses' wants.

Uncle Billy had come out of the war unharmed after his four years on the USNS *McDougal*. Yet the mine in Whitesville, where Uncle Billy and Uncle Frank had worked in the 1950s and '60s, collapsed in the 1950s when Uncle Billy was inside; his legs became pinned under one of the shafts.

Fortunately, he was rescued. Billy was a supervisor who, after a short stay in the hospital, walked out of the hospital on crutches, only to go back into the mines—on crutches. He was afraid of losing his job.

That mine exploded in 2010.

Year after year, politicians ignored safety reports of poor conditions in the mines.

Now a forty-eight-foot-long spiky black granite slab, set up right along the highway into town, is engraved with twenty-nine ghostly life-size images of the coal miners who died in that explosion. There are no coal miners' women left to pray to a silent God in Friendly View.

As young men found little solace in the options of either mining or welfare, they chose a third option: it was time to leave the mountains for the cities where often a relative or someone they knew wrote back that there were jobs outside of Dry Creek and Friendly View. They only returned on occasion to pay homage to their loved ones.

Remembering My Stay with Aunt Betty, Revisiting Dry Creek after a Twenty-five-year Respite

As I grew older, I regretted not visiting Aunt Betty in my late teens and twenties. She continued to smoke, even after being diagnosed with lung cancer, right up until her death. I was thirty-five when I heard. When I arrived at her house, she was taking a nap. I walked across the old swing bridge, now barely functional, to get to the house where I had stayed with my grandmother. The house was still there. It had been white when we lived there, was now red, and there was a trailer on the property with a large TV dish next to it. In the back was what I believed to be our old outhouse.

When Uncle Frank died in his early fifties of black lung, Aunt Betty, like Mary Ann in Baltimore, married a considerably younger man. Unlike Uncle Frank, he had let the grass turn into weeds around the house. The house of seven acres was now surrounded mainly by oat grass. The numerous apple and peach trees, as well as the chestnut tree, were now dying or dead.

1954: The Last Time I Lived in Friendly View

A photo of my cousin Shirley and me, likely taken in Washington, DC, prior to my leaving to live in Friendly View for the last time.

Back in Friendly View at age seven. Being with Joe, Sheila, Frankie, and someone unknown, I fully returned to Friendly View's way of life.

My last trip to live in Friendly View was a short one. My only memory of it was a stray dog I came to call my own. I called my German shepherd Lady.

I taught her to race me around the house, she going in the opposite direction. I could tell how proud she was that she beat me every time. She would stare up at me as if to say, "Let's do it again." I swear, she even put her paw on the pavement as though it were our starting block. I told everyone who saw her, "She's the smartest dog I ever saw."

One day when I came home from school, Uncle Billy simply said, "I had to kill your dog today. Rabies." That was the end of the conversation.

That was the way of mountain folks. Sometimes they were the most loving folks a person would ever want to be related to; sometimes their lesson was "Life is difficult. Get over it."

I didn't get over it. She had always been there to greet me when I'd come home from school, staring up as if to say, "I'm lonely. Let's play." I felt that loneliness then—the only real playmate I had, gone;

the isolation, greater than ever. I never had another dog again. Lady had set that bar too high.

It was 1954. I saw my mother and father coming down that old rutty road together in his rusting Ford. I sensed they had made up. Maybe it was the hope of a seven-year-old boy that they would like each other and we would live together in the kind of unison I had come to know by being around Aunt Betty and Uncle Frank, the kind of hope that could be dashed in an instance, as became the case in short order.

Never to Speak of West Virginia Again

In 1955, the year after I had lived in Friendly View for the last time, Aunt Mary Ann told Mom Tucker it was time to give up keeping house and come live with her in Baltimore. My grandmother griped at the idea but moved there just the same after she had to give up Joe to Bobbie and John. That was when the oldness grew in her in short order. That was the last time she snapped peas.

Mary Ann gave her household chores in her row house in Arbutus, Maryland. Mom Tucker only left the townhouse to occasionally visit one of her children, several of whom lived in the DC area at that point.

She never talked about West Virginia again, or raising seven children and even their children. She just performed her chores for my aunt while Mary Ann was working on an assembly line for Westinghouse.

Almost unheard of for a mountain woman or any elderly woman in the 1960s, in her midsixties, my grandmother entered therapy to work through some of the issues that had caused her pain over the years. It appears that she died at peace in her early eighties.

Mary Ann's life took on a series of nearly unbearable events. While Mom Tucker went on to live with her for another decade, Westinghouse would eventually go under. Uncle Burl, Mary Ann's husband since she was sixteen, died of cancer when he was thirty-two.

A younger man she married shortly after Burl's death left her for an even older woman. Mary Ann died in hospice care at seventy-eight, with only my mother to call her from time to time. The last day of her life, Mary Ann called Mom.

"Nancy, I just want to call you to let you know I'm going to heaven today." She did die that evening.

★★★

Neither my mother nor Mary Ann seemed to be particularly religious. Although just before my mother died, in a clear moment from her dementia, she said, "I'm going to be in heaven with Mary Ann soon."

★★★

Just as Mom Tucker's life would change forever in 1955, my life ended as I knew it when Dad came to pick me up in West Virginia in 1954. Instead of Richmond, this time we arrived at night in Falls Church, Virginia, a suburb of Washington, DC. As Dad drove down the neatly separated streets of concrete and asphalt, I saw streetlamps, traffic lights, and neon signs for the first time in my life. I could hardly take my eyes off the neon signs.

The night people were dressed in fine clothes and milled about like wasps heading to and from their hornets' nests among the stores and bars and apartments. There was a mishmash of skin colors, the likes of which I had never seen before. They clustered in like tones.

In Richmond, I had been mainly housebound other than playing in the yard in a semirural area. If this would become my awakening at seven to the world I was made to join, I would find even more ways to isolate myself internally than I had in Friendly View.

This world was too disorienting for me. The kids were not the kids I knew. The adults were even less so. And if it all seemed too big to comprehend, I wouldn't see the ocean until I was twelve.

Chapter 7

1954-1960: DAD'S WORST DRINKING YEARS

My mother, about twenty-four, circa 1954.

In 1954, we began life in Virginia for the rest of our time as a family, which would last until 1960. For a very brief time, it appeared that we were headed for happier times. My father and mother went out on occasion. Prior to that, I had only witnessed times when he had promised to take her out but rarely did.

My mother, likely in her early twenties,
obviously expecting to go out. (Check out the necklace!)

I had yet to adjust to life in all the technicolor around me in Falls Church. So occasionally, I was happy to spend summers back in Dry Creek with Aunt Betty around the thirty-two shades of green of the mountains.

For the remainder of Mom and Dad's marriage, we moved throughout Northern Virginia or just over the state line into Maryland, in likely stolen trucks. And once again, we used Aunt Mary Ann's row house in Baltimore as a safe house when Dad's kettle boiled. My father came to realize that's where we stayed after he struck Mom at any given time. Evidently, he thought Mom would continue taking his battering.

One weekend he showed up at Mary Ann and Burl's house. Burl was at work. Dad was drunker than usual. In a rage, as he had done when I was four, he grabbed my mother by the hair and ran her into the wall in front of Mary Ann. He had no regard for who saw his violence. Maybe he even preferred an audience.

My aunt screamed, "Get out. I'm calling the police."

He left.

My mother waved her off. "Don't. Let it go."

What my father had wanted all those years seemed to finally come to pass. My mother appeared to be his whipping post, without consequences.

Consequences would take time. She appeared defeated, depressed. She was not the mother I knew, who laughed with Aunt Mary Ann and Uncle Burl on one of our trips into Dry Creek. I welled up inside.

Maybe I was the one who couldn't take it anymore, the one who preferred the loneliness. The occasional feelings of abandonment had been better than living like this. It was easy for my mother and father to overlook that something wasn't right with me. Something was becoming very different with me and would continue into my twenties and thirties.

Let's go back to Friendly View, I wanted so desperately to say to her. She seemed to be a mother without fight. But as my father had continued to miscalculate what was going on inside her, so had I. Mom was changing. Their divorce on September 7, 1951, had been a turning point for her.

She had taken enough beatings, she told him, even as he continued his old ways. She not only internalized his abuse but began to externalize it as well. Her own kettle began to boil. It was a time when neither knew the other's capabilities.

She would not run back to her mother this time but would eventually rise from the *ashes.* And when she did, it was another time indeed. My father had taught her what rage was; hers just needed time to percolate.

★★★

Our stays with Mary Ann and Burl became fewer and fewer. I saw less of my father in what I call his worst drinking years. He had drunk from my earliest memory. But the drinking was by far worse from 1954 to 1960.

When he left for work, driving a bread truck for Rice's Bakery's home delivery or selling Fuller Brush products door-to-door, we never knew if he would come home that night or sometimes a month later. In most cases, they tolerated him for a while. He was an excellent salesman. And when he was sober, people liked him, even gravitated toward him, as I did time and again. Forgiveness came so easily for me.

As the years rolled on and I saw fathers playing catch with their sons, I had reveries that Dad would stop drinking and one day we would be like them. Reality was more the days and years when my father moved us at night, even more often when evictions mounted and seemed inevitable.

★★★

In 1954, I was nearly seven. We lived in an apartment rented out as an attachment to the farmhouse on Gerkin's farm in Vienna, Virginia. There I found a certain serenity, much like I found on Aunt Betty's property. The fields. An occasional black snake.

Memories of Friendly View resonated there. My father often left us for weeks. So along with the peaceful surroundings of cows in the field and my father's absence, it was the nearest thing I felt to having a home.

But as typically occurred during my childhood, my father pulled up to the door after a considerable absence. He was driving a Henry J, a car built and sold by Sears. My mother became furious, not only at the sight of my father after his having been gone for so long but also his driving a car she knew he couldn't afford.

"Tommy, where did you get that car?" Before he could answer, she said, "You get that car off this property, and you get it off right now!" Mom was always fearful that he had stolen vehicles he couldn't possibly have afforded.

It was one of the few times he acted obediently, almost childlike. We didn't see him for a while. When we did see him, he pulled up in a truck my mother sensed he had acquired the same way he had the Henry J. But this time she didn't call him out on it. This time it was her time to act obediently. It was time to move again.

Living among those pastures and forests in the background had for just those moments given me a little taste of my fond memories of Friendly View. From then on, my "pastures" would be those of concrete. The fields of dandelions would turn to yellow stains of the homeless urinating on sidewalks where we lived; the wondrous diversity of birds would turn to pigeons pecking gravel to clear their gullets. The drive on the long winding driveway to the country road would leave me holding on to the one thing I could take with me from the farm—my mother was beginning to show a hint of courage.

My Love for Words and the Magic of Bees Grew

We moved into a small cottage behind the State Theater in Falls Church, Virginia. The cottage was infested with rats. But my mother, as she usually did, saw it as just what life was. She set traps and kept score of the number of rodents she caught in a night or over time. When my father would come in and pass out, she'd go through his pockets for cash as she typically did, even if it was just change.

Life changed for me in that cottage. I was often out of school, always playing catch up when I'd finally register in a new town. I recall my third-grade teacher, Mrs. Klinepeter, spending additional time with me, especially in working with me on cursives. My report card read, "Johnny is very bright, but he needs to spend more time on his cursives." I would receive similar responses throughout my elementary school days, with the exception of another third-grade teacher later that year at another school who wrote, "Johnny is bright and needs work on his handwriting. But I am mainly concerned with the time he spends staring out the window." All my life I would be a writer-wanna-be, cursed with a doctor's handwriting.

I became infatuated with words, the way sentences were formed. Occasionally when my father swore off booze, which was rare and lasted only days or a week or so at most, we visited his sister in Richmond. Her husband, Emmett, worked for a company that made paper. He discovered my love of writing, and he often brought me a couple of reams to take home. He was a loving drunk whom I adored. He had a great smile, and unlike my father, he never showed anger toward anyone.

It rarely took me more than a couple of months, maybe fewer, to go through those two reams of paper. I wrote stories. I have no memory about what. But I can remember distinctly sitting on the floor, writing for hours sometimes. I felt in control of the narrative.

Curiously, it was also a time when I sharpened my math skills. When my mother only had change to give me, she would ask me to go to the store and buy the largest peaches or apples I could buy for the money. I learned fractions on the scales and often learned to cost out the peaches or apples within a penny or two of the change in my pocket.

The most important thing about living in that rat-infested cottage was living within a stone's throw of the theater. The summer was hot, so we beat the heat by going to the movies, where we often watched the same picture three times to avoid the heat. We had no air conditioning. I remember watching *Lady and the Tramp* with interest. The beauty of the colors, the imaginative settings. I didn't know what it would mean to me later in life. I just knew there was something about that film that made me want to be part of it—the story and what made Lady Lady, what made Tramp Tramp.

But we would soon move again, to allow the rats to have their cottage back.

★★★

That year, as the rent came due, we moved to an apartment attached to a house. It was also in Falls Church. Mr. Bowen, who owned the house, occasionally stopped by. He told my mother he would "take care of her," as many of our landlords would offer through the years. These men somehow thought of my mother as vulnerable since my father was mostly absent. She always declined but never showed that she was offended. We needed a place to stay; she couldn't afford to lose her home.

The field beside Mr. Bowen's house was filled with bees. I became fascinated with yellow jackets, bumble bees, wasps, honey bees. I avoided hornets. For me, it was a great place to live. I didn't need to change schools, and there were tall fields of weeds near the house where every imaginable bug lived, including chiggers. I was a walking chigger factory. It was there I began to learn how to roll with the punches, to find new and interesting ways to live my life, no matter what the environment.

It was there I used mayonnaise jars to capture bees. My fascination with bees became obsessive. I found that when I turned the jar over, the bees would rise to what was the bottom of the jar, making it easier to add another. I saw how many I could catch in a jar. I often lost count as their numbers mounted. Occasionally I stumbled or didn't close the lid tightly (where I had punctured holes), resulting in one or more stings. I once allowed four yellow jackets to land on my arm to see what their stings felt like. With every bee sting, my mother rushed me to the doctor. I was allergic to bee stings.

But that never deterred me. There were bees and more bees to be caught, and more trips to the doctor's office to be had. It was the price to pay for something I loved. Yes, I had a fascination for bees, but I also had a fascination to seek my mother's attention, which had so often escaped me during the intermittent months and years I spent in Friendly View without her.

I don't recall the move from Mr. Bowen's house. It was 1955. I was now eight and in the last months of the third grade, I'd never stop staring out the window during class, even later in high school.

Brick and mortar confined me. More and more, concrete (even now) made me feel less in touch with the earth. The culture of mountain folks was well ingrained. But my connections with the river, Friendly View, and the mountains became lost in the fog that time brought in. I missed Friendly View. Terribly. I missed my river. Aunt Betty. The Daltons.

Most of all, I missed the mountains.

The fading times of feeling abandoned, even of my grandmother's silent or sometimes demonstrative rage, were becoming lost in the memory trap of what had seemed most loveless back then.

Photo of Frankie, Betty's son who would die of melanoma shortly after this photo was taken; Benson (eyes covered), Mary Ann's son who would later be shamed by several men in the family to take care of his mother in her last couple of years in Maine; Mary Ann; Bobbie (peeking over Mary Ann's shoulder), who had abandoned my cousin Joe; my mother; me at fourteen; and my grandmother, sitting at the table. Mom Tucker was in her early sixties here, an "old sixties." She would go on to live approximately another twenty years.

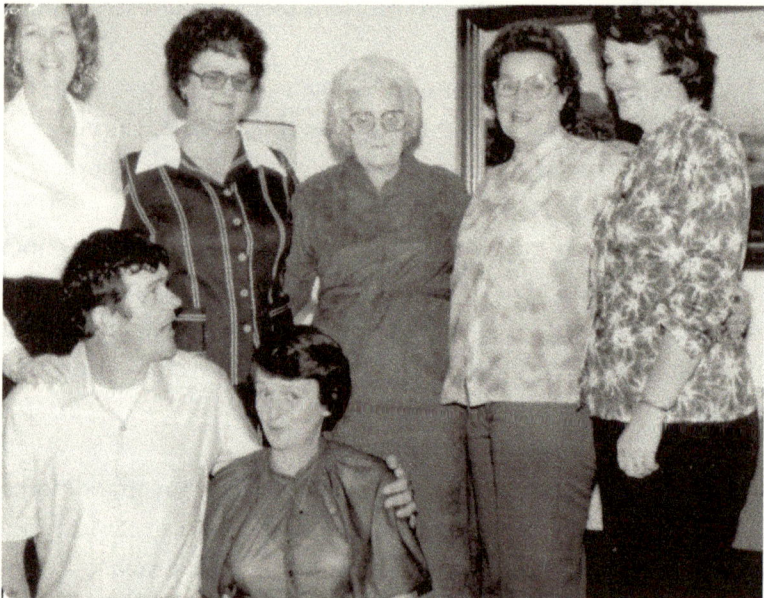

Mom Tucker with six of her seven children. (Uncle Billy rarely had photos taken of him.) Below are Sonny and Patsy, the two youngest. Top row, right to left: Mom, Aunt Betty, Mom Tucker, Bobbie, and Mary Ann in the early 1960s.

1955: My Mother Fights Back

Our move to the Willston apartments in Arlington, Virginia, our third move that year, resulted in my mother acting on her decision to no longer feel victimized when Dad came in with lipstick on his shirt or after a long absence.

One night when one of my father's drinking buddies knocked on the door and ran, my mother opened the door to find my father tucked neatly into the fetal position. It took all one-hundred-plus pounds of her to eventually drag him in with only the least bit of help from his stuporous state. I recall seeing the red lipstick on his shirt and the fury that shaped her contorted face. She brought him out of his stupor long enough to get him into bed.

When he woke the next morning, his face was peppered with brown specks all over that looked like measles.

"Nancy, did you do this to me?" he asked.

"Oh no, honey. Don't you remember? You fell in front of the door."

I don't recall much discussion, only that for years after their divorce, my mother would say things like, "I really got that bastard," referring to that night as she role-played how she'd hammered him in the face with a spike-heeled shoe.

★★★

While Dad was at work one day in 1956, Aunt Mary Ann and Uncle Burl came to pick Mom, my sister, and me up to stay with them awhile, possibly for a few weeks or a month. My father eventually came to collect us. He had been in sales of some sort and did not appear to be selling much.

What little money he seemed to make he'd still spend in bars and on women. His "sincere" pleas to get back together were wearing thin, but as she had done so many times, Mom reasoned that we had nowhere else to go. We couldn't stay at Mary Ann and Burl's forever, she reckoned. So once again, she acquiesced.

Later, I signed up to buy three books at the Willston Elementary school. When I took the form home for Mom to sign and bring in the money, she screamed, "What were you thinking? You *know* we don't have the money!" But she was not going to be embarrassed or bring our family life into the picture by not having the money to pay.

I had ordered a book of photos and descriptions of various fish, a book of stamps, and *Lost Horizon* by James Hilton. It was a novel about a utopia. I never knew what a utopia was before then, but the advertisement for the novel made me feel like I could live in a world like that, and I wanted *desperately* to live in a world like that. As she had done so skillfully over the years, Mom picked Dad's pockets for enough money to pay for the three books—and then some.

1956: Strange Behavior
Orange Peel

I was not quite nine, and my behavior was changing. I had never drawn attention to myself in school. I wanted no one to know what our lives were like at home, and my mother made it clear I was never to talk about our family. Anytime, anywhere. So I remained mainly mute among my peers—with the exception of one girl in our class.

Often, I sat at the lunch table, watching the other kids eat. Some days, my mother didn't have an opportunity to frisk my father's pockets for lunch money. Those days I knew I would smell the other children's breaths of beef and slight hints of chicken while I typically ate mayonnaise sandwiches for lunch.

However, on one occasion as we were sitting in the lunch room, I wanted to impress a girl. I pulled an orange from my lunch bag, peeled the orange, and ate the orange peel. She responded with a number of "ohhhhs" ... but not the positive kind of "ohhhhs."

My face turned colors, my stomach churned, and I became ill to the point that the principal called my mother to come take me home. My sister, Debbie, had been born less than a year earlier, and it was a half-mile walk or so to the school to tote my sister and fetch me.

"What has he done this time?" my mother asked the principal.

The principal shared the incident with her. On the way home, my mother retorted what had by this time become a mantra: "My God, son. You do not have the sense God allowed a mule."

Later in life, I would smile, thinking about my mother's constant berating of that animal, wondering what she had against mules.

My mother had to tote my sister to Willston Elementary School when the principal asked my mother to confer with her. Debbie's teddy bear was as temporary as the place we lived. Our toys were always left behind with each move.

It Must Have Been the Strawberries

The orange peel incident led to another curiosity. After a rain storm one day, I sat on the lawn in front of our apartment building and pulled wet grass and mashed it in a pool of water, making a grass soup. I wondered if the mixture was edible. It had acidic, bitter taste, so I soon gave up the experiment. But not before breaking out in welts.

After attempting to doctor the burning and itchy sores herself, my mother called on Uncle Burl from Baltimore to rush me to the hospital. The doctors were confounded by the welts that covered all parts of my body. Each in turn asked my mother what I had been eating.

"We did have some strawberries one day," my mother said.

"That must be it," one of the doctors said.

I nodded my head. Yes, it must have been the strawberries.

Why Louis Couldn't Play With Me Anymore

My curiosity with orange peels, grass, (and strawberries) never diminished my passion for catching bees. That same year, the passion took a different turn; I was only interested in the behavior of yellow jackets. I was especially interested in how they lived underground and had two holes in their habitats—one as an escape route when the other hole became blocked for any reason. I wanted to test my theory that they would all try to escape if one hole was blocked. From their escape route, I wanted to capture as many as I could. I had two jars—one for each hole.

About that time, Louis, a not-so-clever boy from my third-grade class, asked me, "What are you doing?"

"Capturing yellow jackets," I said.

"Can I play?" he asked.

Somewhat irritated that Louis referred to the experiment as *play*, I brushed off his insolence and decided it would be helpful to have someone ready at the other end rather than my having to run quickly to place the other jar over the escape hole.

"Sure," I responded. I took Louis to the escape hole and instructed him. "When I say, 'Now,' you just place the jar over this hole."

I returned to the first hole and soon thereafter placed a jar over it. I screamed, "Now, Louis."

If Louis had initially gotten the gist of what I had asked him to do, he had clearly forgotten now.

"What?" he asked.

About that time, yellow jackets poured from the escape hole and immediately attacked Louis. He ran up the street, screaming, waving his arms as he went.

But the yellow jackets had escaped just like I thought they would. The experiment was a success.

Weeks later, I saw Louis again. He approached me cautiously.

"My mother said I can't play with you anymore."

I had all but forgotten the incident. The days of experimenting with yellow jackets were over. So I spent the next several years capturing and categorizing as many varieties of butterflies as I could. As I had done for years in Friendly View, I remained a loner.

Moving into the Projects

The rent had only been overdue for a short while, but the Willston Apartments had evidently been less tolerant than most apartment developments where we'd lived. One of Dad's "midnight trucks" pulled up to move us again. My utopian book and my belongings, other than my hand-me-down clothes, were left behind.

After Dad's mother died and her properties were no longer an option, we only lived in substandard apartments and row houses.

For the fifth time between 1955 and 1956, we moved, this time to a row house in Arlington, Virginia, where my father would start a furniture refinishing business after he gave up driving cabs and selling door-to-door. The the smell of varnish permeated the house.

Those next two years were fairly uneventful, save my clumsiness that resulted in more visits to doctors' offices and, subsequently, lots of stitches. When I was nearly ten, I slipped on ice and ran into a tree limb, a small protuberance of wood spikes caught in my forehead. I bled profusely.

My mother said, "You'll have to go to the doctor on your own." She was caring for my two-year-old sister, who had come down with scarlet fever. At the doctor's office, a mile or two away, the doctor said that without a note from my mother, he could do nothing for me. So I made the round trip again, note in hand, before he finally stitched me. I don't recall paying him. In all likelihood, I didn't, and we likely never did. The scar still remains.

About the time my sister contracted scarlet fever, I developed a flu and a fever so high I saw snakes around my bed. I recall cautioning my mother to watch the steps up to my bed where none existed. She continually dampened my forehead with cold washcloths. We couldn't afford a doctor for either my sister or me. Since Dad had started the refinishing business, which didn't go well, there was little money for Mom to frisk. At times, she seemed embarrassed to send us to doctors when we couldn't pay. Other times, she didn't seem to mind at all. Sometimes it just depended on her mood.

Dad drank less during the first days of his refinishing business, but as the business began to fail, his drinking consumed him. Without money, Dad talked our way into the projects in Seat Pleasant, Maryland. Gregory Estates was an apartment development that housed prostitutes, families waiting for their loved ones' release from prison, and an ex-cop who had been fired for physically abusing children.

Even after living through the poverty of Friendly View, I had never been and never would be exposed to more down-and-out people than I witnessed at Gregory Estates. I began to ask myself, *Is this who we are?*

Of the vague memories I have of our time there, one stands out the most. The incident gave some validation that we were on the same decline as the other residents in the projects.

My father and Uncle Burl fought after Dad called Uncle Burl a name. Three police officers showed up. I was playing in the courtyard, and I could hear the screaming and scuffling coming from our apartment. When it was over, two policemen had Dad's arms held behind his back while a third one pulled him along by his unbuckled belt.

I had a sense of pride that this time it had taken three of them to take him down. When it didn't affect my mother, sister, and me, there were times I approved of Dad's bad behavior. This was one of them. When his bad behavior wasn't aimed at our immediate family, I found myself wanting him to "win" just like in the movies when there's something about the bad guys that has some appeal. This may have been about the time the seed was planted. My own version of "I don't give a damn" would soon take root.

We lived on a second-floor walk-up. There were four apartments on each floor. The apartment two doors over from us was occupied by a prostitute. My father would occasionally have conversations with her in the hallway after he came home.

On one such occasion, she showed him her arm, which was covered in countless black specks. My father told her, "You'd better get off that stuff," which I assume now was heroin.

Mrs. Rivera lived below us. She had two sons who took me under wing when we first moved in and asked if I wanted to go on a picnic. I nodded yes. We walked into the Safeway store across the road, where the two boys began to stuff potato chips and other food items beneath their coats. I walked out of the store and avoided them for the most part after that.

My mother saw Mrs. Rivera years later. She confided that her oldest son was in prison and her youngest son was in reform school.

★★★

During the time at Gregory Estates, I became ill. It came on quickly and with a vengeance. The pain felt as though someone were kicking me in the back, and I could only lie in bed in the fetal position. My mother used the little money she took from my father's pockets to take me to the doctor. I later referred to the doctor who examined me as a "ghetto doctor."

"It's just gas pains," he said.

I continued to miss school and outside activities for the next two years, still not knowing what illness plagued me.

One Positive Note

Our stay of less than a year at Gregory Estates resulted in several beginnings for me.

I had been out of school for some time when I started attending a school near our home. I don't recall how long it had been since I'd been in a classroom—weeks, months. What I do recall is my fourth-grade teacher asking me to have my mother come visit her. After my third-grade experience with the orange peels, it was fair that my mother asked me, "What did you do this time?" I shrugged.

My mother was one who always acquiesced to authorities. It was the best way to not bring attention to who we were or who she thought we were. I went with her to the meeting.

"Your son had been out of school for so long and was so far behind in his studies, I thought of asking you to put him behind a grade. But somehow, he has surpassed the other students in his studies. I just thought you would like to know. And I would like to make him the captain of the safety patrols. It would require him getting home a bit later."

My mother was so proud, one day she brought my sister while I was on safety patrol duty and took a photo of me with her Brownie box camera. Approximately twenty years ago, my mother, who over the years had taken thousands of photos, showed me that photo. She seemed about as proud of it then as the day it was taken.

1957–1958: More Moves

We moved from Gregory Estates the end of 1957. Nearly two decades after we left, Fred Trump, Donald Trump's father, purchased Gregory Estates for one dollar after it had been condemned. In October 2016, the *Washington Post* wrote an article describing Gregory Estates as it had been nearly two decades after we left: "Prince George's County inspectors had complained of broken windows, rotted rain gutters and missing fire extinguishers at the 504-unit Gregory Estates."

Their description was little different from the Gregory Estates we left in 1957.

★★★

At the end of 1957, less than ten months after we had moved into Gregory Estates, my mother took my sister and me to live with my Aunt Mary Ann in Baltimore. During our on-and-off visits there, I had met a boy about my age.

His parents had bought him a BB gun for Christmas. He asked me if I wanted to try it.

"Sure," I said.

"Do you know how to use it?" he asked.

"Of course I do," I responded.

"Then see if you can hit that guy's tires."

About that time, a '57 Chevy turned the corner and was just beginning to get away. I quickly pulled the gun up nearly to my chest and fired. Immediately, the driver spun around and came toward us.

Thinking that he hadn't seen us, we ran into an apartment building where we must have been talking too loudly. An older woman came out of her apartment and yelled, "You boys get out of here! You have no business playing in the hallway!"

About that time, a thirty-something-year-old man grabbed me.

"You little son of a bitch, you shot my wife in the head, and she's pregnant!"

He insisted on taking me to talk to my mother, and out of fear, I acquiesced.

"Your son hit my pregnant wife in the head with a BB from his BB gun."

"He doesn't own a BB gun," my mother said.

"Then what's this?" he asked, holding up the BB gun he had seized.

I explained to my mother that it belonged to the kid who lived down the block from my aunt's house.

"I'm going to sue you," the man said.

"You go right ahead and sue us. My husband and I are separated, and we're staying with my sister here because we don't have any money!" With that, my mother broke into one of her wails that would serve us nicely for years to come.

"All right, all right, just keep that little juvenile off the streets. He's dangerous."

It was the first time anyone had ever referred to me as dangerous. Yes, Mom and I often thought of Dad in those terms. But, me? Maybe it was an omen.

That was when Mom felt that we had better hightail it to Aunt Bobbie and Uncle John's house in Manassas, Virginia, before this guy changed his mind. We may have only been at Mary Ann's for a week or even less. But that was the nature of our stays with Mom's sisters.

As before, I would be out of school for weeks, possibly a month or more.

★★★

Aunt Mary Ann lost Uncle Burl to cancer the next year. He had spent most of his time at Johns Hopkins University and agreed to become a beta tester to various experimental drugs.

I loved Uncle Burl, but I only visited him in the hospital once, where he snarled like an animal from the disease and possibly the drugs used in the experimentation. Not only had he been one of my most significant father figures, but also he was the first important person in my life to die.

Dad's mom, Grandma Maude, had died in 1955, but we had only seen each other on several occasions where she insisted on feeding me that castor oil. It was her remedy for all that ailed the human condition.

Although I had never heard the word *grief,* I wailed at Uncle Burl's viewing. That was the first and last time I would ever cry at a funeral. Before that, I had only cried, internally, when my dog Lady was shot.

1958-1960: The Serenity of Friendly View Wanes

After Uncle Burl's death, Mom felt that a time in Dry Creek might help me with my sorrow. As I had at times, I took the bus back to Dry Creek on my own. Mom went back to stay with Aunt Mary Ann to help console her and to help Mom Tucker with the chores around the house. Aunt Mary Ann's home was still not a safe place for me to be in case the man with the pregnant wife lived nearby. Mom contacted Aunt Betty and Uncle Billy to let them know I was coming.

I longed for the serene days to sit along the riverbank. Just sit. Maybe, for just a while, it would calm all the turbulence and emotional pain I had felt back in Northern Virginia.

But Friendly View felt different with Mom Tucker living in Baltimore now. Her old house was abandoned, and the tall weeds had grown even taller beside the old rutty road that led to the river.

Aunt Betty was kind, but it became evident that I was just one more mouth to feed. As much as I hated the frenzy I'd known as my life in Northern Virginia, and as much as I felt that I didn't belong there—whether because of the kids who weren't of my ilk, or life as it was among the concrete sidewalks—I rarely went back to Friendly View after 1960.

Violence Escalated

My mother, age twenty-nine, just before or just after her self-induced abortion. She would divorce my father, this time for good, a year later in 1960.

About the time of the shotgun affair. Christmas was always a dangerous time, bringing on my father's worst drinking binges.

My father asked my mother to come back. For the umpteenth time, he had given up drinking, and Mom felt that for the meantime she had consoled Mary Ann as best she could. Dad was driving a bread truck in Prince George's County, Maryland, and again was paid cash from the revenue he produced daily.

Again, with few options, Mom agreed to go back with him. I came back from Dry Creek but felt there was little to come back to. We lived in a basement apartment in Landover in the Kent Village apartments. Kent Village was a lower middle-class neighborhood, mainly Whites, and was near a middle-class neighborhood where I made friends with a boy my age, John Pulaski.

His father was an engineer, and John would become a star pitcher on the baseball team at the University of Maryland some years later. I used to watch the *Washington Post* for articles about him. I was proud to read that he had four wins and no losses for the season at the time. We were both in our early twenties then.

As twelve-year-olds, we played a game with sponge dice and a plastic bat, and we even developed a strike zone with chalk on the side of my apartment building. I had made up the game, and John took to it immediately. It was always his first choice of things to do when we got together, which was often.

★★★

Dad soon resumed drinking. During the short season when shad were running, he left for a couple of days to go shad fishing in creeks around the area. The shad only ran once a year. It was an excuse for drunks to sit around campfires and drink through the night.

When Dad came home, it was evident that he had rolled over into the charred wood from an extinguished fire. He was wearing only a blackened T-shirt and filthy work pants and was unshaven.

As Dad walked by, John said, "Look at that bum."

For the first time ever, I broke my family's silence regarding what typically went on inside my house.

"That bum's my father," I said.

My family's situation never seemed to affect my friendship with John. Once when we tried out for the same baseball team, the coach called out the names of those who made the team. I wasn't one of them. It was obvious John was going to be the star of the team.

He said, pointing to me, "If you don't keep him, I won't play on your team."

There have been rare instances in my life when I learned what true friendship and loyalty felt like. To this day, none have been as meaningful or heartfelt as that one.

I sat on the bench for a few games until it became evident I would never get to play. So I quit. But my friendship with John Pulaski remained strong, even stronger, until our family left.

★★★

On days when my health issues allowed, I played basketball at a nearby basketball court. To call it a court is a misnomer. There was no blacktop but only a dirt area around the basket. When it rained, at times it was unplayable.

Yet there were several Black kids from a nearby development who played under most conditions. We played together. The rule was unless the *court* was too muddy to play, we played but wouldn't dribble. We passed the ball to each other, and if the ball got muddy, we took time out to clean it off in the grass.

When the sun went down and darkness became evident, I went home. The other kids often stayed and played in the dark. Black and White never appeared to be an issue with us. We liked the game. The game ruled our social conscience. That fact would serve me well four years later when my high school integrated and again six years later when I joined the Marine Corps.

★★★

If the pains in my side and back had been bad in Seat Pleasant, they were awful in Kent Village. When my mother could afford it, she sent me to doctors. One doctor said I had a vitamin K deficiency, typically caused by lacking green vegetables in the diet.

At eleven years old, I was five feet four and weighed ninety-six pounds. I recall the weight because shortly after that, a science teacher asked me how much I weighed, and when I told him, he said to the class, "Slim back there would weigh sixteen pounds on the moon." For whatever reason, even though I tried to *disappear* in class, I was often the butt of classroom jokes. I was an easy target.

My father began leaving us more and more, and as he came home less, we had less to eat in the house. One night my mother said, "All we've got is flour and tomato sauce. So I'm going to make us pizza." We ate my mother's "pizza" for the next three nights.

At school during lunch, I lied to the teacher in charge of proctoring the lunch room, saying I had forgotten my lunch. When I asked to be excused, she said I had to sit at the lunch table. Watching the other children eat made it easier for me to flip that toggle switch, where I was there but not really there. Those times, while not as severe as those three days of eating flour and tomato paste, I learned to check out as I had done staring out the window in the third grade.

***

I learned to caddy at the Prince George's County Country Club, which was only blocks away from our apartment. I had no idea if I could find work at that club where wealthy men and women dined and played golf. But if I had any characteristic that helped us survive, it was that I always *thought* I could find work, whatever it took.

There was a pro master there named Bo. I'm quite sure Bo knew I was in trouble physically; one look would have told most anyone that. At one point about that time, my mother had said we'd run completely out of money. Bo sensed that and took me under wing, and I truly think he saved us.

When a golfer would balk at my age and size, sometimes Bo would acquiesce ... but more times than not he would say, "He's one of my best caddies." I will never forget Bo.

Sometimes, I carried two women's bags on one round. And there were days I would go out again, if I got back to the pro shop early enough. I learned to transcend the pain of the straps rubbing my shoulders raw or my legs becoming rubbery.

★★★

One day, my mother cried because she didn't have a dime to call Aunt Mary Ann collect in Baltimore to tell her we were in trouble. We didn't have a phone, and it would have been three cents for a stamp to send them a letter. Aunt Mary Ann and Uncle Burl, before his death, used to bring us groceries often, just as Grandma Maude had done in earlier years.

I caddied that day. It was around the time we had eaten tomato paste and flour for three days, and even now, I don't think I've ever been that tired. It's something that, even being so young, you don't forget.

I went to the golf course, where Bo sent me out with one man's bag. When I came back in, I told him I wanted to go out again. Two women approached the caddy area. He told me that I looked like I'd had enough for one day, but I told him again that I wanted to go out. He gave me the two women's bags to carry, and I only lasted nine holes. These were not golfers. They took over two hours to play nine holes.

The required pay to caddies was $2.25 for eighteen holes. Usually, the men who played in less than four hours would round up to $3.00, leaving me with a tip. The women often took nearly five hours, and if they tipped at all, they made a bit of a spectacle in front of their friends to give me another quarter. These women gave me a dollar each to show their disdain—less than half the required fee.

I would also wade into the pond to fetch wayward golf balls and sell them. By the time I finished that day, I had made $13.00. I had earned $5.00 from caddying and $8.00 from wading into the pond near the edges to retrieve golf balls that had mostly just been hit into the water. I stood behind a tree and watched as the less skilled golfers sometimes hit one ball into the water and then, showing an unwarranted determination, hit another one into the water. I waited until they were gone and collected their golf balls, only to sell them to other golfers who came up to that tee box.

My legs were shaky after all that activity. Afterward, I went to the Safeway food store in the Kent Village Shopping Center. It's so funny to me now how I thought I was acting like a little man that day. I was taking care my mother, sister, and me. I was going to buy some food.

But when I got there, the boy came out in me. The only food I carried home was cut up watermelon and 7 Up. I bought my mother some cheap, tiny lamps. She didn't have any extra light in her bedroom, and she loved to read, to fantasize about something other than what we had. She kept those lamps well into her forties. I also bought her some stamps, and more importantly, I had money left over to call Aunt Mary Ann.

It was a long walk home with that watermelon, 7 Up, and those lamps. Like everything else I ever did in my life, when I thought I was finished and couldn't go anymore, I'd found a way to go a little bit further. Maybe that was the making of a future Marine.

★★★

During our stay at Kent Village, when Dad would come home to us, he sometimes stopped by in mid- to late afternoon to take me on his bread route. He was typically drunk during those times, and my mother always protested his taking me, but to no avail.

I carried my father's basket, full of bread, cakes, and other confectionary items, up to the doors of existing customers to collect money and attempt to sell them additional items.

In one such instance, my father hadn't realized that I was putting the basket in the back of the truck. My pinky finger got caught in the door hinge and cut my finger deeply into the bone. My father said, "That doesn't look so bad. Let's go to the drugstore, and I'll buy you a Coke."

The Shotgun Affair

As his drinking became worse, so did my father's lack of self-esteem and his increased womanizing. My mother often made threats after he'd come home. "I'll leave you for good," she'd tell him.

And our time at Kent Village ended for good when my father entered the apartment one night and said, "I'm going to kill you all."

He went to the closet where he kept a shotgun and fell in.

As he fell, my mother screamed to me, "Come on. We've got to go!" She grabbed my sister and ran toward the door. She screamed at me again, "Come on. He's going to kill us!"

She ran over to me, grabbed my arm, and we ran upstairs as my mother screamed to the woman who lived above us.

Our neighbor opened her door and said something like, "Come in. Hurry."

By this time, my father was coming up the stairs. After our neighbor locked the door, we could hear him beating on it with the butt of his shotgun. The neighbor said, "If you don't leave, I'm calling the police."

My mother reminded me later that she had been in her night clothes, and the neighbor gave her clothes to go to the police station to file charges. I imagine the woman drove her; my mother didn't drive at the time.

My mother confided in me years later that she had performed a self-induced abortion with a coat hanger during our time at Kent Village. "I wasn't going to bring another child into this world," she said.

★★★

Shortly after the shotgun incident, after having returned to Baltimore to stay with my Aunt Mary Ann for a brief while, my mother went back to my father yet again. When we came back to Kent Village, Mom called Dad's older sister, Turman, to let her know of the incident.

Immediately Turman came. Dad hadn't worked that day. The window to our apartment was open, and I was outside throwing a rubber ball against the apartment wall, when I heard a smack.

"Don't you *ever* talk to me that way again!" Turman exhorted.

Shortly after that, Dad received a letter from his brother Chester, pleading with him to change his life.

Of course, it didn't take long before Dad was up to his old tricks—the drunken beatings my mother took, calling her a slut even, though

Mom never left the apartment unless it was to visit her sisters when they would come to pick us up.

However, amazingly enough, after Turman had humiliated him and Chester made his plea for him to change his life, within the next year, Dad stopped drinking. There is no reason not to believe that his brother and sister's interventions had helped make it happen.

But there was another incident that may have been just as powerful.

A Little Bit of Bleach

Margaret Thatcher once said that if you stand in the middle of the road, you chance getting hit both ways. Mom would no longer stand in the middle of the road. "If he touches me, he's going to pay," she said to her sisters.

She kept her promise. For Mom, the mental scars were mounting— the drinking, the lipstick, the beatings, the shotgun affair—and they required a leveling of the score. For all the pain she had endured at seventeen and beyond, Mom finally said, "I'll kill the son of a bitch. You just watch me." A man can only mess with a West Virginia mountain woman for so long.

Her sisters, who by now lived within a short drive, encouraged her.

"You kill the son of a bitch, Nancy, and we'll watch the children while you're in prison." That tough attitude was the way of mountain folks, especially those of Scots-Irish heritage where nature *and* nurture were at play. Aunt Mary Ann and Aunt Bobbie came over for a "strategy session."

Like a teeter-totter, sometimes Mom had taken what Dad dished out and fallen downward into depression, and other times she'd shown a rage she never knew earlier in life, her temper skyrocketing.

I was never sure how serious they all were about killing my father, but they sounded serious. My aunts always seemed to show up when needed, especially Aunt Mary Ann. And I wanted them to and believed they could save us from the state we were in, but at the same time, I just wanted them to go home. Sure, there were times I loved my father more than other times, but the thought of him being dead made me feel sick inside.

Then, one night after Dad passed out, Mom poured bleach down his throat.

"It was just a little bit," she said later. "I wanted to let him know that if he ever even thought about touching you or me again, I would kill him."

When she recalled the bleach story again years later to my wife, Kate, she told the story with a giggle and always put her hand over her mouth as she did when she was embarrassed.

"Yeah, I did it," she said, embarrassed, yet somehow proud of what she had done.

★★★

We had been in Kent Village for several months. Dad's work was sporadic during that time, and he became antsy when we stayed someplace too long, especially if the rent was due or overdue.

When the midnight truck eventually pulled up, it was time to move again. We left behind all furniture and nonessentials that wouldn't fit on the truck. Again, as was typically the case, those nonessentials included my toys, model airplanes, comic books, baseball cards, and some of my hand-me-down clothes from Joe. I grew faster than Joe, so his clothes had begun to fit less and less securely anyway.

As always, we left abruptly, so I never did have the chance to say goodbye to John Pulaski.

Chapter 8

1960-1961: A FITTING ENDING

D ad had actually stopped drinking.

He started a soft ice cream business and had found a financial partner to help hire several people to drive their trucks. Dad drove one himself. They sold half-smokes, hot dogs, and coffee to construction outfits during the winter. Construction was booming in Arlington, Virginia. So we moved into the Greenbrier Apartments on Columbia Pike, a busy thoroughfare.

I was still suffering from the feelings of "kicks in the back." Dr. Beatty, a physician whose office was only a few blocks away from where we lived, immediately said, "I think you have some kidney issues." He charged eight dollars and later charged nothing when he discovered that we were struggling. He referred me to Dr. Bagley, a well-known urologist in Arlington.

Prior to the appointment, I had taken a series of aptitude tests at Kenmore Junior High School. At some point, an administrator wanted to retest me. I still had a bit of the West Virginia twang and showed little initiative in the short time I had been there.

When the administration read over what transcripts I could provide, it was evident I had gone to schools in undesirable neighborhoods and had missed a lot of school due to illness. It also seemed logical that I had missed some very important elements of my education. I don't know for sure if those were the reasons, but the administration felt compelled to retest me in the cafeteria, alone, with the exception of an administrator who proctored the test.

After scoring the test, the administrator called me to her office. She told me they were going to place me in an advanced math class with only fourteen other students. I felt there had to be some mistake. I didn't feel particularly bright. And I always felt like crap, physically, which took up a great deal of my attention. Also, I just felt different from the other kids. They had friends, and having friends seemed important to them.

I was in the eighth grade. At thirteen, and six years removed from my time living in Dry Creek, much of what had been instilled in me from Dry Creek still influenced how I felt about myself and how I viewed other people and my surroundings. These were not my people.

Boys at Kenmore often talked about going to Steven Windsor, a moderately upscale men's clothing store, to buy high-end Eagle-brand shirts. The gulf between the way they looked at life and the way I had been raised was of a Grand Canyon scale.

All the boys in Dry Creek had either worn their older brothers' clothes or clothes their mothers made for them. I still wore Cousin Joe's hand-me-downs. By this time, he was built like a block of wood; I was built like a tall fence post. So his hand-me-downs barely came to my beltline. And because the boys at Kenmore seemed to put such an emphasis on clothes, I came to believe that clothes should determine how I felt about myself.

Joe fifteen, me fourteen, wearing one of Joe's hand-me-downs

The math class was extremely challenging for me. I felt that if I really belonged there, I must have been the last student to make it into the class. The course was designed to finish algebra and geometry in a single school year. I asked few questions regarding the material. I didn't want to appear dumb.

One day during class, I dropped over at my desk. A surgeon's report stated later that I had malnutrition and an obstruction that required two surgeries at the Arlington Hospital.

I had been selling Christmas cards door-to-door after school, had a newspaper route, and often stayed out late to sell more subscriptions for my newspaper route. Later I won an award for selling the most subscriptions in the DC area.

The Christmas cards came for delivery shortly after my surgery. I felt obligated to deliver the cards to my customers. I hemorrhaged, likely from the weight of carrying all the cards in a large box. It required going back to Dr. Bagley's office for a procedure to remove blood clots that had formed in my genitals.

At the same time, with hospital and doctor bills mounting, my father had disappeared again. One bill after another had come through the mail, some threatening legal action. And his partner had absconded with a lot of the cash from the business, so he was nearly broke. We wouldn't see him again for weeks.

During the visit to the doctor's office for the removal of the blood clots, Dr. Bagley sheepishly said to my mother, "You know, you haven't paid me anything." I could tell from his voice that this was very difficult for him to address.

My mother started crying. It was her wail, as she did often in life when all seemed out of her control. "My husband has left us, and I thought if I told you that, you wouldn't see my son anymore."

I will never forget how quickly Dr. Bagley responded. "Consider it paid."

As we were getting ready to leave, being the sales boy that I had become, I asked Dr. Bagley, "Would you like to buy some get-well cards?"

He had a thunderous laugh. "Son," he said, "can you imagine what my patients would think if I sent them get-well cards?" He reached into his pocket and gave me a five-dollar bill.

He saw me for the better part of a year without so much as asking for a penny. When I became a general manager of a trucking company years later, at a time when I owned three rental properties, I told him I wanted to pay him back with interest.

I was twenty-nine years old then, often working fourteen-hour days and taking care of my rentals as time permitted. The work ethic I had developed as a young boy was still with me.

"Don't even think about it," he said. "I wrote that off years ago."

I would find out later that Dr. Bagley's son had become a prominent urologist but had died of cancer. *Where is the justice?* I wondered. I never received an answer to such questions for the rest of my life. If there was a God, he didn't come to my neighborhood.

1961: Divorce and the Knife Episode

Mom and Dad at Aunt Turman's house in
Richmond just prior to their second divorce

My father came back to our Greenbrier apartment a month or two later with a man who claimed to be his Alcoholics Anonymous sponsor. They say in AA that every drunk has to have a bottom. Imbibing bleach was probably Dad's, along with the intervention from his sister and brother.

He stood slightly behind his sponsor, Ray, with his head down, never making eye contact. Ray told my mother that my father wanted a divorce.

"He says he can't live here any longer," Ray said. It was obvious what his sponsor meant: it wasn't *safe* for him to live there any longer. A little bleach and the man was bailing.

As so often was the case, my father couldn't address his own issues. His mother had been his enabler. Now his AA sponsor was his enabler, if only to speak for him when situations called for it.

My mother fired back. "You go, you son of a bitch! You were *never* the man I thought you were! I was just a girl! I should have killed you long ago! You take this man, and you get the *hell* out of here! Go! Get out of here!"

Debbie was sometimes saddened by Dad's leaving; I was as relieved as I had ever been. I never had to worry about feeling threatened or waking up in the middle of the night only to be castigated. Now at nearly thirteen, I was the man of the house.

Afterward, an AA lawyer went to court for my father. My mother was "awarded" one hundred dollars a month for child support, which didn't cover our rent. Dad pleaded with the court that he was just starting a painting business and barely had money to live on.

My mother's temperament changed rapidly thereafter. During dinner one night, Mom had cooked a simple meal that included stewed tomatoes. "You know I don't like stewed tomatoes," I said.

My mother ran to her kitchen drawer and pulled out a butcher knife. I had seen her lose control of her senses recently but never like this. I grabbed my sister's hand and ran into the bedroom my sister and I shared. I heard a whack-whack against the bedroom door until the blade of the butcher knife splintered the cheap plywood door.

"I'm scared," my sister whispered.

"It'll stop soon," I said.

That was one of many times when I felt it was my job to be my sister's protector.

Soon it ceased. I heard my mother crying and leaning against the door. We would all be able to breathe normally again soon—whatever normal had become.

★★★

Arlington County provided home teachers for me for the rest of the year after my surgery. The following year, in the ninth grade, Dr. Bagley had only allowed me to go back if I opted out of phys ed class. During that time, I was required to rest on a cot at the nurse's station. I had never gone to a school that had its own nurse before.

Meanwhile, outside of school, I added a morning paper route prior to attending classes and also carried an evening newspaper, always adding new customers to my routes. I was so successful that the general manager of the evening newspaper would take away existing routes and give me new routes to increase the newspaper's readership as new apartment developments rose. Developments were booming in the area.

I felt like the man of the house, often telling my mother I wouldn't be in that night, occasionally on weekends. Sometimes I stayed with friends. Sometimes I stayed in the woods in the park until the mosquitos made it too intolerable. Then I went home in the early-morning hours.

I needed time away from Mom, as I had needed time away from Dad during his violent years. Mom's violence was different from Dad's—mainly verbal. But it hurt as much as Dad's belt.

For all my efforts, we were evicted from the Greenbrier Apartments, and the manager refused to give us our belongings that were in storage cages beside the apartment building. Some of Debbie's dolls, my Lionel train from when I was five that Dad had bought me—the one toy I was always allowed to bring on our midnight runs—and many of Mom's winter clothes.

I had failed to provide for us. I would miss my newspaper routes and customers who bought my Christmas cards, all-occasion cards, flower and vegetable seeds. I felt powerless, with the exception of one last act.

I let the air out of all the tires of the manager's old Ford.

Later, I would hear from one of my old friends that the manager had a heart attack. Hearing that gave me both a feeling of power … and shame.

Mom had sold all of our furniture to a junk dealer. Most memorable was the sale of a painting that had been in Dad's family for ages. The frame likely dated back to the eighteen hundreds. It was very ornate. The painting was a pastoral scene that reminded me later of Thomas Gainsborough.

"I'll give you three dollars for it," the dealer said. "I'm only interested in the frame."

"Take it," Mom said. The fact that she was almost giving away one of Dad's prized possessions that he had carried around for years, no matter how many places we had lived, must have given her the greatest satisfaction.

We had no more belongings to remember Dad by; Mom had cleared the deck of any tokens of his memory. And even as we shuffled around from one of Mom's sisters to the next, there was rarely any discussion of Dad.

Only after they divorced would Mom say, "You know your father's crazy, don't you?"

When I visited Dad several years later, he claimed, "Nancy is as crazy as a loon!"

In both instances, I remained silent; there was no room in the middle of the road. In fact, it was time to stay off the road entirely.

Chapter 9

1962-1966: MOM'S WAILING FOR
SUCCESS AND OUR GODSEND

After we were evicted from the Greenbrier Apartments, my mother became more and more depressed, constantly wondering where to go next, concerned about us being a bother to the next sister to take us in. And as her depression rose, so did her erratic behavior.

We went back to Aunt Bobbie and Uncle John's house in Manassas, only to go to Aunt Mary Ann's in Baltimore weeks later after I had finished the ninth grade at Osbourn High School in Manassas.

The administration at Osbourn sent for my record at Kenmore and told my mother they would give me the grades I had earned there. However, my grades were sliding. My own period of depression was kicking in.

Mom received enough money, most likely from my Aunt Mary Ann, to rent an apartment just two blocks from where we had been evicted.

It was obvious Mom was going to have to get a job, and it became just as obvious that as depressed as I was, I was going to have to watch Debbie, who was around five years old at the time, after school if and when Mom got a job.

As Mom scoured the Help Wanted ads in the newspaper, the only one that was within walking distance was a company called Melpar that built components for the government's Minuteman missile project.

One morning, Mom put down the newspaper, put on her best dress, and walked out into the living room.

"Where are you going?" I asked.

"I'm going to Melpar to apply for one of these Minuteman missile jobs."

"What? Mom, you barely made it through the first two weeks of the eighth grade! What makes you think you can work on missiles?"

"I don't care. It's the only job I see in the newspaper within walking distance, and I'm going to try. All I can do is my best."

It would have taken a thousand unicorns and six hundred flying pigs for me to ever believe she could land that job.

Several hours later, however, she came home and said, "I got the job!"

"How?" I asked incredulously.

"Well, they gave me all those tests, and when the tests came back, that man who interviewed me said, 'I'm so sorry, but you didn't pass the tests.'

"Well, I just gave him the loudest cry I possibly could and told him, 'My husband left me with two kids, and this is the only job in the newspaper I can walk to, because I don't drive. And if you don't hire me, I don't know what I'll do.' So he said, 'Okay, okay, if you'll quit that crying, I'll give you the job.'"

Mom started out on an assembly line with work she was very accustomed to doing. And within two years, she was a supervisor in the white coat room where there couldn't even be a speck of dust for fear of interfering with the assembly of parts.

After reading a draft copy of my memoir, my sister, who had been the executor of Mom's estate when Mom died three years earlier, handed me two pay stubs from Mom's days at Melpar. It was a moment we cherished as we looked at each other. That was our Mom; that was a woman who got just about anything she wanted in life, just from that wail.

***

In the afternoons, I took Debbie with me when I went to play sandlot football with some of the neighborhood kids, only to lose her one day. She had wandered off into the woods.

When one of the boys found her, she was sitting in the middle of the woods, collecting dead leaves and throwing up others toward the sky to watch them float down. She was nearly five when Dad left.

That moment stands out in my mind because Debbie has become a woman who can throw up the dead leaves of her life, no matter what is going on, just to move on to what comes next.

Another time I took her to the bowling alley.

"Is that your sister down there?" an obviously frustrated bowler asked me.

"Yes."

"Well, she's taking our balls and throwing them down the alley. Would you please go and get her?"

On the way home, she skipped along, about as happy as any kid I had ever seen. She had had a successful day of bowling. At five years old, she seemed so pleased with all that was going on around her. And all I could do was wonder, *Why?* How could that be, with all that had gone on recently in our lives? If she had felt like a pain in the past, it subsided at that moment. And maybe it was just for the moment, but she was so fun to watch just then, and I was proud to be her big brother.

When Our Savior Arrived
1962: Mom Remarries ...
Someone Else This Time

Mom and Bucky's wedding: Aunt Mary Ann on the left; Jean, Mom's best friend, who would later marry Mom's brother Sonny; Mom Tucker; Mom; Bucky; and Bucky's dad.

Aunt Bobbie said she worried about us. She wanted Mom to start dating again shortly after Dad's and her divorce. Bobbie had worked with a younger man, Bucky, when she worked at the food counter in the bowling alley. He was the mechanic.

She told Mom, "He's such a nice guy. You really should meet him. Just go out with him once, and if you don't like him, you'll never have to see him again."

As happened with so many decisions Mom made in those days, this one had to do with economics. She agreed.

After a dinner date, Bobbie called to ask Mom how it went.

"If you think I could marry him, Bobbie, you're sadly mistaken! I wouldn't marry that ugly son of a bitch if he were the last man on earth! Besides, he's too young for me!" Mom was thirty-two; Bucky was twenty-five.

But when Bucky called again and asked her out for dinner, Mom simply said, "Okay."

The following year they were married in Bobbie's house.

Bucky Crabill, My Godsend

At twenty-five, Bucky was more like an older brother than a father. I was fourteen when they married. We both had a passion for bowling. When Bucky and Mom married, I was able to give up all but one of my newspaper routes—I kept the evening paper route, the *Washington News*, for some months after they were married—and I gave up the weekend job that my father had obtained for me. I had worked for $1.25 an hour for several hours on the weekend to clean the cabin cruiser of the former Commissioner of Rivers and Harbors, who used to bring congressmen and prostitutes out on his Chris-Craft boat for a day of amusement.

Bucky's upbringing was far from Dad's. Rather than being enablers, his parents had felt as though they had more children than they needed to work on their small farm. So they rented Bucky and his brother to a larger farmer in Manassas, Virginia, for ten cents an hour. Bucky and his brother slept in the farmer's barn during the week and were allowed to go home on weekends.

At fourteen, Bucky drove a milk truck through the night and went to school directly from his job. "I could get a license to drive the milk truck, but I wasn't old enough to get a driver's license to drive a car," he once told me.

He was still working as a mechanic in the bowling alley in Manassas when he married Mom. Even on a limited paycheck, one day he brought me a new bowling bag, bowling shoes, and bowling shirt with my name embroidered on the back.

"You need your own ball if you're going to do anything with your game," he said.

Weekly, he took me and a friend of mine, who was also a good bowler, to watch him bowl in a league. After the bowling alley closed for the night and they shut the doors, the manager allowed Bucky and some of his friends to bowl for money.

Within six months, my game had improved enough that Bucky asked, "Do you mind if my son bowls with us?" All approved. I started winning more than my share of the "cash pots" until the other bowlers said that a kid shouldn't be bowling for money.

Bucky never called me his stepson, nor Debbie his stepdaughter. He always called us his son and daughter.

Chapter 10

1963-1965: THE WOMEN WHO CARED

Shortly after Mom and Bucky were married, I began high school at Wakefield High School in Arlington, but I pleaded with my mother to sign the papers to let me drop out. Moving to Arlington, one of the most prestigious counties in the DC area, made my inferiority feelings greater. Congressmen who chose to send their children to public schools often sent them to Wakefield, where I was now a sophomore. A couple of them drove Corvettes.

"If you don't do anything else with your life, you're going to finish high school," Mom said.

Other than simply feeling I didn't fit in, I still felt the curse of wearing Cousin Joe's hand-me-downs. If anyone could understand not wanting to go to school like that, I thought that it would be Mom, who dropped out of school for the same reason, after several weeks of being taunted by other kids in her class because she wore the gray cloth dress that came from CARE packages.

There were nearly three thousand students at Wakefield. It all made me feel small, although by the age of fourteen I was six feet, three inches tall and weighed 153 pounds. I ran just about everywhere when I wasn't in school. The only time I felt a part of anything at Wakefield was running cross country, even though my surgeon Dr. Bagley had told me several years earlier that I could never participate in sports.

Wakefield integrated in my junior year to the chagrin of many parents. The White students kept mainly to themselves. If there had been any acquiescence on the part of the White students, it was that Wakefield had rarely excelled in any major sport. Yet when Hoffman Boston, the Black high school, closed during my senior year and its students joined our team, Wakefield played in the state championships.

★★★

I had become a sports writer for the school newspaper as a result of encouragement I received from the journalism teacher the previous year. I hung around the gym when the Black basketball players were practicing among themselves, even before and after basketball season.

At one point, sensing my inclusion, one of the players said, "Come on, Bird Legs, get in here." At six-three and 153 pounds, my legs were thin, nearly to the appearance of bone.

They did their best to treat me as one of their own. But after ten minutes of poor showing, one boy said, "Okay, Bird Legs," which I gathered meant that they wanted to get back to their *real* game. But in the hallways, they often smiled at me, showed recognition, which I rarely received from my White peers. Looking back, my experience at Kent Village on that dirt basketball court had made my friendship with these young men possible.

To make my feelings of inferiority worse, in my junior year, although I had initially been placed in advanced classes after taking the school-based standardized test, I was moved to a remedial reading class by my English teacher. She sensed that the reason I never read a poem or short story was because I had a reading disability. The reading teacher, Mrs. Jacks, was also the journalism teacher. She had been a reporter earlier in her career for the *Kansas City Star*.

After several reading exercises, she asked, "Why did they place you in here?" She went on to say that my reading retention rate was phenomenal. I don't recall exactly what mine was, but she said that most average students retained reading at nearly a 50 percent level.

She said while my reading rate was slow, my retention rate was significantly higher than average.

Then she asked if I ever wrote anything on my own. It had been a long time since anyone had taken that kind of interest in me. *"Yes," I told her, "I write poetry."* She asked if I would bring in some for her to review. I trusted her.

When she read my poetry, she simply said, "Will you *please* sign up for my journalism class next year?" I did. After reviewing and including several of my journalistic articles in the school's newspaper, she said, "I would like to put you up for the Quill and Scroll Honor Society. What was your grade point average last year?"

"It was 1.0," I said.

The Quill and Scroll Honor Society required a 3.2 GPA. In my senior year, Mrs. Jacks asked me to edit the last edition of the school newspaper. I never showed up.

"Straight Ds." I often joked with my mother. "Do you know how hard it is to carry straight Ds?"

My mother didn't care about my grades. She only cared that I was still in school. I was a year away from graduating. After receiving my standardized test scores, which Wakefield High School and Arlington County required on a regular basis, my guidance counselor and advisor, Evelyn Wilson, used to call me into her office periodically and just ask, "Why?" regarding my grades.

I would just shrug my shoulders. It was not only an answer, it was an honest answer. I didn't know what was happening to me. *Everything* pretty much overwhelmed me.

I went back years later after graduating from college with honors from Virginia Commonwealth University to let the guidance counselor, Evelyn Wilson, know I had made it and how much I appreciated her being there for me at a time in my life when nothing else made sense, at a time in my life when life itself didn't seem to matter. I even confided in her that in those days, I had considered suicide and that she was one of the several reasons I didn't try.

She was packing her boxes.

"If you had come much later, I would have been gone," she said. "I always wondered what happened to you."

Years later, when she passed away, I sent checks annually to Wakefield's student scholarship fund in her memory.

★★★

In my senior year, I saw some of my friends I had known from middle school studying for the SATs. I signed up for the test. By midyear of my senior year, I was carrying a 3.2 grade point average. I mainly wanted to go to college because my friends were going.

Although I never saw a practice test prior to taking the SAT, I tested well enough to get accepted to Elon College at a time when the school was relatively easy to get in. They accepted me unconditionally as long as I graduated, which meant I could quit studying. The 3.2 grade point average became 2.2 by graduation. My overall high school average grade point average was 1.8 for my three years at Wakefield. Elon and Mom had equally set the bar low.

While my aunts had all bought new dresses for my graduation, I went bowling that night instead. I was bowling in the Peterson Point Classics money league at the time. I had started bowling at the age of twelve, and it had become my passion. I really wanted to become a professional bowler. *Who needs college to become a professional bowler?* I thought.

Often, I skipped classes in high school to go bowling. The manager of the bowling alley would ask me why I didn't have school that day. I had myriad excuses, developing much of my mother's manipulative behavior.

A new manager had been a pro bowler at one time and coached me for nearly a year. He'd charge me for one game, and with my own pencil and paper in hand, I could bowl as much as I wanted, sometimes as many as twenty-five games in a day while rubbing my thumb raw.

The Peterson Point Classics was a semipro money league. I made enough off my only newspaper route to pay the weekly fees. I also entered more "pot bowling," where unsuspecting middle-age bowlers divvied up as much as five dollars. I won many of the pots.

Since I was only seventeen, my mother had to sign for me to enter the league, and league members had to agree. One member had said no to my joining but would later acquiesce. The first week, he and I went up against each other in a head-to-head match. In the first game, I threw the first eight strikes in a row and beat him handily in the six-game match. I had bowled 300s, perfect scores, in practice from time to time, but in league bowling when people gathered around me after eight strikes, I lost concentration.

Later that night, he asked me, "Where did you come from?" I only smirked. I would have told him, "the gutter," having developed some of my mother's low-class paranoia. Instead, I took some solace in having placed him out of the money.

★★★

In my lifetime, after achieving seven diplomas and completing the equivalent of over 350 semester hours of coursework, I still have never attended a graduation ceremony. Like so many other things in life, such events seemed petty then when life itself had so little value.

Ironically, including Defense Graduate School later, I attended thirteen colleges for those diplomas—and joined the Marine Corps. I felt that advanced education, after such a poor showing in high school, and joining the Marine Corps, after so many health issues, would make me feel mentally and physically *normal*.

Even today, I feel something is lacking.

1964–1965: Carrie

Prepared for Senior Prom in 1965

When I was sixteen, several of my friends either had their licenses or their learners' permits. I had gone for a learner's permit, even though I didn't have access to a car. When I was asked at the Division of Motor Vehicles during the vision test to tell the tester what was on the sign on the left, I asked, "What sign?"

"Son," he said, "I think you need glasses."

Carrie was a part-time receptionist at the optometrist office. I think somehow she was attracted to my shyness. The chances she would want to go out with me were slim, but I asked anyway. She had been a five-foot-eleven model for Chris-Craft boats, and later I discovered she played classical piano.

"It would have to be someplace where we don't need a car," I said. She smiled.

"That's okay," she replied.

I often went to see her at her parents' apartment. Her father was an RCA engineer; her mother had been a radio personality at one point in her life. They were very much against her seeing me. I came from a divorced family, and they didn't see much motivation when they asked my plans for the future. They set the rules. She could see me as long as I went to college and as long as I graduated.

Without a car, we'd typically go to a local Howard Johnson's restaurant when we first started dating. When we'd walk in, heads would turn toward this beautiful young girl, five-eleven, over six feet in heels, strawberry blond hair that lay gently down her back. I soon learned that my nearly incognito presence took a turn when I was with her.

In our junior and senior years, we went to both proms with the same effect. Students who hardly, if ever, knew of my existence gave evidence when I was with Carrie. At our senior prom, during a waltz, we stared at each other as we turned around the floor as though no one else were there. At one point, I noticed that several couples had abandoned the dance floor as we circled around, even applauded at the end of the dance.

In those moments, we were unaware that our relationship had peaked. The rest of the summer, with foreknowledge that we would see each other less when we attended college, there were at times almost somber moods. I sensed that I hadn't given the greatest of assurances that I would finish college. But there was a youthful regard for wanting to revisit, hold on to, what we'd had over the previous two years.

Near the end of summer after we graduated from high school, we attempted to get married in North Carolina, where the required age was eighteen. Carrie was eighteen, but I wouldn't be eighteen for seven months. I had scraped across my birth certificate and changed my birthdate to a year earlier.

The North Carolina administrative clerk said, "This appears to have been changed. If you'd like, I'll call Richmond," where I was born, "and verify this birthdate."

"We'll think it over," I said, took the certification, and had my friend Lamar, who had driven us there, take us home.

The rest of that summer, I fell deeper into depression. I had no interest in college, yet her parents were firmer than ever that was a condition of our seeing each other.

While ironic that Carrie had gone against her parents' knowledge for us to get married, she occasionally still mentioned my going to college and graduating as a condition for us to continue seeing each other.

So I begrudgingly went off to Elon.

★★★

While attending college in North Carolina, I hitchhiked through the mountains to Radford College most weekends to see her, typically a six-hour trip. My main interest in life was being with Carrie, certainly not studying.

At Radford, she was a music major who wanted to increase her skills of playing classical piano.

The last time I had hitchhiked to see her from Elon, I suspected something was wrong. Carrie was still friendly, but her affect toward me had the effect of a weather report. I told her near the end of the semester that I wouldn't be going back to college. Our visits ceased when I left for Arlington at the end of the semester.

Chapter 11

1965-1966: COLLEGE BOY TO MARINE

My time at Elon College would best be described as a time when I drank wine and played bridge until it was time to go to class, often operating on little or no sleep. I was carrying a D+ average, and that was because I aced many of my first tests at the beginning of the semester and then quit studying. Even my D+ average was in jeopardy.

The dean of men called me to his office.

"I've received interim grades from all your professors and spoken with a couple of them. Your grades aren't going to cut it if you plan to stay at Elon," he said. "It's important that you take your studies more seriously during your finals and next semester."

Leaving his office, it dawned on me that I had no interest in taking my studies seriously the next semester. Still seventeen, I had no idea what I wanted to do. So without taking final exams, I called my father to pick me up. He had paid for the first semester. I had no idea how I was going to tell him I wasn't going back.

I stayed at my father's house and helped him paint houses. His business as a paint contractor was beginning to take off.

When my grades came to his house, he said, "You flunked everything. Son, I'm not sure you're going to ever amount to anything."

"Let me look at that," I said. "No, see, I passed phys ed."

To which he said, "You can't stay here anymore."

My mother couldn't take me in, and later I learned it was because she was embarrassed to tell me she was pregnant. Plus, she didn't have the space. She and Bucky, who had been married for nearly four years at that point, had a two-bedroom apartment, but my sister was nine years old and needed her own room. There was no place for me.

February 3, 1966: "Now I Am a Marine"

I soon lost interest in bowling, as my mild depression became much greater. Living or dying became inconsequential to me during a time when the Vietnam War was going strong.

I applied for a job at the Safeway food store without any knowledge of how I would support myself, even if I got the job. It paid nearly minimum wages. I had to take a couple of tests, mainly testing my ability to add and subtract. I scored a 100.

"I'm going to send you to the Safeway near where you're staying now," the human resources person said. "You'll be placed in the produce department if the produce manager agrees to hire you."

When I arrived, the produce manager said, "Okay, I'll hire you on one condition ... you cut that hair."

It was the Beatles era, and I had let my hair grow near my shoulders. I simply shook my head no. It was the beginning and ending of a potential career in produce.

Without prospects for a job, and soon turning eighteen, I attempted to join the Marine Corps. Initially, I failed my physical at Fort Holabird, Maryland, because of the surgery performed by Dr. Bagley when I was twelve. The physician at Fort Holabird said I would have to get a letter signed by the surgeon before I could join.

Dr. Bagley refused to sign. So I went to Dr. Beatty, my family physician, who said he would rather sign a 4-F form so I would never *have* to go. However, at my encouragement, he signed the form. I enlisted in February 1966, eight months after graduating from high school.

Recently, when my sister heard that I was writing this memoir, she said, "Yeah, I remember when you were making up songs on your old guitar." Then she laughed and sang, "Now I am a Marine. Now I am a Marine. I don't know what I used to be, but now I am a Marine."

Maybe it was a precocious moment, but back then, I really didn't know who or what I was. I only knew the world was spinning around, and I was having trouble keeping up with it. The Marine Corps would fix some of that.

My Aunt Mary Ann, who came to my boot camp
graduation in lieu of my mother.
I would find out later that my mother was eight
months pregnant with my half brother.

I learned only after completing Marine Corps boot camp that my high school girlfriend Carrie had become pregnant by her English professor. After boot camp, my first visit was to Carrie's parents' apartment to ask how she was doing. Her mother replied, "Didn't you know? Carrie is married."

Carrie had sent a letter to my mother's apartment. I assume the letter was to tell me of her marriage. My mother explained later that she had received the letter and tore it up. She said, "You didn't need that problem. I didn't want to worry you."

My first attempts to sign up for Vietnam failed. It was possibly a reverse Catch-22: *If this guy is crazy enough to* want *to go to Vietnam, he must be insane.*

Looking back, there are three reasons I put in for Vietnam: 1) I wanted desperately to get out of Camp Lejeune, North Carolina, because I hated it; 2) I wanted to be with my buddies who I'd trained with (some who later died in Vietnam and some who were mentally unstable when they came back); and 3) I felt I had nothing to lose (à la Janis Joplin). In the scheme of things, life seemed more like a rotten bowl of fruit than those perfect specimens that Cezanne had painted.

★★★

One day, working in a warehouse at Camp Lejeune, a sergeant called out, "Anyone who wants to go to Vietnam, form a line." There were likely over a hundred Marines working in that warehouse. I ran quickly across the floor and was fourth in line.

"We're only looking for three right now," the sergeant said.

My heart sank. Then he asked our ages. The Marine in front of me was only seventeen. Eighteen was the minimum age. I had been eighteen for nearly seven months. I was on my way to Vietnam. So I thought.

One day, just before leaving for Camp Pendleton, California, for my guerilla warfare training, I stopped by the dry cleaners to pick up my uniforms. As I was leaving, Carrie and her new husband were coming toward me.

The look she gave me was the same look she had given me on the dance floor at my senior prom. Not a word was spoken. Maybe it was a fantasy, but I felt that she still loved me.

After some time, her professor husband waved his hand between our faces.

"Hey! Hey!" he said. "I think that's enough."

While I thought that was the last time I would ever see her, I saw her in a department store from a distance after I came back from overseas. She was obviously visiting her parents who lived blocks away from the store.

Her towheaded son stood next to her as she reviewed sewing patterns. She had become a domesticated mother. *So what happened to the piano playing she so dearly loved?* I wondered. Maybe she was living the life she and her parents wanted for her. But it seemed a long way from her youthful dreams.

***

After thirty days of leave at home, I prepared to hitchhike to Camp Pendleton for guerilla warfare training. I had spent my money in bars, contemplating what I had done to sign up for Vietnam and what my mother said to me as I was preparing to leave.

"You're going to die in Vietnam!" she screamed as I headed for the door. "I just know it … you're going to die in Vietnam!"

The night before I took off, I had gone to the Hayloft bar off fourteenth street in downtown DC. I sat next to a Green Beret at the bar. Three guys who'd had too much to drink chided us to fight each other.

After it became too much for both of us, he whispered, "I'll take the two guys behind me. You take the other one." The music was playing loud enough that they didn't hear us.

He coldcocked the two he had chosen; I coldcocked the other one. We ran from the bar before the bartender could call the cops.

The Green Beret revealed that we were both headed for 'Nam, and who knew, we may even see each other over there at some point.

"Hey," he said, "I'd like for you to stop by our house. I know my mother would really like to meet you."

When we arrived, his mother greeted us with a smile. After introducing me, he said, "He's going to Vietnam too."

"I'm so proud of you boys," she said. She went on about how we would protect our country and how it was a shame that so many people were acting like communists, tearing our country down like they were.

I left that house that night contrasting what Mom had shouted and what this mother had said. Maybe I didn't feel like I was going to die in Vietnam, but I didn't feel like I was protecting our country from anything either. At that point, I didn't really know why I was going. I just knew it seemed to be my best option since I had no place else to go.

It would be years before it would dawn on me that the short scuffle in the bar was the first time I had ever started a fight, as brief as it was ... the same as my father had done in those bars when he was in the navy.

Guerilla warfare training at Camp Pendleton, California, nine months after leaving college

One of my buddies in guerilla warfare training at Camp Pendleton was Dave Brace. I called him Surfer Dave. His girlfriend brought him his draft notice while he was surfing on the beach. Only one out of ten draftees were sent into the Marine Corps, and he was one of them.

He became a radio operator in Ripley's 3/3, a company that saw significant fighting in Vietnam. Of four radio operators in his company, he was the only one who would survive.

*Group photo at Camp Pendleton. On the left is Surfer
Dave, holding his rifle high in the air.*

In preparation for going to Vietnam, we trained in guerilla warfare tactics at Camp Pendleton a month or so prior to boarding ship. When the day finally came, we were called to attention prior to boarding the USNS *Buckner*, which had been sunk during WWII but had been restored as a troop carrier to Vietnam.

"Eighty of you have had your orders changed from Vietnam to Okinawa," a colonel said. I was one of the eighty of over a thousand Marines bound for Vietnam who were now going to Okinawa.

Next to me was a man named Pullen who had four children. Later they changed the rules that men who had more than two children didn't have to go to Vietnam. I broke ranks, against Marine Corps regulations, and walked up to the colonel.

"Sir, Pullen over there has four children. He doesn't want to go to Vietnam, but I do. Can you change our orders?"

At the time, I didn't *necessarily* want to die, but living or dying didn't much matter either.

The colonel said, "Get back in ranks, Marine. These things are done at a higher order than you and me."

Okinawa Bound

Once we boarded ship, a corporal named Haas, who I had been on field exercises with during our guerilla warfare training, approached me.

"I'm going to call you P.T. And it's not for physical training; it's for *Probably Touched* in the head. Do you have any idea what you're doing? I'm trying to get over there to be with my brother. You don't have an excuse. This isn't John Wayne stuff, P.T.! John Wayne didn't bleed. Did you ever watch a John Wayne flick? Did you ever see him bleed? No, not once did he bleed. You know why? Because that's Hollywood. This ain't Hollywood." Continuing to avoid eye contact, he flipped the butt of his Camel onto the pier below and walked off.

I would find out later that Haas had been in Vietnam. He had been in what he called the dead-body platoon. His job was to piece together body parts and place them in body bags to send fallen Marines home to be buried.

Me, Nance, and Smitty on board the USNS Buckner, *which had sunk during WWII and had been revived to serve for Vietnam and Okinawa for army and Marine Corps support units.*

One day a guy named Nance got a little pissy with me. "I hear you went to college. I don't like no college punks, you got me?" It seemed to come out of the blue. No one knew when Nance was going to get pissy.

Haas got between us. He stared down Nance. "You fuck with P.T., you fuck with me first … you got me? You got me?" he screamed again.

Nance stared at Haas for a moment. His scowl would have scared most men. It was a scowl that said, *I'll make you raw meat.*

Haas didn't back down.

"I've had guys like you for lunch, Nance. So get that fuckin' frown off your face before I beat it off."

Nance smiled briefly, then broke into a laugh. "You're all right, Haas! Man, I want you in my foxhole if I make it to 'Nam."

We all had that in common. We still wanted to go to 'Nam.

Not one of us was pleased to have been issued new orders for Okinawa. I put in for Vietnam two more times but only got the offer to go when I had just over ninety days left in the Marine Corps. Going would have required my shipping over for an additional six months. I had already had enough of the Marine Corps.

"Now shake hands with P.T., tell him you're sorry, and give him a pack of your Camels," Haas said.

"I'll shake hands, but I'm not going to give him my—"

"Give him your fuckin' Camels! We're family now," Haas said.

Nance shook my hand and handed me a pack of Camels.

Haas was like a big brother who would mainly keep me out of trouble. Ironically, later the company commander would ask for my help to keep Haas out of trouble. He would not get a chance to go back to Vietnam.

Another Marine named Smitty was a mercenary. He loved war. He had been in the Australian Army, the British Royal Navy, and now the Marine Corps. He had also been in boot camp with me. At one point, a drill instructor got up in his face and taunted Smitty. Smitty told him to "fuck off." I never knew how he got away with it. Any one of us other than Smitty would have felt a lot pain for having done that.

Smitty would get his chance to go to 'Nam after several months on Okinawa. We became friends.

★★★

During the trip to Okinawa, the waves often swelled as we did jumping jacks, leaving us three to four feet off the deck. The sergeants who had been to Vietnam and were going back for a second tour seemed to delight in our hitting the decks hard. At one point, the captain of the ship called for all hands to go below. A typhoon was coming. We heard it was going to be a rough one.

As one Marine after another hurried down the narrow gangway, I stood with my arms folded over the railings of the ship, watching the storm brew. The rain came, and I still stood in the midst of a soaking. The waves started tossing the ship about. My staring out at the massive waves, nearly unaware of my surroundings, didn't feel much different from the boy in the third grade who had stared out the window, only to forget what life at home was like or, in this case, living at all.

The merchant Marines started battening down the hatches. One noticed me.

"Are you crazy? If I hadn't noticed you, we would have left you out here. Get the hell down below!"

Even then, I acquiesced. By then, the waves were pouring over me just below the knees, pushing me back. Something about the power of the storm drew me in. It became one of many times in life when I would respect, no, revel in, the dominance of a storm. If the wave carried me over, so be it. Later, a merchant Marine who had seen me above on the slick deck said the waves had been as high as sixty feet.

Down below, Marines were throwing up. One threw up, which led to another barfing, until nearly the entire bunk areas were swimming in puke. I bobbed and weaved areas that were hit the hardest.

"You there, Private," a sergeant called to me. "You don't seem to be affected by all this. All of you ... get to the showers if you got to puke, and you," he pointed to me, "you get in the shower and clean up their mess."

For hours I spent time with a mop and bucket cleaning up one mess, then another, each with a different stench. For the rest of my working career, nothing matched the squalor or the humiliation of those hours.

Up on deck the next day when the weather had cleared, the previous day's experience was punctuated when a Marine leaned over the rails and vomited just as the wind turned toward me. The yellow bile-like fluid splattered against my face and onto my work clothes. Maybe if I hadn't gone through what I had gone through the previous day, that would have been a moment for a conflict. He apologized.

"It's okay," I said, "just leave. Go barf on someone else."

As the ship drew close to the port and the tugboats pressed the ship into place at the docks, one sergeant said, "It's beautiful! It reminds me of Hawaii without the flowers." That would be the last time I heard any Marine speak well of Okinawa, with its benjo ditches (sewers), filthy bars teeming with overly made-up prostitutes, and drugs that no serviceman had ever been exposed to.

Chapter 12

1966-1967: "YOU'RE LUCKY YOU WEREN'T IN THE WAR"

When we arrived in Okinawa, affectionately known as The Rock or Devil's Island, Haas took over the barracks, just like he had at Camp Pendleton, California, during our guerilla warfare training. There were other corporals more senior than him. But they fell in line, just like Nance had.

We were in Okinawa as part of a direct supply unit to Vietnam, Third Marines, Third FSR (Field Service Regiment). There was no fanfare as we docked. We boarded buses and were taken immediately to Camp Hague. At the gate, I could see a tall fire burning in the distance.

"What's that all about?" I asked the guard at the gate.

"Somebody has been growing grass back there," he said. "The company commander ordered it to be burned." I had no idea that grass meant marijuana. I had never even smoked a cigarette before joining the Marine Corps.

Okinawa, and especially Camp Hague where I was assigned, had no saving graces. It was called Devil's Island because most Marines who came there, innocent in life, left after their tour of duty. They were typically jaded, often drug addicts, and disillusioned by their parts in the war. It was our duty to support the war and all its death and destruction. But upon our arrival, none of that sank in for months. But when we would eventually return home, because we had not been directly in the war zone, on those rare times we would mention that we were a direct supply unit to Vietnam fifteen hundred miles away, many unsuspecting folks back home would say, "You're lucky you weren't in the war." How were they to know the toll playing our part in the war would have on us years later?

I lived there for thirteen months, eleven days, and eight hours. It was a camp sparsely populated with the Quonset huts without air conditioning, an enlisted man's club/bar, a small library, and a small shop to buy supplies and some electronics.

Our Quonset hut was about a quarter mile away from the warehouse where we'd work. Behind our Quonset hut, the area was thick with elephant grass, stalks as high as six feet tall. We were told habu snakes resided in that area. Poisonous, they chewed on their predators like coral snakes did.

We found out when we got to our warehouse it had no forklift and no air conditioning. Camp Hauge was the pits of the Marine Corps and of Okinawa. Outside the warehouse, days sometimes approached 100 degrees with extremely high humidity. We had no idea what the temperature was inside the warehouse.

We wore T-shirts that became glued to our skin within minutes of entering the warehouse. The sweat cooled us slightly, but we also took showers in the morning, at lunch, and at night before hitting the rack or going into town. But as soon as we came out of the shower, our bodies were once again riddled with sweat.

Our job was to store and ship machine guns, machine gun rounds, new and used packs, K rations (K-rats), C-rations (C-rats), field ranges, and other miscellaneous items to support the war in 'Nam.

Sometimes when ships came into the port down south at Naha Beach, the officers would round us up on weekends, if we were unfortunate enough to be in the barracks, and take us to Naha where they would send us down to the "hell holes" where cranes hoisted large pallet boxes down to us. The cranes swung wildly. Our job was to steady them.

If it was over ninety degrees around the warehouse; God only knows how hot it was down there. Every half hour or so, they gave us a five-minute break to gather our bearings, then ushered us back into the hole. This went on for hours, sometimes nearly through the night.

Haas rarely got caught. He found places to hide around the base and seemed to know inherently when they were coming for us.

"I told you guys to get out of the barracks. Maybe you'll listen someday!" he would say.

I had been caught twice before I listened.

Binge-Reading Boxer

When not loading ships at Naha or working nearly around the clock when "things got hot" in Vietnam, I spent time at the library. I had hardly read a book in my life. Even in high school, I only remember reading *The Pearl*, a tiny work I found manageable. And although I never read other Steinbeck novels at the time, I found I liked his writing style. He wrote a lot about poverty. I related. Many of the guys in the barracks also came from poverty.

"How many books can I check out?" I asked the librarian. She was an officer's wife who volunteered in order to escape the boredom of being on Camp Hague. The island had little to offer the troops, less so for her. She looked pleasantly surprised. It seemed obvious no one had ever asked that question before.

"All of them," she said. "As many as you think you can read. Just bring them back before your tour of duty is over."

Someone, an American literature scholar, maybe an officer, had left all of Steinbeck's novels. In addition to Steinbeck, the racks were lined with many of Hemingway's works, Fitzgerald's. I started reading at the library on weekends to avoid being taken back to Naha. I even started reading at nights when we didn't have to work late.

Months of Warehouse Sweat

During the "hot times" in 'Nam, we worked through the night. Trucks backed up to our warehouse door, waiting for their turn for us to handload or offload goods.

Crates of machine gun ammo weighed nearly four hundred pounds. Field ranges weighed more. Without a forklift, we had to use what ingenuity we had to get them onto or off of a truck. They usually didn't look the same when they were finally loaded or unloaded. A ding here, a ding there, but goods were loaded and unloaded.

Haas usually sent Terry to the post exchange (PX) to get us some chow before closing around 9 p.m. Terry was a New Yorker with a thick Brooklyn accent. He was fairly nondescript except he hung close to Haas and did anything he asked him to do. But when it came to food, no matter what Haas asked him to bring back, he always brought back what he wanted. Sometimes it was oily smoked oysters in a can. Haas and I passed; Nance had no problems eating nearly raw anything.

"P.T., you've got to keep up your end!" Nance yelled at me as we unloaded or loaded ammo off or on the truck. When I joined the Marine Corps, I was six-three and weighed 153 pounds. After boot camp and on Okinawa, I was 175 pounds. While I had gained significantly greater strength since I'd entered boot camp, I was still weaker than most of the guys. It was obvious Nance still had it in for me. I didn't trust him. This time Haas agreed with him. It was the first time Haas hadn't supported me.

"P.T., you've got to start working out or something. You've got to carry your weight on lifting these ammo crates."

After Haas said it, I knew I was going to have to start doing something. For nearly the rest of the time in Okinawa, I worked out. As so often in my life from then on, I became obsessive compulsive with most everything I engaged in, as it was with working out.

Murph the Machine Gunner

One guy in the barracks, Murphy, was going back stateside. He had few duties—stayed mainly in the Quonset hut. He had three hundred pounds of weights and a bench, which I never saw him use. I bought them from him for ten dollars.

Murph had been a machine gunner in Vietnam. During a firefight with the Vietcong near a village, Murph chopped down what he thought were Vietcong. When he approached the dead bodies, there were four children. Murph freaked.

The Marine Corps had tried to put Murph back together again. He was on a heavy-duty drug, Thorazine. His hands shook incessantly, and his mouth and eyes often twitched.

Often, he lay on his bunk and stared at the ceiling. When he did come to the warehouse, Haas gave him light duty, like keeping records of what came in and what went out. When he checked out, he didn't say goodbye to anyone. When the rest of us were working at the warehouse one day, he just left.

The corps was short on experienced gunners, but it finally gave up on Murph. It sent him back home to do whatever it was that guilt-ridden machine gunners, child killers, did when the war was over for them. For Murph, it was over. I wondered what would happen to him after that. Was that something someone could get over? The war tallied many casualties.

I still think of Murph from time to time. The pain. Whether or not the government abandoned him after the war.

The guilt also set in with me. I was sending machine guns and machine gun rounds to Vietnam that killed men, women, and, as Murph discovered, even children.

"That's okay," Haas said. "He wasn't one of us anyway."

The rest of us were what can only be described as the "Haas clan." We followed Haas's every instruction.

Most of the time, I saw Haas as the big brother I'd never had, someone to look up to. But there were times he could be cold. I wondered if it was what Vietnam did to him. All those dead body parts—Murph must have been a reminder of what Haas had gone through over there.

I was beginning to hear clearly what Haas had told me on the *Buckner*. This was not John Wayne stuff. People changed. I didn't want to, but I was changing. I was living vicariously through Murphy and Haas. My anger over the war, the body parts, the dead children, turned to rage. Just like my father's, my fury needed someplace to go.

Johnson's Haircut

I had a workout partner named Johnson. Johnson was only with us a short while. He put in for and was eventually sent to Vietnam. Shortly after he arrived on Okinawa, an officer came into our Quonset hut and informed Johnson that his father had noticed a number of charges for new clothes at Neiman Marcus just before he had joined the Marine Corps.

It was obvious Johnson came from a well-to-do family, unlike most of the rest of us. And what he thought he was going to need new clothes for, especially from Neiman Marcus, in the Marine Corps, was a mystery. As Johnson's punishment, his father asked the Marine Corps to take the amount Johnson had charged out of his pay until he had fully paid up. The Marine Corps agreed and was merciless. It hardly gave him enough money to pay for basic expenses.

He came to me one day and said, "P.T., I don't know what I'm going to do. I can't even afford a haircut."

Knowing he was used to getting a fine razor cut, I told him that I could give him a razor cut.

"That would be great, P.T.!" he exclaimed. "You know how to do that?"

"Of course," I said with an air of authority.

I had no idea how to give a razor cut but was willing to try to help a buddy. So I took a razor out of my shaving kit and began to cut and scrape his hair. When I was finished, he had patches of hair missing along with a mixture of trickles of blood.

The next morning when the officer of the day inspected us, he looked at Johnson and broke out laughing.

"Corporal, who did this to you?"

Johnson pointed to me. The officer went into a guttural laugh, the likes of which I had never heard from an officer.

"Dismissed, Goddammit," he said. "I said dismissed!"

Thankfully, Johnson was the forgiving type.

P.T. the Enforcer

I continued to work out even after Johnson was gone. I felt a new sense of power I had never felt before. And the guys in the barracks noticed it too. While Haas was still the go-to guy for decision making, I became the guy they came to when someone outside of our barracks was messing with them. In short, I had become our Quonset hut's protector and enforcer.

I didn't know what a protector was then, but for the first time in my life, I felt it was my job to look after my buddies, and that sometimes meant being the enforcer, especially in town. I emulated Haas where I could.

Even for guys I didn't know, when I saw a guy picking on another guy, I felt it was my obligation to step in. Along with my feeling over what Haas and Murphy had gone through, the anger built up over the years from my father's abuse was unleashing.

I don't know how many noses I broke, but I broke a few in bars. And with my new strength, on one occasion, I threw a guy over the bar.

The guys who went to town with me would brag about my antics when we came back to the barracks. I don't recall how it came to pass. Maybe the guys even bragged about it to our commanding officer, Officer Blake, who felt he had to put a stop to it.

"With all that piss and vinegar, I want you to go out for the boxing team."

I balked, but he insisted.

He also made sure I had plenty to eat since I was burning a significant number of calories. I chose to fight at light heavyweight at

175 pounds, and I would actually require some weight loss while still finding a way to maintain my strength. I had been gaining too much weight from eating omelets with eight eggs for breakfast and protein drinks I made with a quart of milk. I had watched the heavyweights work out. I knew I couldn't beat them. There were a couple of light heavyweights I knew I could take on.

I had first learned to box when I was ten at a boy's club at Gregory Estates in Seat Pleasant, Maryland. The police officer who ran the boy's club was eventually kicked off the force for brutality to children. He had boxed my ears plenty of times.

Now as I trained for the team, Blake arranged it with the powers that be to allow me to go into the mess hall at night and eat whatever I wanted to eat, as long as I cleaned up everything before I left.

One night at the mess hall after a workout, a guy in our barracks insisted on a taking photo of me eating my workout reward for going out for the boxing team. So I took him there one night for this photo shoot. I hope he became a photographer. He had a passion for it.

During the first round of my first fight, I nailed the guy, just like I had done in the bars. He was fairly short and dumpy. No more a boxer than I was. He was bleeding from the nose and mouth. I kept waiting for the referee to stop the fight. He didn't.

I took some pity on him and only hit him lightly on what was assuredly a broken nose. He screamed. The referee finally stopped the fight. I didn't feel like a victor. It was just another time I felt like the father who loved barroom fights.

The next time, I fought a semipro boxer from Houston, Texas. I missed his nose but closed one of his eyes. After that he pummeled me for three rounds. I was knocked out on my feet. Every time I saw an opening and I swung, it felt like slow motion. My arms were like rubber.

The next morning, Blake came to the warehouse, jovial as ever, possibly expecting to hear that I had done to this guy what I did to the first one. None of the guys had mentioned it to him, likely embarrassed for me.

"How did it go last night?" He asked.

I turned to face him. My face was a mass of bruises, not a white place on my face, my right eye nearly shut. It hurt to turn. I had totally shut the other guy's eye, if that mattered to anyone.

"My God!" he exclaimed and immediately turned and left the warehouse. My boxing days were over. My days of late-night stopovers at the mess hall also ended. Possibly, the company commander had achieved his ultimate goal. I never wanted to harm anyone again. Ever. But it wouldn't be long until I was back at it again. The next time it was something that could have given me brig time, something that could have ruined my life.

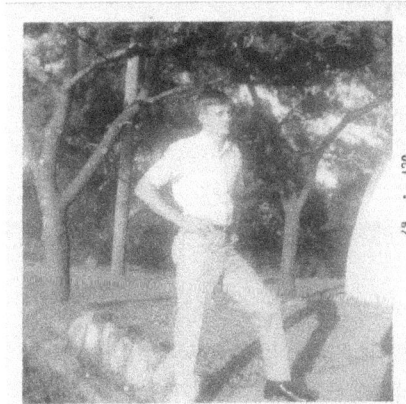

Photo taken two weeks after the second fight. I still had a black eye, which is hard to see from this photo. Also, compared to a photo in the Enlisted Man's Club shown with Haas and the gang, my weight loss for the fights become evident. Sometimes, I blamed the weight loss for my losing the match, not the fact that I had little to no skill as a boxer.

Reckoning with Death

Months before leaving Okinawa, I would learn that my best buddy, Amato, from boot camp and in guerilla warfare training at Camp Pendleton, had been killed by small arms fire. We would have been in the same unit if my orders hadn't changed.

"How could that happen?" I kept asking myself. "How could that happen?"

After my charade as a boxer and learning of Mike's death, I spent most of my free time on Okinawa going to Moon Beach and watching the ocean waves come up on the volcanic rock where I sat. Similar to Buddhist meditation, as I had done as I stared out the window as a youth, I was able to disengage from myself and focus on what was there: the waves. I let the pain of loss weave in and out with each wave. Nothing more, nothing less.

Moon Beach was also the closest thing to Friendly View on Okinawa, though it was opposite BC Street, which was filled with bars, Okinawan gangs, drugs, and prostitutes. Lots of prostitutes. When the naval ships came in, a "short time" with a prostitute went from four to six dollars. An all-nighter, ten dollars.

My experience with death followed me, even after I got out of the corps. Two years later I was working in a Safeway store near the one that turned me down prior to my joining the corps. One of our training sergeants, Irby, from Camp Pendleton walked in. He had gone to 'Nam. His wavy hair that had been dark in color when we were in California was now silvery white. He came to me and shook my hand.

"You remember Lemke, don't you?"

"Yes," I said. Lemke had been a very quiet, gentle soul, very much like my buddy Amato.

"Well, when we were at Pendleton, he said, 'I'm going to get it.' And he did."

The now sergeant walked off. There was nothing left to say. Nothing at all. It was those times I still thought of Haas and what he must have witnessed with all the death around him in the fields—the body parts, the odor of death. I could smell it with him, even as time passed by.

Haas's Brother Visits

Things changed one day when Haas heard his brother was coming to Okinawa on R&R (rest and relaxation). Haas's voice cracked. His palms sweated. His eyes wandered about when he spoke.

"His mug isn't as pretty as mine. So don't think it is," Haas said, laughing softly, somewhat tentatively. Haas had a face that was akin to a bulldog's. Puffy cheeks, square jaw, thick forehead. He was pale skinned and only seemed to burn rather than tan in the sun and heat like the rest of us.

The next day Haas's brother arrived. He wore battle fatigues and carried a sea bag over his shoulder. He looked younger than Haas but otherwise was the spitting image of him. He spoke with the same Chicago accent as Haas, only much faster.

"So why ain't you in 'Nam yet, brother?" He laughed as he stared at Haas. "Haven't gone yellow on me, have you?"

For a moment, Haas only stared at his brother. Haas was teary-eyed. He turned his head away from the rest of us. "Naw, I haven't turned yellow," Haas said, finally hugging his brother. "What's up with the sea bag? Haven't you checked in yet?"

Younger Haas would be stationed at Sukiran, about ten miles south of us. The facilities were air conditioned there. It was like a resort hotel compared to Hauge.

"Naw, I have time. I want to show you something." His brother took out a finger that was partly suspended in some kind of fluid. "I took it from a VC."

I turned away. War. I imagined the way someone would dismember an appendage. Haas was right. This was not John Wayne's war. What was there about 'Nam that I had wanted to go there?

Finally, I looked into the younger Haas's eyes. His eyes were somewhat glazed; his irises were nearly black; his lips trembled somewhat. Possibly he was waiting for his brother's approval.

"Man, I don't know little brother," Haas said, turning the jar around, taking in the finger from every angle. "This is some heavy shit."

I don't recall that we ever found out younger Haas's name. Haas only referred to him as Little Brother. I sensed this took Haas back to his time in 'Nam when he attempted to put together the right body parts in the right body bag to send back to the States. He seemed uptight. The corners of his lips turned down, and his eyes squinted as he turned the jar. "Nine months you've been there now, and this is what it's done to you?" Haas asked.

His brother settled down, sat on Murphy's bunk, and told us his war stories.

The VC (Vietcong) had started firing from a wooded area near a clearing. His platoon returned fire. The VC advanced another unit that had set up at a ninety-degree angle to the other VC group that fired on the American platoon, making advancement or retreat nearly impossible. When the Americans retreated to their right, the VC had set up punji stakes in dug-out pits, soiled with feces and urine, covered with grass. Some of his buddies fell in. The anguish of watching them bleed from their torsos and legs.

Medics did what they could. Those Marines still healthy enough worked around the perimeter and found some laggard VC who were celebrating their victory. That was when the Marines pinned them down and eventually killed them. The one VC was lucky that Haas's brother had only taken a finger, he told us. The Marines had found some of their guys with detached genitals in their mouths. So the VCs got what they deserved.

"And that isn't all," Haas's brother continued, "The VC women would come into camp, put the moves on our guys, and give them the Black Syph."

"What's that?" I asked.

"Syphilis, man. These babes know they're going to die. But so what? They can take out a dozen or more of us before they do. Incurable. I've heard they send these guys to the Philippines to die."

All I could think about was what the military tells their families stateside: *I'm sorry to tell you that your son died of Black Syph.*

Blake gave Haas time off to spend the week with his brother. The rest of us shouldered the workload. Blake had come up through the ranks. He was like one of us and kept us out of trouble as best as he could. We gave him a run for his money.

Now he spent most of his time chasing wives of officers who were in 'Nam. He was good at it. He had that Dean Martin look. All of us in the barracks stood guard duty at the gate from time to time. When an unauthorized person came through, we were supposed to stop them and ask the nature of their business, even if they were with an officer. Whenever Blake came through with another officer's wife, he waved; we waved back. It was the least we could do for him keeping us out of trouble.

When Haas's brother went back to 'Nam, Haas came over and sat on my bunk. I was reading Steinbeck's *Our Winter of Discontent*. I was right at the end when the protagonist walked out into the water, presumably to kill himself.

"What's that you're reading?" Haas asked.

"Steinbeck," I said. I could have gone into the whole thing about this guy's life turning out bad and how he just wanted to end it all. But when I looked at Haas, I thought better of it.

"What did you think of my brother?"

I felt I owed it to him to be honest. "I think he's got some problems," I said.

"Yeah, I guess so. I told him the same thing before he left. I told him just to get his ass back home safely. I told him that he ain't going to see me over there. I don't know what I was thinking. I think he'll be all right if he just doesn't try any John Wayne shit."

Haas Plunges into the Deep End

I had now finished all of Steinbeck's works that were in the library. Five of them. I turned to Fitzgerald. There were three of Fitzgerald's works I had checked out of the library. As I picked up *The Great Gatsby*, I heard Haas scream out, "I am the Chicken Man." He screamed out in a shrill, squeaky voice, then clucked. I left him alone for a while. I read through *Gatsby* that evening. Just before it was time for lights out, I walked over to Haas's bunk.

"Are you okay?" I asked.

"Don't I look okay, P.T.?" He was almost in a fetal position. "What you got there? Another book?"

"*The Great Gatsby*," I said.

"What's it about?"

"It's about a guy who started out as one thing and then decided he wanted to be somebody else," I said.

"Isn't that the fuckin' weirdest thing you ever heard?" he asked in an almost inaudible voice.

I watched Haas from a distance for a few minutes. He hadn't moved from the fetal position since we talked; he was just staring off into space. When we woke up the next morning, he seemed to be fine. We went back to the warehouse to sweat through another day.

One Saturday, two weeks later, I received a surprise visit from Blake in the library. It was well known now that I spent time in the library to avoid officers who might send me back to Naha.

"I need your help with Haas. He got the keys to an Ontos and is driving around the base. If the colonel hears about this, there's nothing I can do for him. Haas will listen to you."

Outside, we got into Blake's car and scoped out the base. Soon we saw an Ontos, a small tank-like vehicle, coming around a bend. It veered from one side of the road to the other. Blake drove off the side of the road to keep from getting hit. We got out of the car, and I ran toward the Ontos.

"Haas, it's P.T."

I heard a muffled, "This is Chicken Man!"

"Okay ... Chicken Man. Can we talk?"

"Any VCs out there?"

"No VCs. I promise you."

"How do I know you're really P.T. and not some VC who talks like P.T.?"

"Do you remember how you told Nance to give me a pack of Camels? Would a VC know that?"

Shortly thereafter, a head with a helmet popped up from the turret of the Ontos.

"I told you 'Nam ain't no place for you to be, P.T."

"Officer Blake is here. We've come to take you back to the barracks."

"Hey, sir," Haas said.

"Come on down, Haas, before some other asshole officer sees you and turns you in," Blake ordered him.

"That just wouldn't be right, would it ... I'm trying to make the world safe for democracy."

"Haas, are you on something?" Blake asked.

"Naw, just a little Naron."

Years later, it dawned on me: the reason Haas began to call himself Chicken Man was because he had felt guilty regarding not wanting to go back to Vietnam, where he had hoped to be with his brother as his guardian.

The Naron Habit

We had all been warned about Naron. It was a synthetic opiate sold in many of the open-air drugstores on BC Street, the main drag in town. Sometimes several of us might take it when the workload just seemed intolerable.

The drug helped ease the physical and emotional pain, the dehydration during the day, the *Stars & Stripes* monthly newspaper that listed the dead from Vietnam, the test of how much we could take when working long hours in the suffocating heat. But up to now, none of us had taken it as a recreational drug.

Our colonel called a meeting shortly after we arrived and told us anyone getting caught with Naron might serve a brig sentence. After the meeting, we went into town to search for it. The officers couldn't afford to throw us in the brig unless we killed someone; we were too shorthanded. And if they were threatening us with a brig sentence, this must be some good shit.

So when Haas was in the Ontos and said he was on just a little bit of Naron, I said, "Come on, Haas, don't be saying that."

"Like I don't know," Blake said, whispering to me.

Haas finally came down from the Ontos. One of the guys at the barracks who worked in the truck pool retrieved the Ontos. It appeared that, as incredible as it seemed at the time, no one had reported the Ontos incident.

The next day, Blake called me into his office.

"Sit down, P.T. I want to request something. I don't think I can rely on Haas to go on leave outside the gate by himself anymore. He's already mixed it up with one of the locals. One of these days, he's going to find himself in real trouble. Most of the time he listens to you. So I want to make sure that anytime he goes on leave outside the gate, you go with him."

I wanted to say no. I had really become accustomed to reading at night. Haas rarely had money to go into town. The prostitutes often got him so drunk that he passed out; then they would roll him for most, if not all, of his cash. He had missed curfew several times, but Blake was always able to make an appeal to his senior officers. It was only a matter of time until they might say enough is enough.

"Yes, sir." I remembered the escape and evasion course at Camp Pendleton in California, the way Haas got us through it, and the way he had taken me in.

"Thanks, P.T."

I left Blake's office feeling like I had betrayed Haas. We had always been straight with each other. All this behind-the-back stuff … it didn't seem right.

★★★

One evening Haas dressed in his civilian clothes, combed back his wavy yellow hair, and stopped by my bunk. "Blake said you and I did some good work this week. He's giving us Cinderella liberty tonight. So you might want to get off your fat ass, put that book down, and get ready."

Cinderella liberty allowed us to stay out two hours after the rest of the military guys had to be back at base. The prostitutes knew about Cinderella liberty and often hung around the bars to turn a few more tricks. At this point, I had little interest in prostitutes or getting drunk or even scoring a little Naron. I had withdrawn into the world of *Across the River and Into the Trees*. Hemingway.

"What's that one about?" Haas asked.

"It's about death and how one faces death," I said. "Give me a few minutes to get ready."

Within twenty minutes or so, we were on our way to the Enlisted Man's Club. After a few rounds of gin, we staggered outside the gate where we hailed a *skoshi* (small) cab to BC Street. BC Street mainly housed a series of bars interspersed by a few open-air drugstores. Like so many bad habits, and unlike the times when I was a teenager and had had to use a fake ID to get into bars, getting drunk was easy; all I had to do was walk into a bar and order drinks. The Okinawan bartenders never said, "You've had enough." In fact, they encouraged more drinking. It made it easier for the Okinawan bar girls to separate Marines and other GIs from their money.

We walked into Haas's favorite bar, where he immediately put his arm around a young Okinawan woman. She was one of the least attractive women in the bar, had a slightly pock-marked face, was slightly overweight, and seemed to scowl at nearly everything Haas said. I could barely hear their conversation over the American music blasting in the background. "Homeward Bound" by Simon and Garfunkel. "Burning Love" by Elvis. "Hard Day's Night" by the Beatles.

Haas and the Okinawan woman danced until it was time for all the other military guys to go back to their barracks. Haas whispered something into the woman's ear. She ran outside, crying as she went.

"God, Haas, what did you say to her?"

"I asked her to put out for free. When she refused, I told her that she was the ugliest thing I've seen for a prostitute, and I wouldn't put my cock in her anyway."

"Jesus, Haas!"

As we left the bar that night, the girl stood across the street. She pointed to us. The higher-ups bristled when military guys mixed it up with Okinawan street gangs. It became obvious that we were about to encounter one of those gangs. To get back to base, there was no other way to go than by passing them.

As we approached, they surrounded us. One had broken glass in his hand wrapped several times over in a cloth. He sliced Haas's forearm. As I spun around to help, they evaded me. It was obvious they wanted Haas.

Within seconds, a guy who it turned out was AWOL from the navy came out from between two buildings, swinging a broom wildly. Almost as soon as he appeared, he disappeared, as the MPs (military police) pulled up in two vehicles. As the one who had cut Haas was being ushered into one of the vehicles, Haas tripped him, sending his face plummeting against the cold steel of the upper step.

"Think you can fuck with Chicken Man? I'll show you!" Haas flapped his wings. I could see he was bleeding pretty badly from the glass cut. I called over the MP.

"He needs something for that cut."

"Chicken Man doesn't need anything!" Haas appeared disoriented. If he had taken Naron, I hadn't seen it.

We were taken to the Criminal Investigation Division, where we were kept until the sun came up. We were waiting to tell our stories, to tell how we had been jumped by these Okinawan thugs, when finally, someone came out of an office and said, "You can go now." We never found out what happened. Had the Lieutenant once again saved us from ourselves? Had the CID driven the Okinawans back to where they first found them and released them? Even now I wonder.

A Few Shots of Gin

Haas says we need to stop at the club
and have a few shots of gin. I'm hesitant.

"The brass can't smell it," he says.
We're checking out, going stateside.

I just turned nineteen, Haas twenty-one.
He tells me his job last year in 'Nam emerged,

recovering body parts borne out by men's
identities, to lay them out in body bags.

Even then he grins. He always seems to grin.
So I concede. He is the experienced one.

I will learn sometime in life when to follow
and when to lead. But today I am sitting

in a bar in Okinawa drinking more shots
of gin than I think I should, following

Haas's encouragement. Our company
officer will say, "You two are shit-faced!"

He tells Haas he will go home by plane.
"You," he says, "for your stupidity, sixteen

days on the *General John B. Pope*, to think
of what you did." On that ship, I learn

to comprehend the detriment of following,
when one thinks he should know otherwise.

But I question if a man's life isn't really
a roll of the dice, one shamed by drinking

a few shots of gin, and how one lives
with his stint as a steward of body bags.

Haas Bails Me Out One Last Time

It wasn't the only time I would be called on to help out one of our own. One of the guys in our barracks, Gilbane, was what is often called among enlisted men a shit bird. As soon as he *earned* a stripe, he lost it by getting himself in trouble in various ways. He not only caused friction among our guys, he constantly created friction between our barracks and Marines across the way.

While we had no idea what caused it, Gilbane said several Marines had held his arms behind his back while another Marine hit him in the head repeatedly with a board. He was bleeding profusely from his forehead when he came back to the barracks.

Among the guys in the barracks, I was still the enforcer, which included trips to town to right a wrong for someone in our group.

"P.T., I know Gilbane is a shit bird, but if we let those bastards get away with this, they may think they can do it to any of us," Haas said.

We all hated Gilbane. He was a truck driver who had pulled out of the warehouse loading dock when Nance was pulling up the tailgate from the truck bed. It turned Nance's kneecap ninety degrees to the side of his leg. Now Nance might have had to wear a knee brace for the rest of his life. Haas was right; this couldn't go unheeded. Gilbane was still one of ours.

I ran into the other barracks, where a guy that met Gilbane's description stood laughing with one of his buddies. It was obvious he was one of the guys who had either held Gilbane down or been the one who hit him with the board.

I ran up to him and sent a roundhouse left to his temple. He fell against the bunk, then lay still on the barracks floor. For one moment, I thought I had killed him. Soon after his eyes opened, partly glazed, Haas, Nance, and Terry arrived.

"Anybody else want some of that?" Haas asked, puffing out his chest.

Gilbane's offender spent four days in the hospital with a fractured arm and a concussion. Blake received a call from the adjutant general's office.

"I'm not sure I can get you out of this one, P.T.," Blake said. "This is just some serious shit. They want you at the adjutant general's office in three days."

★★★

Three days later, I sat in front of the lawyer for the adjutant general's office. He perused my file, then finally spoke.

"The guys tell me you read a lot. What do you read?" he asked.

"Steinbeck, Fitzgerald, Hemingway."

"Not light reading," he said. "I reviewed your standardized test scores, and I have just one question to ask you."

"Yes, sir?" I asked.

"How did such a smart guy like you do something as stupid as this? Do you know I could throw you in the brig, ruin your career?"

"Yes, sir."

"But I'm not. Do you want to know why I'm not?"

"Yes, sir."

"It's because of your buddy Haas. Maybe he'll be a labor organizer one of these days," he said, laughing softly. "But the other guys that he brought here?" he shook his head. "Haas must have rehearsed those guys until the cows came in because they all came in here and told me *exactly* the same lie!

"Now I could refute that. And believe me ... I could. But you don't have to worry. We're not going to prosecute, and I'm going to give you a chance. I've given Blake instructions to give you unofficial office hours. It won't go on your record. You'll cut all the elephant grass growing around the officers' tennis courts ... with a hand sickle. Is that understood?"

"Yes, sir."

"Then what are you waiting for? Get the hell out of my office and don't ever let me see you in here again."

Back at the barracks, Haas sat on my bunk waiting for me. The guys had stopped work until they knew of my fate. Haas had a smirk on his face.

"Well, P.T., how did it go?"

I smirked as well. "I think you know how it went. That could have cost you big time, lying like that. And the other guys? Especially Terry? My God, how did you ever get him to learn his script?"

"Terry might not be very bright, P.T., but I chose him because I knew he would be loyal. To me if not to you."

"We'll stay in touch when we get out of the Crotch, okay, Haas?" *Crotch* was slang for the Marine Corps and was used by most Marines in general. It likely came from times on the battlefield where bathing was nearly nonexistent. One Marine who I met later in life and who had spent much of his time in the jungle as a sniper said, "Even though we were high up in the trees, the Cong could smell us."

"Naw. Chicken Man can't fly. I'm damaged goods. You won't need me, P.T. You're going to be somebody."

Haas and me at the Enlisted Man's Club, 1967

Front left: Johnson; Back left: Terry; Front right: me; Back right: Haas

*The Quonset hut where I lived for thirteen months, eleven days,
and eight hours without air conditioning in temperatures often over 100 degrees*

*Satchiko, our house "girl"/my surrogate mother, and me outside
the Quonset hut where I lived, October '66 to November '67*

The elephant grass was about four to six feet high and spread out about the size of a football field. None of the officers wanted to go outside the gate of the courts if a ball went over the fence. The area was known for habu snakes. My knees buckled from the heat and dehydration. My hands were bloody from the rough wood of the sickle handle.

Blake granted Haas leave on his own for saving my ass.

When coming in from town, Haas asked, "Where's P.T.?"

Someone told him that I was still cutting elephant grass around the officers' tennis courts.

"And you left him out there?"

Haas and his loyalists came to fetch me.

"I came to take you back to the barracks," Haas said.

"I'm not finished," I retorted.

"You *are* finished," Haas responded. He grabbed one arm and put it around his neck and instructed Nance to do the same. Nance, with his bum leg, was hardly in any shape to lift me, but by this time, he had learned not to counter Haas. They stood me erect as best they could. I had little leg strength left.

"I haven't finished," I said again.

"That's enough." Haas repeated, "That's enough."

The next day, Haas smiled at me. It was a smile of brotherhood, of what seemed like a bond never to be broken. Haas said again how he was damaged goods and how I wouldn't need him. He could never have been so wrong.

Later in life, the people I'd need the most and the people who would need me were all damaged goods. And of those people, I would become more damaged than most. I just didn't fully know at that time how damaged I already was.

I contemplated all that had happened to me after the Gilbane incident. I didn't even know what marijuana was when I arrived on Okinawa, and now I was having a tough time giving up the Naron. Like all the other Marines who went into town looking for Naron when the officers threatened us with a brig sentence, I too went on and off Naron most of my time on Okinawa. Reading novels was one of the ways I could get my mind off of it.

I had hardly read an entire book in my life. Now I had read much of Steinbeck, Fitzgerald, and Hemingway and had studied a foreign language, Japanese.

I had never been strong in my life. Now I was considered the enforcer in the barracks.

No one had ever seemed to listen to me before. Now guys in the barracks came to me for advice—even if Haas had the last word.

And all I could think about was what a fucked-up leader I'd become. I had jeopardized my career. I had placed my buddies in jeopardy for lying for me. And what if I had killed that guy who'd messed with Gilbane? What would my life have been like then? But it wouldn't be the end of my fury, not by a long shot. I had become Tom, my father. Only difference was I had never hit a woman and never would.

***

Our house "girl," Satchiko, approached me one day as she handed me my clean work clothes. Each of the twenty-five guys in the barracks paid her six dollars a week to clean our laundry and polish our boots. She was about forty years old and was like a mother to me, always giving me unsolicited advice.

"Why do you do this to yourself? You're not like the rest of them," she whispered to me.

I wanted to tell her how Murphy's story had affected me, how I also felt guilty for sending those machine guns and ammo to Vietnam, where they were killing children. But I just nodded and silently wept inside. I would learn the art of weeping inside, especially as it pertained to that time and experience, for the rest of my life. To this day, I think I was partly responsible for the killing of Vietnamese children.

***

The Marine Corps closed down Camp Hague in 1972 after Okinawa was turned over to Japan after twenty-seven years of American rule. Much of Devil's Island would become only a bad memory for many servicemen and women.

No more would a Marine warehouseman have to take in a pack at Camp Hague and wonder if it signified good news, that a Marine was safe and on his way home, or news that by then would have reached his family, that he didn't make it.

I could just envision a fellow Marine in a warehouse in Vietnam surveying packs to see which were still serviceable and which would go into the burning field ranges or other furnaces.

When I left Okinawa, I thought I would never have to wonder about those sorts of outcomes again. But it was all about to become a part of my mental Rolodex. The kaleidoscope that wouldn't, won't, stop turning over the years. The words, images of an active mind, of those days, of my memory, turning over again and again occasionally at night, even now. Memories like surprise visitors some nights when I try to sleep.

Chapter 13

1967-1968: COMING HOME ... TO THIS?

Our departure time on Okinawa was drawing near. A month or so had passed since Haas's and my Cinderella liberty. Blake, after thinking over the stories from one of the guys in the barracks about the skirmish with the Okinawan gang, and my going up before the adjutant general for my hurting Gilbane's attacker, just shook his head. But he had a greater concern.

Several days before we checked out to go back to the States, I got a call to come in to see Blake. "You're probably aware the other guys are going to fly home. I'm going to put you on a troop carrier. You and I both know you're still hooked on Naron. I don't want to send you back home to your parents as a fuckin' drug addict. But you and Haas ... my God! What am I going to do for excitement?"

I remember most everything about the trip *to* Okinawa on the USNS *Buckner*. Haas making Nance give me the Camels, the physical training as the waves swelled, the time we were caught in a typhoon and I was one of the last to go below, so fascinated by the waves coming up over the deck. The main thing I remember about the trip going *home* was that it was on the USNS *General John B Pope*. And I do remember finding a corner near a box on deck and shaking profusely.

Also, I recall a time reading pages from *Typee,* one of Melville's earlier works. It was about a sailor who landed on the island of Typee and saw beautiful fruit trees, only to find, as he drew closer, that the fruit was rotten.

It wasn't John Wayne land where a young Haas would ultimately become Chicken Man, and I was confused about who I might be in the future. I wasn't the same person who had arrived on Okinawa. I was even more depressed than I had been prior to joining the Marine Corps, and certainly more disoriented.

Several hundred yards from the San Diego port, I witnessed hundreds of apparent well-wishers with their placards as we drew nearer. The placards were too far away to read. I could hear the people chanting from a distance.

For a moment, a brief moment, I wished Chicken Man had been with me, to observe the crowds waving their placards in a nation where a young Haas could dream of something other than dead bodies and inhumanity.

As we drew near, it became apparent the signs, among other things, read Baby Burners. A Marine standing next to me, his arm in a sling, holding a rifle he had taken off a VC, just said in an almost inaudible tone, "I'm coming back to this shit."

The frenzy going on in my head needed to be quieted, but it didn't stop just then. Instead, something happened as I arrived home on the *General John B. Pope.* The fury of war and an ungrateful nation seethed.

When I mentioned that I had been in the Marine Corps and had spent my time on Okinawa, listeners would often say, "Aren't you glad you weren't in Vietnam?" Afterward, for years, I never mentioned my time in the Marine Corps or tried to explain what those months in Okinawa were like. I built a fury that would remain most of my life.

Even if I had *only* lost my buddy Mike Amato, wouldn't that have been enough to stoke the anger? Mike was a meek guy who was more suited to become a priest or minister than a Marine. Prior to our departure from Camp Pendleton on the USNS *Buckner* bound for Okinawa and Vietnam, Mike gave encouragement to those in the barracks he sensed were frightened. "Everything will be okay" was his mantra.

The USNS *Buckner* departed for Okinawa and Vietnam in October 1966. Mike was killed in action in May 1967. His passing was one of several reasons I didn't take up the Marine Corps's offer later. Haas was right; this was no John Wayne movie.

Years later I tried to look up Haas on the internet, to no avail.

Last Days at Camp Lejune: 1968

I had ninety-three days left in the Corps when I arrived at port in San Diego. If I had had less than ninety days left, I would have received an automatic out. When the Marine Corps gave me a preferred duties list prior to going home, what we affectionately called a wish list, they gave me three choices. I put in bold letters across the page, ANY PLACE BUT CAMP LEJEUNE, NORTH CAROLINA!

They sent me to Camp Lejeune, North Carolina. Part of the reason I had applied for 'Nam was to get out of Camp Lejeune.

Back at Camp Lejeune, to bide my time as a short-timer, the corps placed me in a warehouse to show new Marines recently released from boot camp how to build storage bins that were approximately 7'x4'x4'. (My wife Kate will tell you the last thing you want to put in my hand is a hammer.) When we moved to Davidson, North Carolina, the driver of the moving van said, "You have some really neat tools here!"

"Those aren't my tools," I responded. "Those are my wife's tools."

For the corps to find light temporary duty for me to while away the remainder of my ninety-three days after thirty days of leave, the commanding officer called me into his office and said, "I notice that you are unqualified in swimming."

"Yes, sir," I said. "I can't swim."

"Well, no man is going to leave my Marine Corps if he can't swim!"

It quickly brought to mind that I was originally assigned to go to Vietnam, where troops had to physically navigate river crossings. And it was now, in my last days, the Marine Corps was going to teach me to swim.

I was assigned to a swimming instructor who would teach a five-year-old colonel's son and me to swim.

First, the instructor addressed the youth. "Go up there and jump off that platform and try to make it back to the beginning of the pool. I'll be nearby to help you if you can't make it."

Immediately, without thought or provocation, the boy climbed the ladder and jumped from the fifteen-foot-high platform. With some help, he easily made it back to the beginning of the pool.

"Okay, Marine, up you go," the instructor said, staring at me.

When I arrived at the top of the platform, it looked more intimidating than it did when looking up from the ground. I hesitated.

"Okay, jump!" The instructor chided me at my hesitation.

When I finally jumped, I sunk to the bottom, and he let me stay underwater forever—or probably just a few seconds.

When he pulled me up, he said, "When I tell you to go up on that platform and jump, you jump. Hear me?"

Eventually, I learned to swim the length of what was an Olympic-size pool. At the end of two weeks, he passed me as a "Second Class swimmer."

In addition to my swimming instructions and attempting to teach new on-the-job trainees to build storage boxes, I was approached by a Marine who came into our barracks and asked me, "Do you know how to handle a basketball? With your height, we need another center for our basketball team." So I became a third-string center for the Marine Corps and had to borrow tennis shoes to get into the one game I played.

The Navy Seabees were killing us, and we were possibly behind by forty points when I was told to go in. I scored occasionally only because by that time, the Seabees had sent in their third-stringers. Later I went on to play city league basketball in Alexandria, Virginia, until the guys on our team asked me to be coach that year. I was thirty-three.

Finally, the Marine Corps recruiting/administrative office called me in for my re-up talk.

"We want to send you to Naval Academy Prep School." It was evident that, true to the adjutant general's lawyer, my unofficial office hours resulting in my cutting elephant grass around the officers' tennis courts had not become part of my permanent records.

I snickered and thought, *I'm guessing this isn't because of my carpentry abilities or my ability to handle a basketball.*

I had a fairly exemplary record, on paper, in the corps. Based on the fact that during boot camp, the Marine Corps had offered to send me to computer school if I extended for two years meant that I had scored well on their standardized tests.

Maybe it was the insult of having to come back to Lejeune after I had specifically made it clear I wanted to be stationed anywhere but Lejeune, maybe I had just had enough of the Marine Corps, maybe because the death of my buddy Amato was still fresh in my memory, but I declined.

Looking back, I would say the Marine Corps helped give me direction, although the path would be a circuitous one. Paranoia, for whatever reason, seemed to dictate who I was and how I handled myself. And it seemed to come and go. Something no one would wish on themselves. My mother's paranoia had been well established. Mine was soon to follow.

Chapter 14

At my twentieth high school reunion, seventeen years after leaving Okinawa, my female bowling buddy, Sue Frye, ran over to me. I introduced her to my wife, Kate, the third one. I would stay with Kate the rest of my life. It had taken me some time to "get it right."

"He was such a sweet boy in high school," Sue said. "The girls used to call him Sugarfoot because he reminded us of a TV cowboy who was like that, sweet. But then when he came back from overseas, wow!"

Sue was the first person I visited after getting off the plane in DC. She had a menial government job and lived in a small row house by herself. When she saw me, she hugged me tightly but soon backed off.

"What's wrong?" she asked.

"Do you mind if I stay here for a day or so? I don't want to go home to my mother yet."

"Sure," she said. She had a single mattress on the floor in an extra bedroom where I spent most of several days while she was at work, in part staring at the ceiling, in part watching birds outside the window chirping, just chirping. But after three days, she said, "You need to go home."

Shortly after that, I walked into a Sears, Roebuck store to buy civilian clothes in preparation for getting out of the corps but had to leave after vertigo set in. The aisles started spinning. I wanted to scream. Everything about the store was agitating me. Something wasn't right, and I didn't have a clue.

Years later, I cleared out an electronics store, yelling with a loud guttural scream because a manager had sold me a TV that didn't work and laughed about it. I could see the security guard from the corner of my eye. He remained still. It was as though he were thinking, "Hey, man, they pay me five dollars an hour. I'm not getting involved in this!" The same click that went off in my head when I took down Gilbane's attacker was still there. It didn't seem to take as much to set it off then, but it was still there.

Kate had been parking the car during the electronics store incident. She ran into the store and said, "Come on. Please? Let's get out of here!" But like my father during his barroom fights when he was winning and the MPs were on their way, I was willing to chance that the manager or a clerk had already called the police. I waited until the manager gave me a new TV set before I left. He did. I walked casually out of the store. The police were the least of my concerns.

Illusory Lifelines

Maybe it was the Naron, maybe it was taking in packs of some Marines I knew must have been killed in Vietnam—it had all seemed like too much for an eighteen-year-old, but a Christian Navigator mission group I had come in contact with in Okinawa gave me great comfort from time to time when I was trying to get off Naron. The Navigators had taken me in like family. And if ever I needed a family, it was on Okinawa.

I loved those people, and back in the States, I wanted to duplicate those feelings. When I returned home, I was depressed, extremely agitated, and just like the occasion at Sears, I often found that when I walked into a crowded building, vertigo continued to kick in. I had to leave immediately, never really understanding what was happening. (I still have issues at seventy-four when being in crowded and confined areas, which never occurred prior to my going overseas.)

Like Melville's protagonist in *Confidence Man*, I was looking for a life raft, only hoping to avoid latching on to an anchor instead. Too many anchors inhabited my life now.

I had only been home from the Marine Corps for about a month when a minister visited my mother to entice her to come to his church, but she turned him down and pointed to me instead. "He needs that a lot more than I do," she said.

I'd hardly been able to get up from the couch since I'd come home from the Marine Corps. It was obvious my mother, who had my brother shortly after I graduated from boot camp, now had more than she could handle looking after him.

"I know a seminary that will help you get over some of those things you're feeling," the minister told me.

While I was not terribly religious, I decided to attend the seminary to sort out my feelings about Amato's death, humans killing humans in general, *what it all meant*. If I had gone on to 'Nam, Amato and I may have been in the same company. And the deaths of other Vietnam-era brothers dominated my thinking.

There was no peace in that headspace. No peace at all. I had come home searching for serene places and beliefs. Yet the alteration between fury and depression refused to be denied. My introduction to Buddhism and the Navigators' brand of Christianity while in Okinawa had given me hope for pulling myself out of that space.

At the seminary, I was criticized by other Vietnam-era veterans for my lack of faith. Most had memorized pages of scriptures. I had memorized a few scriptures based on my time with the Navigators. (I still know those verses today—can't get them out of my head.)

A couple of the brothers in the seminary who had been in the army in Vietnam were particularly tough on me. I was working part time at the Safeway food store in Arlington, and my seminary grades were suffering as I spent less time studying the Gospels and more time contemplating what I was going to do next in life. Most of the brothers knew I had performed poorly in Christology/Theology, one of the most important classes at the seminary. It was a course that showed a seminarian believed in the tenets of religion as it was taught in the seminary.

My prayer life suffered too. One day, one of the brothers, Brother Tony, an excellent musician, had been "trumpeting for the Lord" when his lungs collapsed at the Washington Cathedral. The Brother Chancellor gathered all 250 of us seminarians together in a room that typically was designed for a hundred adults. He asked us to kneel in a position with our calves tucked behind our haunches so that all brothers and sisters would fit "comfortably" in the room.

Within a matter of minutes, I began to tear. It wasn't for Brother Tony. I prayed to God as only a man in considerable pain could pray. More than ever before, I wanted God to hear me, answer my prayer.

"Please, God," I prayed, "*please* resolve this thing one way or the other." I still didn't have a strong belief that prayer really worked, but shortly after that, Brother Chancellor came in and exclaimed, "Praise God! Brother Tony's going to be all right! Our prayers have been answered!"

Two hundred and fifty seminarians praying for the same thing left me more in doubt than ever. It reminded me of religious boxers who claimed victory because of their faith in God after they pulverized another man.

The seminary, for entertainment, created "verse clubs." For those who could memorize at least fifty bible verses, they were in the *50 Verse Club*; 100 verses, the *100 Verse Club*, and so on. Many of the former Amish from eastern Pennsylvania could just about quote the entire scriptures. For them, the seminary was a sense of freedom from what had surely been a very restrictive practice.

For me, there were more rules than required by the Marine Corps. The Marine Corps had threatened that if I didn't abide by their methodology, rules, and regulations, I might die in combat. At the seminary, if I didn't follow their ways, I might go to hell. But the Brother Chancellor said it with kindness.

While attending seminary, I attended a Baptist church in Arlington. It was during that time a woman named Ms. Joseph asked me if I would teach a Gospel of John class at her house for singles. (Looking back, it was a setup.)

I had attended the church when I was twelve years old, again not because I was religious but because the church belonged to a basketball league for its youth. I was five feet four, and in this twelve-and-under league, I was the tallest player. The minister had had one condition in order to play: the child had to attend church on Sunday in order to play during the week. Ms. Joseph had been one of the women in the church back then who was in charge of social events. Going back to the same church now gave me a sense of familiarity, some sense of belonging.

When I arrived at Ms. Joseph's house, the class was small—all young single women. One in particular, Linda, always stayed after and questioned me thoroughly about my time in the service, how I became involved with this particular Baptist church, and so on. She was a secretary at the Pentagon, had great organizational skills, and showed more interest in me at the time than I felt I deserved.

I married her after only knowing her for seven months, one more attempt at finding a life raft at near twenty years of age. I had days when gentle waves carried me along, other times when the tide nearly drowned me. I thought marriage would provide me with some mental stability and relief from thoughts of machine guns and the death of buddies who I had trained with and who had been killed in 'Nam. The depression for the moment seemed more manageable, partly because I had a wedding to plan for, although Linda made most of the arrangements. I felt like a spectator during the preparations.

For a while, the paranoia subsided. But it was only for a while, as I had once again become a follower. Linda decided that she preferred living near her parents in a rural area in Tennessee. I sensed later that her desire to become the alpha in our relationship was fostered by my lessening aspirations. Like with the gin episode with Haas, there would be unpleasant consequences to follow.

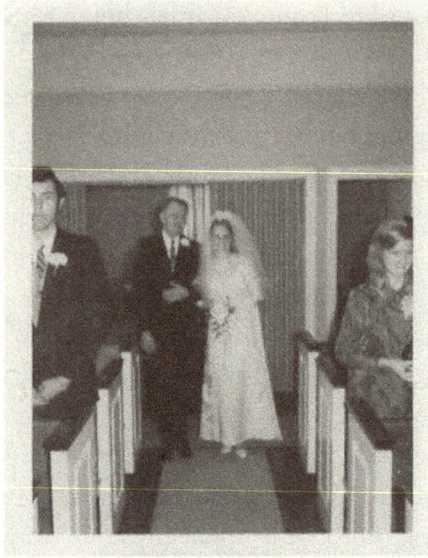

Linda coming down the aisle.
My sister on the right; an old friend, Chuck, on the left

Linda and our wedding party, November 1968

No Lifeline Here
1968-1969: Carson-Newman University

The retired minister of the Baptist church convinced me that if I were to become a minister, I needed greater breadth than I was getting at Washington Bible College and suggested I attend Carson-Newman University in Tennessee where, coincidently, Linda was from. She had been an esteemed member of the church. And later I sensed that she had talked with the minister about attending Carson-Newman, which was only twenty-five miles from where her parents lived.

After our wedding ceremony in Arlington, Virginia, we left immediately for Tennessee, where I had been accepted as a religion student at Carson-Newman. On our wedding night, when we stopped at a hotel nearly halfway to Jefferson City, just before we readied ourselves for bed, Linda said, "I don't want to be married to a minister."

We negotiated an agreement by the time we arrived at the college. I would become a doctor and a medical missionary, one much like the Navigators.

Linda came from a small town in Tennessee called Maynardville. Her father had been a machinist, barely eking out a living. It was the same community Chet Atkins came from, her father would tell me.

"We thought he wouldn't amount to anything. All he did was sit on the corner and play that guitar."

Linda found a job working for the head of the Philosophy Department for fifty three dollars a week. I made $210 each month from the GI Bill, which didn't quite cover my tuition. Just before school started and during breaks, I worked in a Magnavox warehouse loading TV/record player consoles that weighed well over a hundred pounds.

Men weighing nearly three hundred pounds and I loaded the consoles stacked four high in tractor trailers destined for retail stores up and down the East Coast. I made five dollars an hour.

As a result of our poverty, Linda and I found public housing within a series of cinder block duplexes. The walls provided little to no sound reduction. We could hear when the couple next door was having sex, likely they could do the same. Many of the residents were housed there while their spouses served prison time. The project reminded me of Gregory Estates when I was ten.

Soon upon arriving at C-N, my kidney issues recurred from childhood. An internist informed me "You will likely lose one or both of your kidneys."

The thoughts of making it into medical school crumbled.

I had quit drinking upon arriving back in the States from Okinawa, but after receiving the news about my kidneys, I immediately went across the street to a grocery store and bought, ironically, two liters of Christian Brothers wine.

Linda had never seen me drink before. I drank both bottles after arriving back at the housing. I had stopped drinking altogether when I arrived back in the States, but now new demons were in the making.

★★★

Linda and I met another couple at C-N who we expected might become friends for life, Alan and Gail Smith. When we got together for dinner, we often split two chicken breasts, each of us getting a half a chicken breast.

Alan was the science-student star of C-N. He had won an award from Hamilton Beach as Small College Science Student of the South. Final exams for the first semester were typically given after the Christmas vacation. So Alan and I stayed at C-N to study histology slides.

We found a first-floor window in the biology building that didn't lock. We crawled through it every day during the break and tested each other on slides. When the other students returned, none of the other histology classmates scored nearly what Alan and I scored on the slide tests.

Alan was by far the superior of the two of us in the sciences. Studying chemistry came as easy to him as eating. I received Bs in all my chemistry classes, although I outscored him on a couple of tests in biology.

At C-N, science classes were all graded on a curve. Word seemed to get around that Alan and I had "busted the curve" in histology. When students came into a biology class afterward and saw Alan and me sitting together, often they left and dropped the course, only to take it a different semester.

There was one area in which I excelled over Alan. He used to get copies of *Reader's Digest* somewhere and bring over the twenty-five-word vocabulary test. He seemed amazed at my scores on those tests. In most instances, I answered twenty-two out of twenty-three multiple choice questions correctly, on rare occasion more.

"How do you do that?" he asked.

"The same way you blow away the curve in chemistry classes," I said.

Later, on his MCAT exam for medical school, Alan scored on the 99th percentile on the science portion. However, he dropped to the 60s on verbal skills. Of nine medical schools, he was accepted into only one, George Washington University Medical School, where he received a partial scholarship. Coming from a small college, Alan felt, had hurt his chances. During an interview with the Georgetown Medical School, the director said to him, "I don't think I've ever heard of that school." No one had ever completed C-N with a 4.0 average. Alan finished close to a 3.9 GPA.

Around 2014, after a successful career as a pediatrician, Alan and his wife Gail moved to Richmond, Virginia. I saw him on a regular basis after he retired. My mother was in a progressive care unit a few miles from where he lived.

Alan died of brain cancer in February 2020. He was seventy-two, the same age as my cousin Joe when he died. Joe died in September 2019, two months before my mother died in memory care at eighty-nine. In a period of six months, I lost three of the most important people in my life.

1970–1972: When Up Is Down?

My wife and I decided to leave C–N in the middle of my junior year. I was nearing my twenty-third birthday. Both my wife and I had lived in poverty as children when it wasn't an option, but now it was within our control to find a more stable financial existence.

In 1970, we moved to Richmond, Virginia, where I enrolled in the University of Richmond for one semester. For that semester, I developed a nominal relationship with my religion professor. After one class, he said that he had to be out of town the next class and asked if I would share some of my seminarian experiences and lead the class that day.

During the class, I had often wanted to present a hypothesis that had been working on me over the previous few years. I provided the class with a list of similarities between Karl Marx and Jesus.

When the professor returned the next week, he laughed nervously and said, "I understand you gave quite a controversial talk last week." When the dean of men found out about my theory, he made it clear that the University of Richmond wasn't for me.

I dropped out prior to the end of the semester and before grades were recorded.

Besides, the tuition became more than my wife and I could pay.

My University of Richmond photo, age 22.

The next semester, I began attendance at Virginia Commonwealth University and worked twenty hours a week as an orderly in both the emergency ward and radiology at the Medical College of Virginia. The tuition was $257 a semester, and I could take eighteen to twenty-one semester hours without additional charges. So I took overloads nearly every semester. I attempted to make up some of the ground for the time I had spent at Elon College, seminary, and the Marine Corps. It had now been five years since I had graduated from high school.

I enrolled as an English major. I had always wanted to pursue my love of language. I took two semesters of story writing and two semesters of poetry. Nearly all my courses were literature and writing classes to meet the requirements for an English degree.

I published poetry in VCU's literary magazine, which was as selective as most major magazines, and published poetry in several issues of a New York magazine entitled *Bitterroot*, which paid fifty cents a poem and provided several free copies.

The pain from my kidney disease continued to escalate, as did my drinking. Looking back, it is difficult to tell how much I drank to alleviate the pain and how much was from inheriting my father's genes. My temperature spiked to over a hundred from time to time.

During a Shakespeare class where the professor was new and boring, I went to the cantina, poured out the soda I'd brought with me, and went to a female classmate's residence who always had wine available. I filled the cup with wine and drank in his class.

After one class, obviously drunk, I walked up to the professor and said, "Professor N., that was the best lecture I've ever heard."

"You need to go home immediately," he said, "before someone in the administration finds you like this."

I drank through one of his exams and still managed to fill an eight-page blue book. When he handed back the graded exams, my exam read, "See me after class."

He called me into his office. I had been drunk several times in his class but always came in prepared and had participated more than most students. Shakespeare resonated; it was the professor who didn't.

"I can hardly read a word of this," he said, pointing to the exam book. "Can you decipher this for me?"

I looked at the first page. "Not a clue," I said.

"I'm going to give you an A-, just based on what you've said in class."

***

My favorite professor, Dr. Maurice Duke, was also the book editor for the *Richmond Times Dispatch* and had helped me publish a major article in the newspaper about my days of hitchhiking. The short bio at the bottom of the article stated truthfully that I had started hitchhiking at the age of twelve. I had hitchhiked around ten thousand miles by the time the article came out and likely hitchhiked another three thousand to four thousand miles afterward.

I wanted so much to please Dr. Duke. He was the most supportive professor I had ever had up to that time. Yet mentally, something was going on with me that I had never felt before—powerful ups, significant downs.

Yes, I had felt plenty of downs in my life. But these ups were energizing and made me feel more mentally powerful than I had ever felt. And other students seemed to notice, even gravitate toward my newfound energy. They seemed to mistake my increased energy as brilliance. It was true that I could do several times the amount of coursework I had done previously and somehow make sense of it all, but at the same time, I hardly slept at all. My mind was abuzz with connecting dots that may or may not have existed. There was no road map to where my thoughts would go next.

I took a Hawthorne/Melville seminar course with Dr. Duke. During that time, there was an English Department student/faculty party near the end of the semester when a number of English majors would soon graduate. I only had one paper left to write for Dr. Duke, which was due the following Monday after this late Friday afternoon party. The paper was worth 50 percent of our grade. I showed up drunk at the party with Linda.

Dr. Duke tried to engage me in conversation, obviously so other professors wouldn't approach me. I had become popular among the English professors, always prepared, albeit a bit quirky at times. They seemed to like my quirkiness about as much as they liked my preparation—never knew what I would say next. I showed novel approaches in interpreting literature.

"How is your paper coming along?" Dr. Duke asked.

"I haven't started it yet." This was a paper he would expect to be no less than twenty-five to thirty pages.

When I arrived home, I began to sober up and realized what I had said to Dr. Duke. He was like a father to me, someone I desperately did not want to disappoint. I fixed a pot of coffee and sat down to read, skim, and evaluate Melville's earlier works *Typee* and *Omoo*, his midcareer work *Moby Dick*, and one of his last works, *The Confidence Man*. I continued to pour down the coffee.

And at one point, I didn't need the coffee. My mind was in extremely high gear, never before to such a degree. While I couldn't explain it, I loved it!

The idea that I needed time to heal from the kidney issues and reconcile emotionally was inconceivable then. I just kept thinking how I *loved* this newfound energy! I soared above any human understanding of what I could accomplish, and in general, those I came in contact with thereafter in years to come would also gravitate toward that energy on and off for nearly a decade.

I was able to stay awake under my own volition for more than two days. Shortly after my review of Melville's works—I had written part of the paper as I read—I completed the paper. The class would end at 4 p.m.

I entered the classroom about fifteen minutes before the end of class and handed in the paper. Dr. Duke first looked at me with a scowl and then a smile. *What has he done this time,* I sensed he was thinking.

The next class, Dr. Duke handed out all the other student papers first. Then he came to me and gave me a stern look. I had written about how Melville had concentrated on physical impairments in life in *Typee* and *Omoo* and then had gone on to deliberate man's struggle between the mental and spiritual demons in life in *Moby Dick*, something I was beginning to understand so well. And finally in *The Confidence Man*, Melville had focused on man's struggles with what appears to be the help of the spiritual world, only to find its demonic mechanisms at work. The paper was fifty pages.

"You son of a bitch," he said, finally breaking into laughter. "This is publishable."

★★★

Years later in the late eighties, I went back to his office and told him how much he meant to me philosophically and personally. Looking back, the late eighties was near the end of my worst mental struggles. It had been some time since I'd had a manic episode.

"You know, you reminded me so much of Tom Wolfe, your writing and your outlook back then," he said. "Tom and I were classmates at the University of Iowa. He was an alcoholic and bipolar. I'm so glad to see you're doing better now." The comparison shocked me. I had no idea that Dr. Duke had envisioned me in that light. Looking back, it was an obvious social and psychological comparison.

I continued to send him thank-you notes over the years until he retired. Recently, I emailed him again as I thought about him while writing this memoir. I discovered online that his wife had passed away six months before. I received his email address through VCU. After passing on my regrets for the loss of his wife, I wrote:

> *You mentored me through some rough times. I was going through a divorce in the summer of my senior year. In addition to helping me get an article published in the* Richmond Times-Dispatch *on hitchhiking when you were the book editor there, you gave me recommendations for graduate school at Purdue in 1972 and again for an MFA program at the U. of Oregon in 1982.*
>
> *I stopped by your office in 1990 when I was taking courses at Ft. Lee for a Federal Gov't job to let you know once again how important you were to me.*

He responded:

> *John,*
> *It was great to hear from you after all the years. It's always good to have an old man stirred when he hears from someone he's influenced in the past. I'm in pretty fragile shape now. I can't walk or drive and writing is out of the question. But what do you expect at 87?*
> *Maurice*

How Many Fingers?

So much of what occurred at VCU appeared to be the beginning of my worst manic episodes. Those years and the next eight years to follow were significantly volatile, the ups, the downs, when the possibility or even probability of suicide seemed imminent.

Yet on my best days, I considered a writing career might be in the works for the future. Even during a period of thirty-five years when I gave up writing to concentrate on a different career, I liked to think I would return to writing, to the degree my aging hands would take me.

One area when I seemed most capable of keeping my volatility under control was my time working as an orderly part time at the Medical College of Virginia, which is now Virginia Commonwealth University Hospital. But my ups and downs began to create a gulf between Linda and me, and it was growing wider. And my drinking had become an issue.

I spent time at MCV working both in the emergency ward and radiology, wherever I was needed most. In the emergency ward, there were times one or more of the orderlies didn't show up. The administrator often asked me to stay on past the early-morning hours when I typically went home. I almost always volunteered to stay.

We hardly had to look up at the clock. At nearly 11 p.m., the shotgun wounds and knife stabbings started coming in. The times I remember most can never be forgotten: the man who needed the paddles to bring him back around and the intern who laughed hilariously out of nervousness and fear at the sight.

"I've never seen anyone turn that blue before," he shouted.

Remarkably, the doctors brought the man back around. But what happened next was even more remarkable.

"I'm hungry," he said.

"What would you like?" his wife asked.

"A hamburger."

His wife stared up at the doctor as if to ask permission.

"If he wants a hamburger, get him a hamburger," the doctor said.

While she was out, he went into cardiac arrest again. This time, he did not come back.

The sight of the wife limply holding a hamburger bag—unforgettable.

Then there was the guy who had killed his wife with a shotgun and turned it on himself, placing the barrels under his chin.

The emergency staff brought him in with a blood-stained towel over his face. The doctors asked me to stay by his side until they could get him into surgery. There was nothing I could do to prep him for surgery.

It was one of the few times I felt squeamish. I desperately wanted someone to take him away.

Finally, an administrator came over. I felt relieved that she was going to offer him some comfort, give him an idea of how long it was going to be before he went into surgery.

Instead, she said, "I want you to listen. Raise one finger if you have insurance, two if you don't."

Sometime later, I watched a George C. Scott movie called *The Hospital*. There was a scene very similar to that in the movie. As I watched the movie, I wanted to call out, "This really happened! It was real!" Instead, I remained silent.

I recall the neurosurgeon coming in. He was on call, and it was obvious he had been drinking quite a bit, which was against hospital policy for an on-call physician.

This guy's a goner, I thought. Later, I would find out the surgeon has saved the man's life. It made the expression "doing it in his sleep" come to mind. What would that patient ultimately do? Live his life like that? Maybe try again? Sometimes, I still wonder.

There was also the time a man came in on his own volition with stab wounds all over his chest cavity. The surgeon came down to see him.

"Prep him for surgery, but keep talking to him to make sure he doesn't go into shock."

As I prepped him, I asked him, "Did your girlfriend do this to you?" to which he responded, "She ain't my girlfriend no more."

He came from the Churchhill district, which was known for its violence and where most of the stab wounds and shotgun wounds came from. At times, the violence found its way into the emergency ward. MCV had a plainclothes policeman on duty in the emergency ward to protect against such occasions.

Near the time for the man to be taken upstairs to surgery, a woman came through the entrance. She was holding her stomach. I noticed a flash of something between her arms. I approached the policeman and said, "Something isn't right over there."

He approached her, and after a few verbal exchanges, he placed her arm behind her back and slipped what appeared to be a butcher knife from her skirt. Apparently, it was the man's girlfriend coming to finish him off.

My time working in the emergency ward was at times fretful and at times provided more of a sense of excitement than even a bipolar person could garner. While my manic episodes were fewer than usual there, the staff offered to let me sleep on the interns' bunks when they were available and other orderlies hadn't shown.

But I rarely slept. Sometimes I just walked the hallway when times were relatively silent, and at times, I studied. And there was material there for a young writer. Lots of material.

Story Writer? "I Don't Know"

During my early days as a writer, I wrote for the high school newspaper, and at fourteen, I had published an article in a local newspaper about a youth bowling league. I published nonfiction articles occasionally while at VCU. But at VCU, my poetry professor had also given encouragement for some of my poetry.

My poetry writing classes at VCU were taught by Ms. Troubetzkoy, a published poet, owner of a newspaper, and wife of a Russian prince. Later I discovered she was also a well-known patron of the arts. How fortunate I was to have had her as a professor.

At the end of my second semester and nearing the end of my degree requirements at VCU, Ms. Troubetzkoy called me to her desk and said, "I do hope that you'll continue writing poetry. I look forward to seeing you published in the future." After taking two graduate-level poetry classes the next year at Purdue with less success, I gave up writing poetry for thirty-five years.

I had taken a short story writing class for two semesters at VCU under Gertrude Curtler, who had published two novels, had been a flapper in the 1920s, and who smoked constantly during class. It was an evening class and met once a week.

Ms. Curtler often said how much she looked forward to reading my classmate Lee Zacharias's stories. We were required to complete a new story for every class. Anyone could be called upon to read at any time.

Every week, Lee read a story. Lee went on to publish several novels, teach creative writing at the University of North Carolina at Greensboro, and edit the *Greensboro Review*.

At the end of the second semester, I approached Ms. Curtler.

"Ms. Curtler," I said, "we all know Lee is going to publish and become a star in the fiction world. But I have to ask, what do you think of my chances?"

She turned her head, took a drag off a cigarette, and finally turned to me. "With Lee, I know. Honestly, with you, I don't know."

As soon as I had asked the question I had wished I hadn't.

1972: The Separation

Trouble brewed between Linda and me. Similar to the discussion we had the night of our marriage, when I changed majors from pre-med to English, she said, "I didn't work this hard to be married to an English professor!"

My drinking and kidney disease also contributed to the anguish between us. One night during the summer of 1972, I convinced her to have dinner at a Shakey's Pizza Parlor. A band played on their stage and asked for audience participation.

Early that evening, I drank a small pitcher of beer only to decide it wasn't enough. Sometime during the second pitcher of beer, the band asked if anyone would like to sing along on stage.

Without further convincing, I walked quickly up on stage, took the mic, and asked them to play "Old Man River" in the key of G. I had no idea what the key of G was. They humored me momentarily, and as I sang, I saw my wife walking toward the door. I handed over the mic.

I caught up with her, but she wouldn't look at me. She walked quickly away, trying to outpace me.

"You have humiliated me for the last time," she said.

"Can we talk about it?" I asked.

"We'll talk about it tomorrow. For now, just *don't talk to me.*"

The next morning, she said, "I want a divorce."

"You want a divorce because I sang 'Old Man River' at a Shakey's Pizza Parlor?"

She shook her head, said nothing. Clearly I was clueless.

I had coursework to finish up that summer, but we decided that she would move out while I was in class. I told her to take whatever she wanted. When I came home from school that day, she had left me a small table and chair, and a single bed.

The Divorce

Our marriage as we knew it had ended. I fulfilled the degree requirements by that summer of 1972. The degree was conferred in 1973.

While we discussed getting a divorce, I didn't know at the time that our decision was really permanent. I suggested getting back together in six months to see if there was any reason to pursue our marriage further. Again, Linda was silent.

A photo taken around the time my manic behavior intensified.
Linda took the photo to show me how crazy I looked.

Chapter 15

1972-1973: "I DON'T WANT TO DIE IN INDIANA"

After we made a decision to part, Linda accepted a job in Arlington, Virginia, where we had first met. I had been accepted to Purdue University but was on the waiting list for a teaching assistantship. Without the assistantship, I couldn't attend.

I called Purdue's registrar and asked for an interview. The person called me back and said she had set up an interview with the head of the Graduate English Department. I had no money to speak of, so, as I had done so many times in my life with little or no funds, I hitchhiked to Purdue for the interview.

I met with Dr. Jacob Adler, who asked me as many personal questions as he did questions about literature. For that, I was extremely grateful. I had been a pre-med student most of my college career and had taken as many creative writing classes as Virginia Commonwealth University would allow (four courses). I was weak in most any authors' works other than the Fitzgerald, Hemingway, and Steinbeck I had read in Okinawa, and I felt comfortable with a bit of Melville and Hawthorne.

At the end of the interview, Dr. Adler said, "You need to hurry. The last plane out of here will leave soon."

"I didn't take a plane," I said.

"How did you get here?" he asked.

"I hitchhiked," I said.

Several days later, I received notification that I had been accepted for a teaching assistantship, which allowed me to teach two English classes for $3,000 a year, all tuition paid with the exception of my health insurance which cost sixty dollars a semester.

During my stay at Purdue, I often hitchhiked to Richmond and back. During a semester break, I went to Richmond to see some old friends. Two areas where I cautioned hitchhikers were Richmond, Virginia, and Columbus, Ohio, where there was strict hitchhiking enforcement. Columbus was especially tough on hitchhikers. By that time, I had hitchhiked over ten thousand miles.

"He's With Me"

Columbus police were especially tough on hikers who had been caught hitchhiking on the interstate. During my first vacation, a Columbus cop pulled over twice to warn me. I knew the law: no hitchhiking directly on the interstate. However, I took my chances.

"If I catch you here again," the cop said. "I'll take you in. You can use the exit ramp," he said, frowning. But that was like thumbing for no ride at all. I said okay, but when he was gone, I moved back onto the interstate.

A third time before he could return, I sensed I'd get a ride, but the cop quickly returned and pulled over beside me, cuffs in hand.

"What'd I tell you?" He shook his head, as if to say he'd seen the likes of me before.

Even if I didn't believe in Jesus, I might have just then. A young hippy in a VW van pulled over and screamed, "He's with me." Was this really happening?

The cop released me and said, "I better never see you here again."

I nodded respectfully and climbed in the van of my newfound friend.

"Where you off to?" I asked.

"Fredericksburg, Virginia," she said.

"Richmond here."

I tossed my seabag in the back seat and listened to the radio, "Me and Bobby McGee" blasting until the speakers shook. I started to speak, but she was so stoked, she wasn't listening to anything but Joplin and obviously had no interest in me as her Bobby McGee. She was only doing what the Dope Gods wanted her to do.

"I'm hungry," she said finally.

All I had to offer her was dinner on a Texaco credit card. They were honored at Holiday Inns. And in those days, Holiday Inns had restaurants. At the end of the meal, when the waiter brought the check, I couldn't find my card. It was evident this charitable woman felt duped.

Then it dawned on me: I had put the credit card against my foot in case someone tried to rob me along the way. I took off my boot and sock and handed the waiter a sweaty Texaco credit card. I saw the sigh of relief from my road angel. Then she laughed relentlessly.

At the end of the semester break, the same woman gave me a ride back as far as Columbus. That night she asked me if I wanted to stay over with her and her roommates. After we both had a few tokes of dope, she gave me a pillow and blanket and pointed to the sofa. The next morning, she gave me a ride to the interstate not far from where she had saved me before. The trip back to Purdue was uneventful.

I was popular with my students, likely because I wasn't that much older than they were. I prepared (and over prepared because much of the coursework was new to me as well), and I was very creative in my approach. I received one of the highest ratings of all the professors and other teaching assistants in the department, which did not go well with my faculty advisor and several of my peers. Whether true or not, I sensed my advisor was jealous of my success. We rarely saw eye to eye on anything. I rebelled against his authority.

One unexpected supporter was the assistant head of the English Department, Dr. Miller. I had thrown a party for the English graduate students and faculty. An elderly woman came up to me. It was Dr. Miller's wife. She said, "You are really keeping my husband on his toes. But I just wanted to say, whatever you're doing, please keep doing it! I haven't seen him this alive in years."

Dr. Miller was a mild-mannered man nearing eighty who always had a smile for me while teasingly shaking his finger as I walked down the hallway, especially for the havoc I was causing Dr. Kierce, my assigned professorial mentor. Later when I applied to other graduate programs, Dr. Miller gave me glowing recommendations.

I was friendless other than my story writing professor, Arturo Vivante, a former medical doctor from Italy, now living in the US, who published regularly in the *New Yorker.* He tried to help me publish there as well with no success.

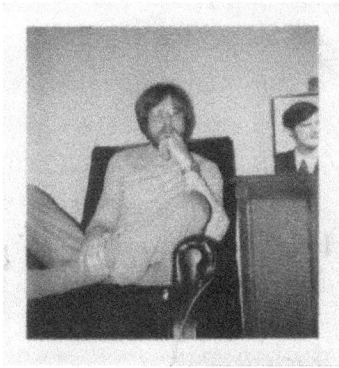

At my mother's house on semester
break from Purdue, 1973.
After six months, I hitchhiked from Purdue to
Virginia to ask Linda to go back with me.

My health was failing, I had no one in my life, and if my request were to serve any purpose, it was to add some stability back into my life. We walked to the old park where we used to go when we wanted to be alone before we married. I thought that was a good sign.

"Linda, I want us to get back together," I said in a moment when everything seemed to be going well. We had even laughed a little.

Her smile became stern, tight-lipped. Even though we were technically still married, she responded, "I wouldn't marry you if you were the last man on earth."

Her anger puzzled me. Yes, we had lived mainly in poverty, and it was apparent from the high-dollar high-rise apartment building where she was living that was no longer the case for her.

With my $3,000 a year teaching assistantship, free tuition except for medical insurance, and one last semester of the GI Bill, I was doing okay, but on the fringe of poverty still.

On the way back to her Arlington apartment, Linda mentioned she was enrolled in a community college music class. She told me her favorite composer was Rachmaninoff. I said I didn't care for Rachmaninoff. She said emphatically, "Well, I *really* do."

My dislike for Rachmaninoff only increased that day. I had plenty of time to think about it as I hitchhiked back to Purdue. It felt like my longest hike ever. I would only see her one more time; that was to sign the divorce papers.

When we met to sign the papers, in what was her most compassionate moment the entire time we had been separated, she asked, "Are you okay?" She showed real concern.

I found out later she was in a serious relationship with a young major at the Pentagon. I was jaundiced by that time, thinking I had only weeks, possibly days, before getting the call from the VA hospital in DC that they were ready for my surgery. Instead, it took months. My jaundice continued to increase.

Photo of me at a Richmond museum just before the divorce,
age twenty-three, three years after completing my time in the Marine Corps.

1973: Journal Entries

I began a journal my second semester while teaching at Purdue.

10 January, 1973

Once again, I am pressing myself. But to what end? Even when there seems to be no goal, I press on until I reach some point at which I am exhausted. Then I rest. A week, a month, two months ... and begin pushing myself again.

I have often wondered if it's not a form of self-punishment, or even living out a life of symbolic crucifixion and rebirth ... When I become introspective, I become suicidal ....

My thoughts have become confused, and I want to quit thinking.

25 October, 1973

My first book of poetry will be called Moods. *It will be divided into several categories: Happy Moods, Suicidal Moods, Ironic Moods, Exuberant Moods.*

In every sphere of my life, there is a mental war. It is inevitable. And within the microcosm of self is the greatest of wars, between the parts of the self, divided between existence, and non-existence.

1973: The Physical Pain Becomes Mental

While at Purdue, the kidney issues worsened. My ureters turned out to be twisted and weakened, causing reflux into the kidneys, damaging kidney cells.

Beyond the physical pain, I constantly thought about the failures. I had been a seminarian just four years before with a marriage that now had been dissolved. The guilt of becoming a divorced seminarian overcame me. And now I faced a possibility of losing both of my kidneys.

I had rented a house from a professor who was on sabbatical, and I asked two undergraduate male students if they wanted to share expenses. It was a three-bedroom house in a fairly upscale neighborhood. I rarely saw the undergraduate roommates and spent most of my time in my office at Purdue at night, working on a novel while teaching two early-morning classes twice a week. Page after page began to consume me. I had turned my days and nights around—taught early-morning classes and slept in until early afternoon. As always, even in my time in Friendly View, I preferred to be a loner.

The novel was about the dysfunction and the odd behavior of folks in our family. The main character was based on my mother, who found creative ways to make the men in her life miserable for their womanizing and drinking. The main male character was based on characteristics of my father, especially his drunkenness, and my mom's second husband, Bucky, who, by the time of my writing the novel, had also taken up heavy drinking.

The narrator was a *Great Gatsby* Nick-like character who both entered scenes and participated in the insanity at times, which brought about considerable depression. The title of the novel was *The Little Bit Berserk Blues*. Later I would change it to simply *Berserk* and completely change the theme to dealing with my anger against God. That anger was a common theme of mine during the worst of my mental states.

Later, I changed the title back and wrote and rewrote *The Little Bit Berserk Blues* as it was originally intended. It would take ten years to complete a 250-page novel while working full time in the mid-'70s to early '80s. I had written well over several thousand pages to arrive at a final product.

My intensity began causing me severely increased anxiety. Pills helped but increased my depression. During the time at Purdue, I entered a meditation class. Maharishi Mahesh Yogi had started a movement that was meant to quiet the mind and heal the body. One of my roommates joined me in attending the sessions.

During one of the lecture sessions, I saw a woman several rows in front of me in an aisle seat. My mania had come back in spades.

I whispered to my roommate, "I really want to get to know her." He whispered back, "That looks like her husband sitting next to her."

One day shortly after the meditation classes had ended, my roommate came in from class just as the woman was walking out of my bedroom.

He laughed nervously. "You're going to burn in hell!"

It didn't feel much like a conquest. Having sex with another man's wife was a line I had never crossed before. It drove me deeper into remorse, deeper into a psyche that had already been damaged by my physical pain, divorce, and the sense that I was falling further and further into something I couldn't stop ... sex, no matter what the consequences, no matter what lines I crossed. Sex had become like alcohol and drugs: a temporary fix, the effect ending nearly as soon as it was over.

I continued to work on the novel and wanted few interruptions. Sometimes I even slept into the early-evening hours. I took various drugs to help me get to sleep, wake up, or just for recreation. I had accumulated amphetamines, sometimes acid, mushrooms, and antidepressant drugs I had collected from visits to counselors' offices or from my roommates, who were both dealing drugs. I went to a counselor at Purdue, never mentioning that I was considering suicide but claiming that I needed something to calm my nerves. I knew the drill, how to get the meds I wanted.

I had been building up the nerve. Finally, I took a sizeable cocktail of drugs. It was time to end everything. I suspect the results of the overdose came mainly from the antidepressant drugs prescribed by the counselor. After nearly twenty-four hours, I came out of a stupor, my bedsheets a pool of sweat. As I came out of my room, my roommates laughed and said, "We thought you were dead!"

I attempted suicide again in my office, on an overdose of meds collected from my Purdue counselor. I assume I had changed my mind at some point because a Farsi Ph.D.-candidate couple found me in the teachers' lounge on the sofa. They had come back late from a party and were checking their faculty mailboxes for students' papers or memos from the administration, which we often did.

While it was late at night, I was positioned in a very visible place, leaving it to fate whether or not I would be found in time. They walked me around the room for what seemed like several hours until it appeared that I would be okay. By the time they left, it was light outside. They never reported the incident.

*Around the time in 1973 when I had attempted suicide. Often
I just stared at this painting during "drug nights."*

As my medical situation grew worse, the second semester one of my students wrote on her student evaluation, "He's a great instructor when he's feeling well." I began sweating profusely, even during class. On several instances, I called the secretary for the department and asked her to write on the board, "Class dismissed today."

I felt that it was only a matter of time until I was successful in a suicide attempt. As Arturo and I were standing outside of his classroom, waiting for another class to exit, he whispered, "You're thinking about committing suicide, aren't you?"

I simply answered, "Yes."

He went on. "My religion says that if you commit suicide, you have to come back and do it all over again."

Hearing that, I felt more trapped in mind and body than ever. I didn't respond. Arturo's belief, if true, made me more depressed.

One day after class, one of my students, Steven, came into my office and told me he was contemplating suicide. Had the mindset that brought on my own attempts been that obvious?

He explained to me that he had *only* been accepted to Purdue, while his brother had gone to what his parents considered to be a more prestigious university. At first, I said, "Steven, do you realize Purdue is among the top ten engineering schools in the country in *every* type of engineering?"

I could see he didn't consider that noteworthy. What he thought his parents believed was the dominant issue.

"I'm not a therapist, Steven. My first inclination is to tell you that if you're feeling this kind of pressure, drop out. This isn't worth it. But I want to suggest that you see a counselor. I do myself on occasion."

Steven did see a counselor, my counselor, and brought me an Add/Drop slip. "The counselor agreed with you."

★★★

After the spring semester, I took my own advice. I dropped out. I needed help and I needed it quickly. There had been no mention of my health on my student evaluations the first semester. There were several the second semester, even though the evaluations were still some of the best in the department.

Becoming an English professor would have to wait. Maybe even in another lifetime. It had been nearly a year since I had all but pleaded with Dr. Adler to award me an assistantship. Now I went back to his office one more time.

He looked up from a pile of papers, likely new applicants. If I had a modicum of compassion for someone I would never know, it was that I didn't want him or her to wait for the news, as I had, of receiving *their* assistantship.

"May I help you?" he asked.

"I need to talk with you about dropping out."

"Why?" he asked. "Didn't we offer you a nice increase for next year?"

"Yes," I said. But why I said what came next, I would never know. "I don't want to die in Indiana."

Chapter 16

1973: BUCKY'S "ENLIGHTENMENT"

After leaving Purdue, I had a brief relationship with a woman who at one point insisted on meeting my mother. I had mentioned some of my mother's antics, which she found amusing. Finally, I acquiesced. I always feared that my mother would "show herself" when she was "in the right mood."

By the end of 1973, Bucky began drinking almost as heavily as my father had. The difference was he was not abusive. In fact, he was often abused by my mother for coming home drunk. That was reason enough for my avoiding visits.

Bucky had been drinking the night before and had come home late. He slept in his easy chair nearly the whole time the woman and I were there. My mother seemed happy to have company, so had been pleasant enough. We even took photos of Mom and Bucky where Mom gave one of her "Isn't this funny" looks. Bucky continued to sleep.

At one point, Mom walked over to the windowsill and picked up a lighter. I found it curious that there was a lighter there since neither she nor Bucky smoked. While continuing her conversation, she lit Bucky's foot.

Bucky bolted from the chair and started hopping on one foot. Mom clapped as if Bucky were performing a Russian dance.

"It's time to go," I said. The woman followed me out the door. I don't remember her name or even what she looked like. The event, however, is burnished in my memory. I never contacted the young woman again, nor did she reach out to me.

After reading a draft of my memoir, my sister, Debbie, said, "You know Mom poured bleach down Bucky's throat too. And she said the same thing you wrote about her doing that to Dad ... that she poured just a little bit."

I became an advocate for Bucky. Mom was beginning to act toward him as she had toward Dad. Yes, Bucky had developed a drinking problem. There was no doubt about that. But he was still a kind man, one who looked after all of us and never said an unkind word, even during Mom's most fervent attacks on him.

In return, in one instance, Bucky and I had gone to Hillbilly Heaven, Bucky's favorite bar that played only old hillbilly songs, like those of Patsy Cline, Merle Haggard, and Hank Williams. From the time Mom and Bucky were married, I was raised on hillbilly music. On the way home, Bucky passed out at the wheel and ran us into a ditch. I ran around to the driver's side and somehow persuaded Bucky to get into the back seat. He curled up into the fetal position in the back.

Soon thereafter, a police cruiser, blue lights flashing, pulled over near our car.

I sat behind the steering wheel.

"What happened here?" he asked.

"Someone ran us off the road."

I had been drinking, but much less so than Bucky. I risked having to take a Breathalyzer test. For all that Bucky had done to support me over the years, it was the least I could do.

"Why don't I see any tire tracks?" The officer asked.

I shrugged my shoulders.

Then he turned to Bucky.

"Sir ... sir! You're going to have to get out of the car!"

Bucky didn't respond but remained in the fetal position. When the officer was able to rouse Bucky from his stupor, the officer said, "Sir, I'm arresting you for public drunkenness."

In my condition, I was in no position to refute the officer's arrest— that Bucky was not in public but in the back seat of his car.

"Come down to the station and get him after he sobers up," the officer told me.

I don't recall Bucky ever having to go to court over the incident.

But another time Bucky and I had gone out to listen to hillbilly music, when we arrived home, Mom had deadbolted the front door. When we went around to the basement door, the door appeared stuck. Bucky and I both rushed at the door until the door buck splintered and opened. Mom had nailed the door shut, nailing every couple of inches between the door buck and the door.

"Don't you think I won't do that again!" She exclaimed.

Bucky spent the better part of two days rebuilding the door buck.

A photo I took moments before Bucky's "Enlightenment"

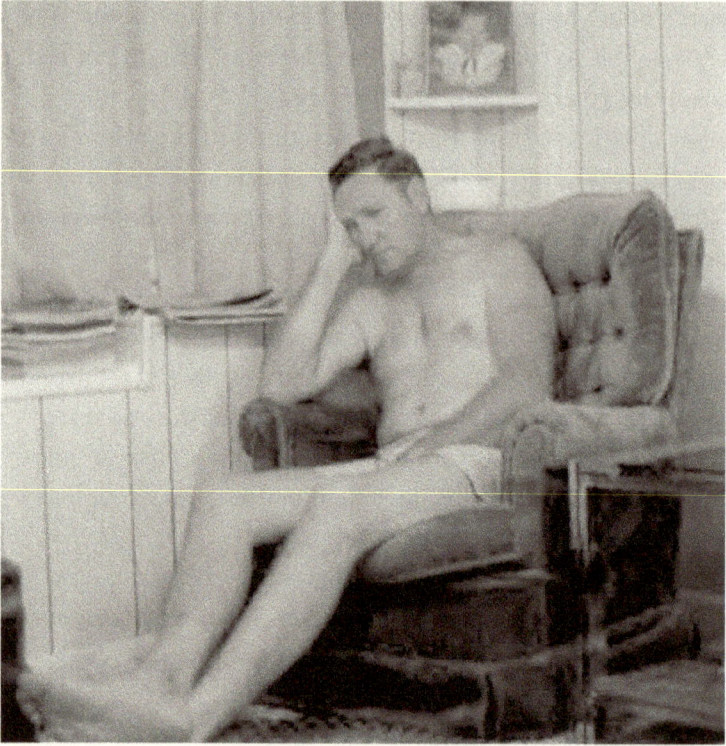

An unsuspecting Bucky moments before aroused from his easy chair

"I Never Gave You a Teddy Bear"

That Christmas, my mother surprised me with a large teddy bear.

"I never gave you a teddy bear when you were young. So I want you to have one now."

I had become well acclimated over the years to go along with any silliness or game Mom wanted to play. She could quickly turn from playful to annoyed.

"Teddy Bear wants a ride," she said.

I went along, getting down on the floor on all fours. She sat Teddy Bear on my back.

Just before her death, Mom had two small teddy bears. She thought they spoke to her. She placed them on her assisted living bed, facing her dresser mirror.

"Isn't that sweet the way they stare in the mirror?"

"Yes," my sister and I said. She carried them with her in her walker's basket when she took walks down the hall. "They liked to go for a ride," she said. "I've tried to feed them but they don't want me to."

I sense she owned the teddy bears for the same reason she had bought one for me as a Christmas present: she likely never had one when she was a child. She had her own way of amusing herself. Always. And it required others to be part of the show.

★★★

Before Dad died, he had been missing for a couple of days from his mountainous Georgia home. When a state trooper found him driving down the road in Alabama, the trooper asked, "Tom, where are you going?"

"I'm going to a football game."

My father had never been to a football game in his life. He never learned to play. His life was all about work from the time he was fourteen years old. He even scoffed at those of us who took time out for play. Totally unnecessary, he felt.

As with my mother and her teddy bears, he seemed to try to correct something missing in his life, something one only misses when it's too late to correct.

Chapter 17

1974-1975: CHECKING IN OR CHECKING OUT?

Nearly a year had passed since my students at Purdue thought of me as someone they trusted and regarded me as someone they connected with. What would their student evaluations say now? No doubt, they would scoff at who I had become.

Also, for all my efforts to entertain Mom, our relationship seemed to head south. I became distant and in no mood to be around anyone as a result of an increasingly deteriorating physical condition and melancholy that came from my long wait for surgery.

Just after the "teddy bear Christmas" of 1974, I became badly jaundiced, had lost considerable weight, and was living off an occasional can of Campbell's Chunky Beef soup while waiting for the VA hospital to call to bring me in for a nearly four-hour surgery.

When the call finally came, I called an old classmate I hadn't spoken with in several years to bum a ride to the hospital. There was no one else in my life. Years later, I joked that if I had died during surgery, I wouldn't have had one pallbearer, much less six, to see me off.

I had no sense of *poor me*; I was too far gone for that. Even *going through the motions* would have shown more cognizance than where I was at that moment. Maybe *zombification* would be a more accurate depiction.

The surgeon, Dr. William Yarborough, had patched up countless soldiers and Marines in Vietnam, he said, over a hundred surgeries. Later Dr. Berger, my urologist who had taught Dr. Yarborough at Georgetown University Medical School, said of him, "We used to call him Wild Bill." He came across as a regular guy but wanted to do things his own way. Some of his ways most medical professionals would have found unique.

"I'm not comfortable with the anesthesiologist who will help perform my surgery," Dr. Yarborough said. "As a result, I'm not going to put you to sleep during the surgery."

He would administer an epidural. I had no idea what that meant regarding the pain I would feel or how it would affect me in general, but I came to trust Dr. Yarborough implicitly.

It became obvious that he was more concerned about my general health than I was. Initially, when he had asked for a private room, the administrator balked.

"I'm the doctor here! I know what's best for my patient!" he screamed.

The administrator set aside a private room for me.

"This is going to be a very complicated surgery," he said. "I want you to have the best chance for recovery."

During the procedure, the operating room nurses and doctors told jokes, played music, and asked me from time to time if I was okay. I nodded yes with the exception of when they were sewing me up at the epidermal layer. It stung. Badly. The anesthesiologist hit me with a few tokes of gas. It was enough to get me through it.

Afterward, Dr. Yarborough told me my vitals were weak. I had refused to give the VA my next of kin. I hadn't talked with my father for some time, and my mother had recently had a hysterectomy and was as crazy as ever. The doctor came into the recovery room after discovering my refusal.

"We really need the phone number for your next of kin. We're having trouble getting your blood pressure up."

Finally, I gave them my mother's phone number.

Back in my room, several hours later, my mother stormed in.

"Why did you do this to me?!" she screamed.

She stayed for close to an hour and then claimed she needed to get back home to her son. She and Bucky, married for ten years, had a child named Keith. He was now eight years old.

Our years of trapsing back and forth to Friendly View were a distant history. Our history was no longer a bonding event. Dad became a rare memory; she had a new family now. Her attention was drawn to raising Keith.

Even her bonds, or lack thereof, had changed with Debbie from how they were during my early childhood years. Debbie was about four when Dad and Mom divorced. Now she was a teenager who Mom claimed gave her all she could handle.

Other than during Mom's brief stay, I continued to collect pain medication while at the hospital. As Mom nearly screamed at me for my "lack of consideration," I popped several pain pills. Nothing seemed to help from her wailing. She was a wailing expert.

Typically, the nurses' assistants left the pills on my tray without watching me take them. Several days later, a nurse who had just come on duty looked into my eyes and said, "Somethin' ain't right here." She opened my drawer and found a stockpile of pain pills tucked away. I was nearly there. I nearly had enough to end the pain forever.

I think I would have if it hadn't been for her. She gave instructions that she was the only one to give me pills when she was on duty. She watched me take them.

"Open your mouth. Lift your tongue. That's it. Honey, it may not seem like it now, but you have a lot to live for."

As I look back, there were so many instances of life-giving causes and effects. The Farsi couple at Purdue who found me in the lounge, Arturo's suggestion that I would have to do it all over again if I were successful, and the nurse who came on duty and showed the initiative to open up the drawer.

I sensed that she was the one who called representatives from the Disabled Veterans of America (DAV) and wanted to give me some hope. Three men from the organization came to see me.

One of them said, "We think we can help you get a twenty percent disability. We'd like to pursue it. We think your health issues were made worse by your time in the Marine Corps."

I declined.

"Nobody told me I had to join," I said.

I cut the conversation short, indicating that I was tired and needed rest. If I had joined the Marine Corps to prove to myself that I was physically *normal*, it hadn't worked. Physically and mentally, I felt spent.

Journal Entry – The VA Hospital

I entered Veterans Hospital, Washington, DC and found the truth! It is more blinding than Plato's sun at first, but now I see it and I must realize the alternatives more perfectly—the alternatives of existence or nonexistence, ultimately to struggle through the darkness without a path pointing the way to a merciful outcome.

1974: Lonely Strangers

What I thought and what I revealed to others were two different things. I still bore the memories of Mom instilling in me that "what goes on in our house stays in our house." What I felt deep in my gut rarely reached the surface. Life was a series of compartmentalized *boxes*, little of it right for sharing with others.

I dwelled on the notion of losing both kidneys, as the doctor in Tennessee had claimed might happen. And socially, nothing seemed permanent, especially relationships. Linda had made it clear that I had been an unfit partner. And at times, it was as though I had set out to prove her right.

Before my entry into the VA hospital, I had met a young woman when I worked briefly for an employment agency, prior to getting fired for showing up partly inebriated from the previous night.

Amber came from a wealthy family in New Jersey. Her parents rented an apartment for her in Georgetown, an upscale neighborhood, and paid her tuition to Georgetown University.

"I'm worried about you," Amber said. "Have you given any more thought to moving in with me?"

For nearly the whole year I had seen her, typically showing up at her apartment after a night of drinking, the topic of moving in was a constant theme. One night after a drinking bout at the Pall Mall Club, my nightly hangout, I showed up at her door. She was in her night clothes. I vowed that I would move in with her.

The next morning when I woke, she greeted me with a toothbrush she had bought while I slept in. I was occasionally still haunted by Linda's depiction of me as unworthy, even as "the last man on earth."

"I'm sorry, Amber. I was drunk last night when I said that. I wouldn't wish my being around you on anyone right now."

She was hurt over the encounter but still saw me from time to time. When I showed up at her door after drinking binges, she fixed me meals and tucked me into bed. I was growing thin, looked more pale than usual, she said.

I continued to lose weight and had little mental or physical stamina for a long-term relationship. I especially regretted that with Amber. Mentally, hope quickly lessened, like a winter tree without leaves, never to bloom again.

She was one of the sweetest people I had ever met, then and now. Maybe there was more to her attraction to me, but I detected she felt I was a stray who needed help, a stray who needed healing but ran at the first instance of intimacy. I suspect that over time, Amber would continue to find other strays who were caught up in her desire to heal them.

Shortly thereafter, when a therapist asked me who in life had shown me intimacy, Amber was the first person I thought of. She cared.

Amber typically got off work in late afternoon and would come to see me at the hospital shortly thereafter. I felt a tinge of hope around Amber, as fleeting as it was.

Another woman who was a regular at the Pall Mall Club was a music teacher at a high school in Alexandria. We also saw each other a few times prior to my going into the VA hospital for surgery. The music teacher (I can't recall her name) typically visited me at the hospital in the early afternoon after school. If I had been more perceptive, I would have realized that she was more snippy than not. Still, she showed an interest in me, and my bar for ephemeral encounters was set low.

Joyce, an infrequent visitor to the club, worked a full-time job with the federal government. We attempted to have a relationship, but she was concerned that she didn't want her four-year-old daughter to see me until our relationship was further down the road, which meant coming to see her after she had put her daughter to bed. I sensed that she had had a number of false starts with men.

Joyce typically came to see me at the hospital during evening visiting hours. She was considerably matter-of-fact. Her former husband had been a blacksmith. I'd have thought they'd have been a good match. I could actually see her pounding an anvil. But for all that, she seemed kindhearted.

For all I knew, none of them knew about the other two.

I always knew there was a possibility of overlap visits. But when I was drugged, nothing seemed to matter. Although what happened next is still beyond my comprehension.

The nurse who had discovered my stash of pain pills walked out of my room after watching me take my pills and immediately poked her head back around the side of the door.

"Oh Lordy," she laughed. "My boy, you are going to get it now!"

All three walked into the room at the same time. I could only surmise that I had left the phone numbers of each on the nightstand next to my bed.

I often nodded off when each made their brief visits. It would have been like Joyce to organize the "get-together." She had great organizational skills, as had been shown during my late-night visits to her house.

Although all three appeared deceived, they all wanted to know who I was going to go home with when released. Drugged as I was, I learned something about loneliness at that moment: even under deception, each was willing to put all this behind them if it meant having someone in their lives.

Like Amber, the music teacher came from a well-to-do family. Her grandmother had bought her a fairly large house on a hill in Fort Hunt in Alexandria, located just a couple of blocks from Roberta Flack's house.

Visibly upset, Amber took what little money I had in my drawer and simply said, "My bus money" and left. I decided I was going home with the music teacher. Joyce only shook her head. She lingered for a bit to see if I would change my mind. I didn't, and she left.

During my stay with the music teacher, she assigned me to a small bedroom on the first floor and occasionally brought me one or two meals a day. She also brought other men into the house, and I could hear them having sex in her bedroom on the second floor. I made calls to find my own place, even though moving about was still painful.

1974: Failure and Agitation

I hadn't worked in a while, so I applied for welfare at social services in Alexandria. I stayed on welfare for two months, just enough time to save enough money to rent an apartment in Carydale East, a moderately priced high-rise apartment building in Alexandria.

Maybe I wasn't a poor, starving student at Purdue anymore, but welfare? It felt as though the pieces of my life's jigsaw puzzle had never come together, even before joining the Marine Corps. A piece here, a piece there had seemed to come together at times prior to my kidney issues in Tennessee and were now scattered about where none of them seemed to fit. Without a framework, the rest was beyond scattered. Starting over was little different from the thirty-plus times I had swapped one house for another for shelter over the years. Each movement gave me new riddles to solve.

I started a part-time job as a telephone solicitor but found myself falling even deeper into depression. I often missed my scheduled times to take my shift, or I showed up late. One day when I was running late, I called the supervisor to let him know.

"Don't bother," he said. "You're fired."

Several blocks from Carydale East was a McDonald's that typically had a sign in the window asking to Apply Within. During those days, I wore my old Marine Corps overcoat and was rarely clean shaven.

Six years had passed since I had left the corps. What if I had taken the Marine Corps up on Naval Academy Prep School? What would have happened if the kidney issues had come up then?

When I asked for the manager, as he approached, he didn't make it to the counter before saying, "We're not hiring today."

★★★

I still visited the VA hospital for Percodan and other drugs to deal with the pain. The doctor had warned me about drinking while taking Percodan.

"You're not out of the woods yet. Your surgery may or may not succeed."

I didn't heed his warning. I drank on Percodan and was rushed to the hospital. I lost most of the function of my left kidney.

The doctor had told me it would be months before I could lift heavy items. Yet as I had done during summers so often, I showed up at a motel in the early-morning hours where moving company truck drivers stayed when they came to town. It had only been two months since my surgery.

I found daily work for five dollars an hour. It was a several-mile walk to the motel each morning where most of the truck drivers stayed.

Feelings of unexplainable agitation settled in. I had cut off all relationships with people I had known. At least when I was young in West Virginia, I had had the river to go to. Now I was surrounded by concrete and fumes from traffic all around me. And people were just passersby.

I had discovered in those Friendly View days that isolation was a sensation I felt when no one else was around, and I felt loneliness when I was around people. In both instances I felt hollow.

When the Ups and Downs Have a Name

The hollowness encroached on nearly every thought in 1974. I thought about what I told my student Steven at Purdue, "This isn't worth it. I want to suggest that you see a counselor."

My occasional visit to a counselor became self-instructive over time, even in my denials. It was time to visit a therapist again. The fact that I admitted needing a counselor steered me to believe I was wading in some serious shit.

I answered the therapist's questions in streams of consciousness, unable to piece together a coherent thought: my *father's violence*, and my purposeful, psychological failing at all aspects of life—a divorce from a beautiful, intelligent woman, giving up my idea of success as a potential medical student for a failure-prone writing career. I'd certainly made it easy to fail. Those were somewhat occasional rational thoughts. Then came ...

"I seek out certainties for reasons to existence and am not pleased with *maybes*," I told her. "I'm not good enough to have success, huh? I have been *suffocating* since I had the surgery. But I'm *alive* now! So hurrah for surgery! I must think about it in that light. But I have discipline now. There will not be the hyperactive workings as in the past ... I am going to begin leveling off—I can feel it ... I have always looked at life from the underbrush. I'm going to clear the underbrush of life soon so I can have a good look at the sky. The light."

On my third visit, she said, "You have bipolar tendencies. I want to send you to our psychiatrist who can prescribe lithium for you. I think you'll feel much better after the regimen takes effect. It will take a while. And I would like to continue seeing you."

It would take months before I saw her again. I was not bipolar, I thought. *That's for crazy people.*

***

I continued to work for moving van drivers. My frenetic moments worked well for them. I loaded trucks lickety-split. In the days when refrigerators were smaller but nearly as heavy, I took my hump straps and carried refrigerators out to the van by myself. As I began to heal from the surgery, I had started working out with weights again, as I had done in Okinawa.

But I was always behind on my rent. The rental clerk at Carydale East was nearly twenty years older than me, and there was a glass front to her office, between me and the front door. She would often wave me into her office before I could slip out.

At one point, she said, "You're more than two months behind on your rent. I'm having trouble finding excuses for you with the owners." She liked me. I wasn't sure in what way. What I did know was she was the only reason I wasn't on the street.

"I'm working now," I said, which was only partly true. Loading trucks was a day-to-day proposition. And soon summer would be over, and there would be fewer trucks.

But when I had saved some money, when faced with the choice of whether to pay the rent or buy an old VW bug convertible, I bought the VW. Both the engine and transmission were nearly unfixable. But a guy who lived next door to an old friend and used to work solely on VWs agreed to repair both the transmission and engine if I would pay him later when I was on my feet. He always had spare engines and parts lying around the side of his yard. I agreed.

We used to say of Bill Bezick that he probably wasn't going to amount to much. All he seemed interested in doing was taking apart and putting back together VWs. He later became a Porsche mechanic making more than any of us were ever likely going to make.

With a car, I was able to get a job selling accident insurance to both businesses and residences. It was basically an ambulance-chasing job. Follow the sirens, see where they lead. Sell to business communities in fear.

I was poor at the job. I lacked motivation and felt the job was beneath me. The days of teaching freshman English at Purdue still percolated at times, but the manager said if my sales didn't pick up, he was going to let me go. That sparked an instinct to survive.

I took a debit package to collect on policies due from former salesmen and attempted to sell those policy holders more insurance. I went to every garage I could find and even tried to sell accident insurance to a race car driver.

At a massage parlor, the owner required all his massage therapists to buy my coverage. There were maybe fifteen or so scantily dressed women who signed up for my policy, along with policies for their children. A couple of them wanted to barter for a massage, but I declined. I was never sure if sex was part of the offer, but the county checked on their business from time to time, likely sending agents who would ask for sex to see if the women would comply. I had policies to sell and rent to pay.

One Saturday, I called the sales manager at home while he was having a family barbeque with his brother and family.

"I need your help," I said. "My hand is stiff from writing policies. I need you to come and help write the policies while I sell them." I didn't expect him to do it, but at one point he said, "I'll come and write them, but if you're lying to me, I'll fire you on the spot."

My mind was spinning *out of control*. I found when I was manic, people gravitated toward me when my mania was manageable, typically at the beginning of an episode.

I had written eighty-nine polices. I would go on to write a new company record for that area, dating back to the 1930s, of 103 policies. I was recognized for my big day at the insurance company's convention. I quit shortly thereafter.

I had enough money to catch up on my rent and buy a better car.

On my way back from the convention, the car caught on fire. It was a sign that better things were coming, I thought. The old VW had served its purpose.

Until I found a better job, I returned to the Pall Mall Club, where I mainly stood in a corner drinking Tequila Sunrises. It was a place of familiarity yet a place where unhappy people came and went. I felt lonelier there after leaving than when I came, always alone among masses of people as I had been since coming back from Okinawa. I felt less vertigo among those masses when I drank. Yet I envisioned good things to come that month, and that's why I wasn't upset about my car burning up.

Sometimes after a night at the Pall Mall Club, as I tried to get to sleep, I saw unfamiliar faces I couldn't get out of my mind. It was like dreaming while I was awake. Most of the faces were distressed faces, even when they tried to smile.

I tried Transcendental Meditation like I had learned at Purdue. But whoever they were, they wouldn't go away. And drunkenness was no remedy for sleeplessness.

I shared what I was going through with Joe.

"Joe, I think I'm going crazy."

No matter what I said to him, he typically answered, "You'll be okay."

While our days in Friendly View were well beyond us—I was twenty-six and Joe was twenty-seven—both of us had put our conflicts back in West Virginia behind us. We had become like brothers.

He had married his childhood sweetheart. His wife, Gloria, became pregnant shortly after graduating from high school. They had twins—two boys—and within two years had another son and daughter. During those early years, he delivered a rural mail route, waking at 5 a.m. and off by 2 p.m. After work, he sold old cars from what can only be described as a shack.

Later, Joe's real father, whom he had hardly known, had died in Florida and left him enough money to turn a small struggling auto dealership into a much larger successful one. Joe became a respected car dealer in Manassas, Virginia, and gave money to charities in town regularly. When he passed away at seventy-two, there were two viewings for two days, which resulted in nearly a thousand people who came to pay their respects.

Even though I had never owned one, Joe knew I was fascinated with fast cars. When I went to him to buy a newer car, he said he knew a man who was dying of cancer. The man owned a souped-up Chevy that had been modified for the Manassas speedway and was willing to sell it for a few hundred dollars. The ill man was afraid if his son took the car after he died, he would surely hurt himself. If I wanted it, Joe would pass on it and tell the man about me.

I bought the car for three hundred dollars. Late at night, after the bars closed, I took it out on Interstate 95 long before it became a crowded thoroughfare and wound it out as far as the needle would go, 120 miles an hour.

Sometimes I drank into the late hours of the night/early morning and never felt the effects of the alcohol. I felt exhilarated. Other times I drank very little and felt totally wasted and depressed. The depression sent me back to the therapist, who once again told me I was probably bipolar. I was finally beginning to believe it.

Chapter 18

1974: A CURE FOR DEPRESSION

One night at the Pall Mall Club, two guys were harassing a petite young woman. I walked up to them and suggested they move on. I was still wearing my Marine Corps overcoat. That was possibly the reason they left, or maybe they just didn't want any trouble in this popular bar.

Her name was Rene, and I offered her a ride home. Turned out, she was a governess who had come over from Germany because she wanted the experience of living in the US. She had followed an American GI she had dated in Germany.

She was five-two and weighed just over a hundred pounds. As I was dropping her off in front of the house where she was governess, she asked if I wanted her phone number.

"Yes," I said.

She told me what it was. "Don't you want to write it down?" she asked.

"I don't forget numbers," I said.

It had been a game a high school friend once played, to give me a series of numbers and have me recite them back to them. Without fail, I did.

The next morning, I called her.

"I'm in shock that you remembered!" she exclaimed.

"Like I said, I don't forget numbers."

The following month, she moved into my apartment while I was out scavenging for better work. It was an efficiency apartment. No bedroom. Just a pullout sofa.

There had been several bags of garbage that I hadn't yet taken to the trash chute just twenty feet or so from my apartment door. When I came home, the trash was gone, the room smelled like ammonia, and there were flowers on the windowsill.

"I don't have enough money to support both of us," I said. "I can't even support myself."

My debts on May 21, 1975

"I have money," she said. "I have four thousand dollars I've saved from working for the Johnsons." She pulled the cash out of a small bag. When I looked in my closet, she had already hung up many of her clothes. Her toothbrush was in the bathroom.

When she took off her clothes that night, I saw she had stab wounds covering her body. Her former boyfriend was a Black serviceman she had had an affair with near Stuttgart. She had lived with him a short while when a tall Black man knocked on the door while her boyfriend was out and asked for a cup of sugar.

He stepped inside and stabbed her more than twenty times with a barber's knife. She crawled out to the stairwell, where a couple stepped over her. She believed they were the ones who called the police.

Later I went to court with her and heard that he only got fourteen years but could be released after seven for good behavior. During the trial, the detective assigned to her case testified. It was Roger Simpson. We had been in boot camp together and stared across the aisle at each other for two months. It wasn't lost on me that Roger had worked his way up to detective in the eight years since boot camp, and I was living in a subsistent world.

"I thought you would wait for me," he said to Rene. He had visited her in the hospital on a regular basis. It was obvious he was enamored by her.

★★★

Rene and I married after only knowing each other for three months. She would wake up screaming at night. I held her and comforted her back to sleep. I needed to care for someone. I sometimes screamed on the inside.

Rene was a governess for a former White House professional photographer. She asked him to take photos of us just after our marriage.

Soon afterward, I stopped drinking. I felt Rene needed my full attention when I wasn't working. I had gone back to work for the insurance company. While I was modestly successful, with fewer ups and downs as I'd had previously, we were living to a large degree off her money.

At one point, she said, "I have to go back to Germany to clear up some loose ends."

I had no idea what that meant.

She sent me a letter informing me that she was having trouble with her green card and that it was going to take months for her to get back to the States. I worked with the federal government to try to get her back. As it turned out, they had misplaced her file.

When she left, I felt my reason for giving up drinking had disappeared with her absence.

Lie Still, Young West Virginian

Lie still, young West Virginian. You, lifeless
in an alleyway behind a DC bar, far from the land
of bobcats, rainbow trout, and blue-green mountains,
partly hidden by the fog and morning dew.

Lie still, young West Virginian, the city isn't done
with you yet, you in your tattered blazer, the only
coat you own, pebbles in your pockets.
How did they get there? you may ask.

Lie still, young West Virginian, on this steel gurney
which holds your gangly frame. You look so feeble,
pale. A doctor will finally say, "A couple found
you, blue, almost without pulse. You're free to go."

Walk gingerly, young West Virginian, past cracked walls
of commerce, Lafayette Park where the homeless reside,
Four Georges restaurant where presidents dine, Mass
Avenue where diplomats unravel foreign policy.

Walk gingerly, young West Virginian. This is not the land
of rainbow trout and mountain streams but of brick barriers,
urban sprawl, where the rhythm quickens, you
don't understand. One you will never understand.

Down and Out: 1975

I went back to the Pall Mall Club. Harry, the bartender, said he was purchasing a bar called Winston's and wanted to share his good news with me. He poured peppermint schnapps until I felt close to passing out.

I had quit the job at the insurance company again. The psychologist I had been attending quit talking about my need for lithium. She became very practical. Rather than dealing with the many issues of my psyche, she wanted to talk with me about getting another job. She often talked about interview techniques, how I would dress, etc.

The morning after sharing Harry's good news, I found myself on a gurney in George Washington Hospital. I pulled the file attached to the gurney. It read that a tall disheveled man had been brought to the hospital, had been blue and in an epileptic condition.

Finally, a doctor walked up to me and said, "You were very fortunate. It was freezing last night, and a couple happened to find you in an alleyway. I found a card in your wallet from your therapist. I phoned and told her what had occurred. She said she wants you to come in later this afternoon, bring your briefcase, and be prepared to go out looking for work."

As I walked out of the hospital, I looked down at my favorite blue blazer, and the first thing that came to mind was that I would never be able to wear it downtown again.

Recently, as I thought of that moment, it struck me how two people I would never meet had been there at an opportune moment to save my life. Maybe it was just another matter of cause and effect, but while I'm still not particularly religious, it gives me pause to believe in guardian angels, guardians who had designs on me to be a trainee to later ease the burden of others.

★★★

When I showed up at the therapist's office, I had done as she had asked. I cleaned up as best I could but was still unshaven. I was carrying my briefcase.

"What do you have in the briefcase?" she asked me at one point.

"Nothing," I said.

"Do you think that's what I meant by asking you to bring your briefcase?"

I remained silent. She returned to my mental issues.

"I'm quite sure you're bipolar."

My meek behavior that had been with me since those days in West Virginia became internal fury. I excused myself and never went back. Maybe I was going crazy when I saw faces at night when I was trying to get to sleep after a drinking binge, but I wasn't *that kind of crazy*.

I was too depressed to work full time. I tried working part time as a telephone solicitor again but, again, was fired after not showing up twice.

Unshaven and wearing my old Marine Corps overcoat, my uniform of the day, dusty as it was, I tried again to answer to a hiring sign at McDonald's near Carydale East. Again, the manager simply said, "We're not hiring today."

A short time later, I went to Winston's, where by this time Harry had bought out the previous owner. Again, we drank until the wee hours. I had no recollection of time, but the fury in me had taken over much the way my father's kettle boiled. The idea that I was bipolar continued to percolate. I had little interest whether I lived or died.

On my way back to Carydale East, I reached Duke Street in Alexandria and challenged fate once again. As I had done several times before, I floored my souped-up Chevy until I could see the needle at 120 miles an hour on what was usually a busy thoroughfare during the day. It was likely around 2 a.m. I hit a truck that came out of nowhere. I spun around and took off.

Smoke was coming over the hood of the car where the truck had collided with my left fender. My fender slightly cut into its left front tire. Behind me I could see and hear sirens. There were two police sedans in chase. I kept it floored. I hit a large hump in the road near the Masonic Temple and went airborne. The police cruisers pulled back.

I spun around the corner to a dead end and ran from the car to my apartment. Cousin Joe told me later that I called him around 3 to 4 a.m.

"Joe," I said, "I think I killed someone tonight." At the time, I thought I had. I would later find out I had hit a farmer and had injured his leg.

The next morning, I heard a knock at the door. Two police officers stood outside talking. They knocked for a while. But instead of getting a search warrant or asking the manager for a key, they just left.

"It's too bad," I heard one of them say.

Perhaps they knew I was a former Marine. I had been stopped several times before for swerving on the road. When officers saw my Marine Corps overcoat, they typically followed me home without giving me a citation.

That morning, I called the Alexandria Police Department. Corporal D. answered the phone. I simply said, "I think I hit someone last night."

"What's your name?" he asked.

I told him. "I think I have a drinking problem. I want to get some help."

"Yes, you did hit someone last night. Come on down to the station and let's talk."

It would have been easy for him to feel that I was trying to manipulate him, but at the station, the corporal sat me down and showed me his report.

"Do you see where it says 'Had the subject been drinking?'?"

I nodded yes.

"I left that blank," he said. "You can do what you want with that. But I want to tell you something ... I have a brother who had a drinking problem. He went to AA. I hope you'll do the same."

I signed the report without indicating that I had been drinking.

"Okay, you're free to go."

I had fully expected to be cuffed and spend time in jail. Instead, I lost my license for a year. That was not resulting from court actions—I never had to go through a trial or see a judge. And I didn't have the money to pay for insurance. It would take a year for me to gather enough funds to pay for SR-22 insurance, a policy for high-risk drivers.

Rene and I had been away from each other for three months. I was angry with the US government for keeping her from me. It didn't make sense. I even thought about selling everything and moving to Germany.

But for the meantime, going to Alcoholics Anonymous seemed like a better option.

Chapter 19

1975: "WE'RE BOTH CRAZY"

I started going to AA meetings. I had doubts that I would stop drinking. I went to meetings at night, and I found in the early going that I had a similar response to detoxing than I'd had detoxing from Naron on the ship back from Okinawa.

I remembered every night what had gone on the night before. Somehow, I functioned during the day. But at night after the meetings, I didn't socialize. I walked over three miles to get to meetings and then three miles to get back home.

When I came home at night after the meetings, I would sit in a corner and shake. The shaking seemed to worsen only at night, as did the paranoia. Paranoia that made me fearful that some unknown horror was about to occur. Fearful that someone would knock on the door. Anyone. It didn't matter.

I thought of Rene regularly. I wondered how she would react to the program and my stopping drinking. After all, we had met in a bar. She considered that a social outlet. But my attention turned to getting clean.

At one meeting, I met a guy named Homer. He had been a colonel in Vietnam and had to be medevacked out for psychological reasons.

He was paranoid schizophrenic, fluent in five languages, and played several instruments.

Homer with his Airborne wings attached.

He was also feared by many of the AA folks. His reputation had preceded him. In one meeting, as he walked into the room, several members ran out another door. He was sweating profusely and carried a towel to wipe his forehead from time to time.

Homer was huge. He weighed upward of three hundred pounds, was approximately six foot six, and had arms that were nearly twice as round as mine.

He stared at me with a cold glare. It was obvious he did not like surprises. As a new guy, I was a surprise. As an added surprise, I walked over and sat next to him and stared back.

He broke into a deep guttural laugh that I would come to know for nearly forty years. He became my best friend. Whatever the case, he was always there for me, and if he didn't hear from me for a time, he called to ask my whereabouts and ask if I was okay.

Fearful that I might slip, I began attending several meetings a day, day and night. In the beginning, when I went to meetings, I seemed physically—and even mentally—okay.

Then one day, I went downtown for some unknown reason and found myself in an affluent neighborhood in DC, There was hardly any place in DC I didn't know, but at that moment, the area was unrecognizable.

It could have been a different state or country at that moment, for all my ability to recognize landmarks. I found a phone booth and called Homer.

"Homer, I don't know where I am!" It was obvious to him that I was in a panic, possibly a psychotic break. If anyone would understand, it was him. By that time, even getting out of the phone booth seemed to be a chore.

"Go down to the corner. Look up at the street signs. Then go back to the phone and tell me where you are and wait until I can come and pick you up."

Like a child, I did as he requested, and when he picked me up, he said, "I called Dr. Burbach. He's my psychiatrist. He's going to fit you in. I'll wait for you."

In the session, Dr. Burbach said that some officers during World War II with "[my] intelligence" had had the same problem. Then he said the same thing the Ph.D. psychologist had said months before. "You're bipolar. I'm going to prescribe lithium," Dr. Burbach said.

He gave me samples that would see me through the worst of it and until I could get a prescription filled. On lithium, I felt significantly drugged, a sense of heaviness where it seemed that when I spoke, I had to wait a moment to understand what I had just said. But the anxiety, the mood swings, dissipated. Homer called me every couple of hours to make sure I was all right.

He asked me to stop by his apartment, where his wife, Marie, often left while he counseled me. She was used to his talks with other "pigeons," as those of us who had sponsors were called in AA.

"I want us to co-sponsor each other," Homer said. That was not typical of AA sponsorships, but nothing about the way Homer approached life was typical.

Homer told me his story in detail—his evacuation from Vietnam, where he had been in charge of building a bridge in a country where

US troops were not supposed to be, his time in a VA hospital in Salem, Virginia, where doctors gave him cocktails of drugs to see what worked. For years, hardly any did.

Dr. Burbach had given Homer the diagnosis of schizophrenia *and* bipolar disorder, a diagnosis rarely given for both illnesses to coincide.

At one point, he stopped telling his story and said, "You know, you and me? We're both crazy."

Chapter 20

1975-1983: THE TURNING POINT

Without a permanent job or a driver's license, I walked to Mayflower Van Lines, nearly three miles from Carydale East. Instead of standing in front of a hotel as I had done in the past, waiting for drivers to come out of their rooms, I stood in front of the Mayflower building, where more drivers came and went. Drivers would hire me to load and unload vans in residences or corporations rather than Mayflower's helpers because Mayflower was union and cost them more. Besides, I was getting a reputation among drivers as a good worker, *and* I was non-union. Over-the-road drivers using non-union help was unallowed by Mayflower management.

One day, a manager came outside. I thought of running but decided to hear what he had to say. I had been chased away by a Mayflower dispatcher before. I had been told by other non-union laborers that as long as I stood off the curb, I wasn't on their property. The union loaders saw us as competition and often harassed us.

"I hear you have a college degree, is that true?" the manager asked.

"Yeah, I graduated from VCU and taught at Purdue as a graduate student."

Suddenly, I felt a deep sense of angst. I hadn't given that part of my life much thought recently, or how far I had fallen, partly because of my physical illness, partly the way I had responded to it, but mostly because of my mental issues. Instead of becoming an English professor, teaching and writing my books, I was loading moving vans in nearly 100-degree heat during the summertime.

"Shit!" he said. "You don't belong out here. You belong inside. I have an inside sales position that's open. It pays $8,500 a year plus insurance. Are you interested?"

"That's great," I said. And after thinking for a few seconds what this manager had really offered me, I almost screamed, near tears. "That's really fuckin' great!" For at least that moment, I allowed myself to think, *All this shit I've been going through ... can it really be over?*

I wanted so much to believe that this was a turning point in my life, at least financially. I was still going to AA meetings regularly, often multiple times a day. My doubts that I could stop drinking were beginning to subside. But now I could have a decent job, and I wasn't going to screw that up. The lithium seemed to be working, and the drugged feeling was heavy but manageable, although I was gaining weight I had never felt before.

Working inside the Mayflower office in the early days after losing my license, some of the union laborers at Mayflower came to know my story and knew I didn't have a car. Now that I was one of them, they had become forgiving.

After I told them what I had gone through, I rarely had to walk to or from work again. Many of them had stories of their own and openly told them to me.

"Nobody here is a Boy Scout," one of them told me after hearing my story one day.

Every evening before leaving, whether it was the white-collar workers in the office or the laborers on the trucks or in the warehouse, they all ensured I had a ride to Carydale East before they left at night.

When one year had passed, I bought an American Rambler for $600 that had a manual transmission that didn't require a clutch to change gears and an engine that often sputtered and had to be restarted from time to time. I kept a case of oil in the back seat. It took more oil than gas—two quarts every fifty miles. As a result of the accident with the farmer, I had to pay SR-22 high-risk insurance for $2,200 the first year.

★★★

It would take just under a year for Rene to get clearance to come back. When she arrived at the airport, she looked somber, almost angry. And later, she seemed angry if I didn't want to go to the bars with her.

"You can just have one or two drinks. You don't need to get drunk every time."

"I can't do that," I said. My joy over seeing her turned to anxiety. I had heard the message over and over again at AA meetings that AA came first, no matter what. That meant marriages as well.

Shortly after she came home, she said, "I have something to tell you. I had an affair with an old boyfriend when I went home. And I got pregnant and got an abortion."

I stared at her briefly and walked out of the room. I had already gone through one divorce that had almost killed me with guilt. I had been a drunk. My behavior had been erratic and intense. Linda had looked almost relieved when she first said she wanted a divorce. I thought about her often, and regardless of the steps in the AA program that strongly suggested making amends with people—except when to do so would injure them or others—I wanted so desperately, even now, to know that she was okay and that in some way, she had found a better life for herself.

The program said I needed to stay sober one day at a time, sometimes one minute at a time.

A couple of weeks passed.

"I'm moving out," I said. "I thought I could handle this, but I can't."

Facing another divorce, I became less stable, even on the lithium. I picked up the phone.

My voice quivered. "Homer, I think I'm in trouble."

I was twenty-seven.

I met Homer for lunch at his apartment. His wife, Marie, prepared lunch for me and left us to discuss how to deal with just about everything life had presented to me. If Homer hadn't been through it, he had been through much worse.

Homer and his wife, Marie. Their apartment became like a second home to me in my early days of sobriety. I looked to Homer often for his sage advice. Marie was, and is, one of the kindest people I've ever known.

Mainly, Homer reminded me that AA came first above everything. Homer could say things other AA people said, and yet when he said it, it resonated much more deeply with me.

He was concerned, he said, that in addition to separating from Rene, I was working so many hours. He agreed that I should get my own place, that I needed some space away from her.

★★★

I internalized the hurt, the anger, the feelings of stupidity that I felt from marrying Rene. I had opened up to her like I hadn't to any other woman since my marriage to Linda. But she wasn't who I thought she was. I had been played for a fool.

Later in life, I felt that, while marrying her seemed like a foolish thing at the time, I had been there for her in one of the worst moments of her life, and she had helped me understand that taking care of someone else in need could provide some means of getting outside myself. To call it a win-win situation? I'm still not sure, but I lean toward yes.

1978–1982: Success and Failure

One day, one of the senior executives from Mayflower's office in Carmel, Indiana, showed up at my desk. "Someone told me your story," he said. "I'm in the program too. See this guy here?"

Beside him sat the top Mayflower salesman in the country.

"He needs our program. So here's what he's going to do. He's going to pick you up at your house each morning and give you a ride home at night. Then he's going to go home, have dinner, and pick you up again so you can both go to a meeting. Got that?"

I nodded but felt very uncomfortable. It took me a while to even look Jack Smith, one of the best salesmen Mayflower had ever known, in the face. When I did, he just nodded, almost sheepishly, like a little boy. He was known nationally for the accounts he served—IBM, Xerox, the World Bank, the International Monetary Fund, and on it went.

"By the way," the corporate executive said, "I've seen your sales numbers. You're outselling most of our outside salespeople over the phone. People obviously trust you. I've talked with your manager. You'll be an outside salesman soon. That will come with a company car." The role also came with paid gasoline and several other perks, including better insurance. The legal write-offs on my taxes with the IRS became incredible.

Jack took me under wing. He picked me up and dropped me off at home each night in his new Cadillac. He taught me the dos and don'ts of corporate selling. I became the number two salesman in the office, but well behind Jack. I went from making $8,500 my first year to over $40,000 the following year, money that I couldn't even have dreamed of even months before.

Immediately upon beefing up my checking account and starting a savings account, I bought a house on a VA loan and started renting out rooms to fund the purchase of another property. Shortly after that, I purchased a townhouse rental property in Manassas, Virginia, twenty-five miles away, with a VA/FHA loan.

During the busy season, I worked twelve-hour days and went to meetings at night, sometimes taking off for a noon lunch meeting.

When I was on the road, I often stopped by the national bank to take out funds for expenses. One day when I stopped by, the bank clerk said, "Sir, you don't have any money in your checking account."

I had recently asked Rene for a divorce. We had been married over a year and a half but had only lived together just over eight months.

"Well, take it out of our savings account." We had just over $14,000 in our savings.

"Sir," the clerk said, "you don't have any money in your savings account either."

I recalled that Rene had bailed me out when we first lived together. But this was considerably more money for only having lived together for less than a year. Once again, I felt like a fool. Why hadn't I seen this coming after telling her I wanted a divorce?

I went to an AA lawyer to begin divorce proceedings. With the income I had coming in from the rental properties and the fact that my sales were booming, I was able to build up reserves fairly quickly in a new account.

The AA lawyer made a peculiar request after knowing Rene had taken all of our funds weeks before.

"We need to take care of our women folk," he said. "You want the house and the rental property. You keep those and let her keep the cash she took out of your checking and savings accounts. Over time, you'll come out ahead."

Ill-advisedly, I bought into his reasoning, only to find out later that he was a friend of the AA person who Rene would marry when our divorce was final. Yes, I was angry with Rene, but the lawyer's dereliction of duty made me angrier.

The program taught that anger was the greatest enemy of sobriety. I had to let it go.

Months later, after marrying the guy in AA, Rene called and asked me for a loan. She told me how much she missed me and complained about her new spouse's lack of sexual prowess.

"Don't ever call me again," I said. That was the last I heard from her.

★★★

It would soon be 1979, and I was often alone except for Jack, Homer, and the other people I saw at the AA meetings. As I had done at age seven when Uncle Emmett had given me reams of paper, I started writing again to keep my mind off the reality that I had failed again.

I hadn't written anything since my college days years ago. I had completed a short novella when I was at VCU entitled *God's Puppet Play*. In 1972, Dr. Duke had read it. That was when he said, "Your writing reminds me of Tom Wolfe. We were classmates at the University of Iowa. He was an alcoholic and bipolar." His words resonated over the years. It dawned on me of those later years at VCU that he had become aware that my behavior was what had led the psychologist to make the call of bipolar several years later.

I didn't feel nearly as manic on lithium, but sometimes I wrote through the night, unaware that it was morning until the sun came up. Then I showered and went to work.

It felt like eons since I had stood in front of a classroom and toiled to make Ben Johnson interesting to a group of engineering students.

One night on our way to a meeting, Jack asked, "Do you ever have a drink now?"

"I don't have any interest anymore. Just want to stay sober," I replied. Maybe it was just a test. Who knows? What I do know is that he took well to the program. And we became work friends, and after a year or so of sharing our Marine Corps stories, just friends.

Jack had been a sergeant in the corps. He had been in Vietnam. He said he used to have a superior, a staff sergeant, who always got on his case. The staff sergeant had grown a vegetable garden and commanded Jack to kill all the red ants in his garden.

"They were called fire ants, and they would attack at the drop of a hat. Their sting was bad. So I just took some gasoline, poured it on his garden, and lit it," Jack said. "I told him, 'I killed your fire ants.'" He bellowed as he told the tale.

I believed his story. Jack was not a guy to reckon with when someone got on his bad side. He told me he was a member of Mensa, something we'd also have in common after I later passed the Mensa test (98th percentile on a standardized test) and Intertel (99th percentile).

After some months, Jack had an offer to leave Mayflower Van Lines to become a vice president for a United Van Lines agency in Alexandria. He said one of his first calls would be to call me and make me an offer. He made good on his promise.

Yes, the job was still in sales, but he gave me a percentage of sales that was 80 percent above what I had been making at Mayflower, plus a $700 a month expense account.

Later, the United Van Lines agency was found to be shipping goods other than those for the World Bank in World Bank containers. Jack held a meeting to let us know the company was going under. While Jack claimed he'd had nothing to do with it, the scheme became public. The company lost business.

"Why didn't you let me know?" I asked. "You knew I was purchasing a third property to rent."

"I couldn't," he said. "But when I get to where I'm going next, you're the first person I'm going to call."

In the meantime, I went to work for a small moving company, making about a third of what I had been making. Rene and I had divorced. In the settlement, I had let her keep the cash she had taken since she already had it anyway. Funds were running out quickly as I made payments on three properties. The rents and my meager commissions weren't enough to cover my mortgages.

1979–1980: The Last Psychotic Episode

Another divorce, falling behind on my mortgage payments, a poor diet, the damage likely done from taking drugs, and having drunk heavily for five years all came caving in on me. A woman from the program, Betsy, checked in on me from time to time.

"I don't like what I'm hearing from you in meetings," she said. She explained that I had seemed so positive early on, and now my tone of voice and what I had to say seemed so depressing, so negative, and sometimes nearly uncompressible.

I hadn't been to a meeting in a couple of days when I heard a knock at the door. It was Betsy. As I had done in some of my first meetings, I stood in a corner and shook.

"Please let me in! I know you're in there!" she pleaded. Her knocking seemed to go on forever until I finally rose and answered the door.

"My God! You look awful!" She smiled in relief that I had opened the door.

I went back to my corner.

"Betsy, I really don't feel like seeing anyone right now, even you."

She sat down next to me in the corner and put my head on her breast.

"You don't have to do anything. You don't have to be anyone. I just want to be here for you."

I wept. She came daily. Several days later I started back to meetings. I had remained sober, but I had stopped taking my lithium.

Weeks later, a used airplane salesman came to a lunch meeting I was attending. Betsy was there as well in her tennis outfit. She was a member of a social club where she played tennis almost daily. She said she was a Class B player. She sat next to me with her legs pointing toward my chair.

I approached the used airplane salesman after the meeting. I had begun to feel particularly energized as I hadn't in months.

"How much would a used 707 cost me?"

"Depends on the quality and mileage," he said.

"Would I be able to buy one on credit?"

"Of course, as long as you're a good risk," he said.

As my debt began to pile up, I had read several "How to Get Rich" books. They all said the same thing: spend other people's money. During the next weeks, I approached people who had been in the airlines industry and who were now in AA. I wanted to start a travel vacation company, I told them. One woman who had worked at the counter of American Airlines and was now retired said she would be interested in working on my new venture for nothing. All she wanted were the "fams."

She explained to me that *fams* were free trips paid for by destination companies vying for vacationers—island resorts, etc. I agreed that I would make those arrangements with her once we were up and running.

Betsy was so impressed with my idea, she convinced a bunch of her wealthy friends to see how many wanted to invest in it. One guy told her after my presentation that "He's really going to be successful." I was about thirty-one at the time and four years sober. There had been a lot of "reasons" for drinking back in the past: bipolar disorder, physical kidney pain, genetic disposition. At times, getting sober hadn't immediately solved the bipolar problem.

In fact, in some ways, my condition grew worse because I didn't have the alcohol to help reduce the agitation and/or mania.

The guy who said I was going to be successful was a psychiatrist who didn't recognize my symptoms. But before long, my depression started kicking in again.

The used airplane salesman came back to one more meeting. I approached him again. I wanted to discuss the terms and conditions of buying a 707.

"Do you realized if an engine goes out, it will cost you about a half million dollars to replace it?"

It was the perfect reason to tell those who were ready to invest that the price was too high. I told them so. We wouldn't be able to afford a new engine if one went out on us. I was coming down from a manic episode, and as so often happened when I came down, I asked myself, "What have I done?"

I was nearing the last of my manic episodes. In my last therapist's notes, she wrote "last manic episode 1980." I would see her for another three years.

1980–1983: A Gradual Return to Sanity

If there was anything going right in my life, I had become respected in AA. I was often called on to go on what were called twelve-step calls to clean up "drunks," as some of the old-time AA members called them. Sometimes, the person was inebriated; sometimes they were sober and had just had enough of broken promises to themselves, spouses, or other significant people in their lives. If they were willing, the AA member calling on them would either take them to a meeting or to the hospital, whatever seemed most appropriate. I had stayed up all night with some who had "made it" in the program "one day at a time"; others I never saw again.

A former used-car salesman named Al had started an "AA Social Club" where people could come any time of the day to get a cup of coffee or go to a meeting, day or night. He kept the club open until midnight for those who needed late-night help.

Prior to that, there were people in the program who had made fun of Al. Even when he wasn't selling something, it always felt like he was.

One day in the middle of a meeting, he disrupted the meeting by coming over to me.

"Come on. We've got a twelve-step call, and I need your help." I sensed he had chosen me because I was one of the biggest guys who came to the club, plus he saw that I had been less stable of late. Thinking about it later, the situation reminded me of what Mom Tucker had said: "We get what we need, not what we want." I felt uneasy about going with Al; I had no idea what I was in for.

When we arrived at the man's house, his wife answered the door. The stench even from the outside of the door was overwhelming.

"You want to help that son of a bitch, you go right ahead," she said. "I've had it with him." This would prove to be a normal response for spouses who had lived through the worst of it.

When we went into the bedroom where the man lay, we discovered he had rolled over in his feces. Some of it was caked on his body. Obviously, he had been in bed for quite a while.

"Take off your clothes except for your skivvies," Al said, directing me to remove all but my underpants.

"Why?" I asked.

He just stared at me, then smiled. "You'll get used to it," he said.

I undressed down to my skivvies.

"We've got to get him into the shower," Al said.

This reminded me briefly of the time on ship in the Marine Corps when I had to clean up other Marines' puke, but this stench was much more pungent.

Without touching the man, Al got down near his ear.

"This is Al from AA. I'm here to help get you to the hospital. You're in pretty bad shape. We're going to need for you to help us get you into the shower."

The man seemed semicomatose. What seemed impossible to me at the moment turned into a possibility when the man said, "I don't want to go to the hospital."

"Well, what you want and what you need are two different things," Al said. "Now come on." The salesman who so many people had seen as amusing I now saw as a man possessed to use his skills of persuasion to help someone else.

I was prepared to do anything Al asked of me just then. And what dawned on me most at that moment: Al wasn't the least bit interested in himself. He was there to help a human being who had obviously lost hope. If there have been few awakenings in life, that moment was one that shed light on who I wanted to be in the future.

The man struggled to get up. Al looked at me.

"You're a strong guy. Get over on the other side of the bed and help prop him up." Now in my early thirties and having grown weak from surgery and years of drinking and drugging, I wondered if I could do my part and wondered how Al was going to support the man from his side of the bed. Al was in his sixties. I pushed the man's back to help sit him up.

"Now come over here," Al said. "Sit down beside him and wrap his arm around your neck. When I push, you lift."

Al went back to the position I had held previously, behind the man.

"Now," he said. He pushed the man's back, I lifted, and the man fell to the floor.

"I didn't say it was going to be easy," Al said.

Al started the shower. After a couple of minutes, we half-dragged the man into the shower. His legs were like rubber.

As the man became more respondent, his legs seemed to gain more strength. We toweled him, then toweled ourselves. Previously I'd had on my suit for work. My suit trousers became soaked from my skivvies when I put them back on. It didn't matter.

It was a price I was willing to pay to be more like Al. He never had to ask me again. Anytime he got the call from the AA desk for a twelve-step call and I was at the club, I volunteered. It was the beginning of something. The club began to feel almost like a home, much more so than my house. My personal issues, marriage and financial, all began to feel trivial.

The man's name was Robert. Two or three days later, he came to a meeting at the club. He was dressed in a clean sports shirt and trousers. His hair was slicked back, and he looked like a man who was in the beginning stages of respecting himself. Helping people like Robert became infectious. It would become a lifetime commitment.

These twelve-step calls affected who I would become in the future when it came to helping others, not just in AA but also as a Big Brother in the Big Brothers Big Sisters program, helping with foster care children and food pantries, and hiring and/or mentoring forty interns when I was an executive in the federal government later in life.

1980–1982: "What Contract?"

The contrast to what it had been like to work for Jack Smith previously became evident. He was in it for himself. Appearances were everything to him. "Do what it takes to get the sale," was his conviction. I needed the funds that I made working for him, but more and more I was torn by being around his attitude. As soon as I could, I would find a way to sever myself from his way of life.

I was still struggling to make ends meet when one day, as I was in a home performing a residential estimate for a move, the resident's phone rang.

"It's for you," she said with a curious look. It was Jack.

"How did you get this number?"

"Never mind," he said. "I want you to come up to Lansing, Michigan. I'm VP of a company up here. I can give you a sweet deal as a sales manager, and I have designs on canning the current general manager and putting you in that position."

It sounded dicey. "Let me think about it, Jack. I go to meetings and have a lot of support here."

"Don't think too long. Give me a call back this afternoon."

That afternoon, I called back. Working for the small moving company was nice from the standpoint that they were reputable, but I needed the money to keep my properties afloat.

"Okay, I'll do it."

"I knew you would," he said. "I have a van on its way down right now to pick up your furniture."

As promised, Jack fired the general manager and made me his general manager for the Lansing office. What he didn't tell me is that he was going to attempt to bust the union. Members had been stealing from the warehouse and shifting goods around in pallet boxes so none of the goods inside a pallet box matched up with the inventory slips.

I started by writing up employees for the least little discrepancy, but it quickly became apparent to the workers what I was doing. Three write-ups meant an employee was gone. The warehousemen had been dissatisfied with the treatment they had received for years from the agency owners. Now the workers were *really* angry.

The union wanted to let me know it was *game on*. The union bosses posted a small guy I called Louie, who rolled up his cigarette package in his T-shirt and sat on the hood of my car, looking up at the apartment I had been renting to let me know they knew where I lived.

During that time, the moving company owners required me to load the workers in a van in small groups and have them polygraphed to see who had actually been stealing and/or moving goods around and also who knew about it.

We fired a number of employees based on the results of those polygraphs. One fairly meek but good worker knew about the behavior, as showed on the polygraph, but refused to take part in it. I called the owner to plead his case.

"Fire him," the owner said.

"I think he's worth saving."

"Fire him, I said," the owner repeated, this time in anger.

The employee had four children and not much chance of finding work immediately. The times were becoming recessionary.

I got a knock at the door. Jack stood in front of me with a smirk on his face.

"Come on, sport. We're going to spend the night at the warehouse. Pack your gear." I followed dutifully, not exactly knowing where this was leading to. Jack acted like we were two Marines on bivouac in the field.

At the warehouse, Jack said, "Those sons of bitches thought they could steal this warehouse blind. Well, let'em think that tonight."

Within a couple of hours, a white pickup truck began backing up to the warehouse. Jack took a pistol out of his bag and shot over their heads. The tires squealed as two men hauled out of the parking lot.

Jack chortled, "I don't think we're going to have that problem again."

There were trees in the background that separated the warehouse from an apartment development. Fortunately, I never heard of anyone having been injured that night.

The next weekend, Jack asked me to go duck hunting with him. He hunted. I rowed.

"I need police protection," I said.

"Can't do it, sport," Jack said. "We can't afford to bring attention to what we're doing. This is union country."

The polygraphs were probably illegal. "If you don't have police protection for me by Monday afternoon at one o'clock, Jack, then I'm on my way back to DC."

Jack just smiled at me. We didn't see any ducks that day.

One o'clock came and went. My secretary asked, "Do you want me to call the home office, or do you want to?"

"Go ahead and call," I said. "I'm going back to the apartment to start packing."

I had only been there for six months. But after tiffs with the union and Jack's antics with the pistol, it felt like years. It would not be the last I would see of Jack Smith. He left that job approximately a year later. He came back to the DC area several years after that.

After he'd moved back, he said, "I've come to know the Lord. I would like to get together with you for lunch."

He was taking over as vice president for an ailing Allied Van Lines agency. He offered me another position, just not as lucrative. I would find out later that the agency was nearly bankrupt. They laid off their employees just before Christmas without pay for several weeks but gave each an eight-pound frozen turkey.

While I took the job for about six months, my time making money with Jack and our friendship waned. Any time we were together, we sat in his car, and he would pray for my soul, that I would come to know the Lord like he had.

I returned to Mayflower, where I earned approximately what I had earned years before. I remained there for several years.

One last act by Jack, possibly in consolation for not having protected me in Michigan, resulted in a call from an owner of a United Van Lines agency in the same building where I had started working before the company had gone under.

"I need a sales manager, and Jack Smith recommended you." She said she would pay me $35,000 a year and provide me with a $700 a month expense account and 2 percent of the net profits as a bonus if I could turn around the company's losses. I accepted the offer.

It was a similar deal to what I'd had in Lansing, with the exception of no company car. I sensed Jack had negotiated it for me. Since deregulation years earlier, moving companies were going bankrupt by the droves, and those that survived were paying less than they had in previous years.

I had sold my three properties shortly after coming back from Lansing and was living in a two-bedroom apartment. I rented out the second room to newer AA members for nearly nothing to give them a chance to get their feet on the ground.

Interest rates were beginning to skyrocket. Companies and families moved very little during interest rate hikes. I turned around this

United Van Lines agency by bringing in corporate accounts that had followed me. But I knew that wasn't going to last much longer.

A year had passed, and the owner hadn't mentioned the 2 percent bonus of any profits she made. The truth was, she had been unprofitable for years. I thought we had established the bonus contractually; her recent profitability was mainly based on my accounts.

"Dot," I mentioned one day, "we haven't discussed my bonus for two percent of the profits we agreed to in my contract."

"What contract?" she asked.

"The one we wrote up when I came here last year."

"I never signed it," she said and turned back to the work she had on her desk. It made sense to me then that she was made up of the same fabric as Jack Smith.

Several weeks later, I approached her. She looked up curiously.

"Need to let you know, I'm firing myself. And I would suggest you batten down the hatches until this surge in interest rates passes over. I doubt that my accounts are going to do business with you."

Later I found out she hadn't heeded my warning. She had to sell her agency for what I would have guessed was a fire-sale price. As for me, I was Oregon-bound.

1982: The University of Oregon and Eugene "Everybody's Crazy" Redux

Once asked near the end of his career about his insights into the human condition which had been so often captured in his cartoons, a political cartoonist, Ralph A. Hershberger responded, "We're all nuts."

After ten years of writing numerous revisions, I finally finished my novel. Everything about our crazy lives seemed like fair game when I wrote *The Little Bit Berserk Blues*.

Based on submitting several chapters from *Berserk*, I was accepted to the University of Oregon's MFA program where Ken Kesey of *One Flew Over the Cuckoo's Nest* fame often came to class to listen to students read their works. Kesey's works were very much in the theme and mood that I wanted to write about: insanity with a touch of humorous relief.

At McKenzie Pass in Oregon, I picked up hitchhiker. Unlike its current environment, McKenzie Pass was a remote location then. I had been in many situations while hitchhiking when someone had dropped me off in an isolated area. Besides, I was ready for some company.

"Are you really going to take that car over Three Sisters mountains? he asked.

I nodded. "It got me this far."

I learned quickly that driving over Three Sisters mountains was not for novices.

"Don't use your brakes! Downshift!" the hitchhiker warned me several times.

I continued to use my brakes until they began to smoke.

"Christ," the hiker said, "if I had known it was going to be like this, I would have waited for another ride!"

It took nearly two hours for my brakes to cool down enough to start out again. Even then, I had no idea if I had done permanent damage to them.

On occasion, going around sharp curves, I could see the valleys down below. The drop-offs from the road were steep. I could see where if someone hadn't been watching and tumbled over the side, they may never have been found again. There were no guardrails anywhere.

I dropped off the hiker not far from Portland, where he was headed. He just shook his head as he exited the old Audi. Not a thank-you. Nothing.

Once I arrived in Eugene, a few blocks from the university, I took one bag into a hotel room and left everything else in the car. I was exhausted from the trip.

One door wouldn't lock in the old Audi.

The next morning, I came out to the car to find that all my manuscripts—two unpublished novels (including *Berserk*), three poetry magazines where I had been published, and a major newspaper article I had written for the *Richmond Times-Dispatch*—had all been stolen.

Ironically, the thief had left an Indian rug in the back seat that was worth several hundred dollars, while all my other goods would have been worthless to the pilferer. If I had learned anything in AA, it was, no matter how unsettling life became, to take it one day at a time, sometimes one minute at a time.

After ten years of working on the *Little Bit Berserk Blues* novel at night while working full time, I had a blank slate to begin working on my poetry and fiction again.

Prior to the semester beginning, I crossed county by county to every moving company within fifty miles, searching for a part-time job. The recession in Oregon had become similar to the Great Depression.

Georgia Pacific had pulled out of the area, so the lumber business, so vital to the area, had fallen on hard times. Without the lumber businesses, restaurants and businesses where lumber employees had spent discretionary money also fell by the wayside.

I watched from my window as people picked through the trash can of a deli just across the street from our group house. When the owner noticed people rummaging for food, he placed wide boards over his trash cans, and every day at the same time, he placed sandwiches on the boards on the cans.

The owner reminded me of Al, the used-car salesman in AA who helped so many people unselfishly. The owner's business was obviously suffering, but he was taking care of people who were more unfortunate than he was.

At the Eugene Mission nearby, there were a lot of people like Robert, the man Al and I had helped. Maybe their issues were different from his, but the people who circled the mission waiting for a meal were every bit as needy as Robert had been.

During my job search, one manager of a Mayflower agency nearly fifty miles from the university said, "I would be curious to see what other moving companies in the area will do with your resume. Very impressive. But I'm family, and they're thinking about laying me off."

Back in Eugene, I went to the employment office on campus and stood in line with dozens of out-of-work folks. The *Animal House* movie had been filmed within several blocks from the group-house room I rented, and there was talk that the producers might make *Animal House 2* there. As a result, lots of beautiful and handsome young women and men had enrolled that semester, just in case that the rumor would turn to reality.

A man approached me and stared at me for a few seconds.

"Have you ever done any acting?" he asked.

"I haven't," I responded.

"Well, it's my job to find people to audition for a Miller beer commercial. Are you interested?"

I said yes, and then he asked me if I had any *slicks*, photos that were typically used for auditions for would-be actors and actresses.

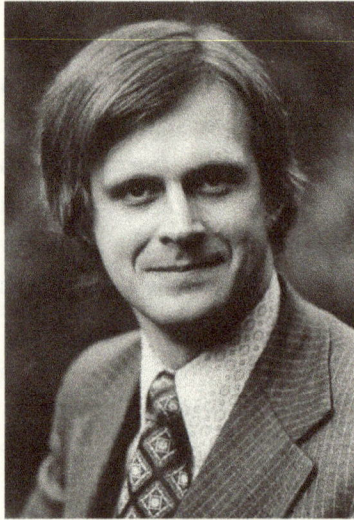

1975 slick photo taken by former White House/
Congressional photographer, Maurice Johnson

*1982 A photo taken by a woman I had been dating
on and off after Rene and I divorced. I also
provided this one for the Miller beer commercial.*

It just so happened that when I married Rene, she had been a governess for a White House photographer. She asked him as a favor to take some photos of us. He must have taken close to a hundred photos. At least one of them had survived my losses from the box that had held my creative works. I provided that photo and another nonprofessional photo that I thought might be apropos for the beer commercial.

I was one of forty or fifty people chosen to audition for the commercial out of hundreds of applicants. We were jammed into one motel room, where we waited for our names to be called. I was one of the first five or six auditions to be called.

The cameraman sat me in a straight chair about six to eight feet from the camera and said, "Okay, I'm going to ask you a few simple questions, and all you need to do is answer them."

"Okay," I said.

"What do you think of Miller beer?" he asked in a most enthusiastic tone.

"I don't drink," I said in the greatest of monotone voices.

He shut off the camera. "Why did they send you here?" That was question number two. He didn't ask any more questions.

Within a day or so, I received a call from the agency that they had another commercial for me. This time I didn't have to try out. I got the part. But I was to wear my best suit.

In a room with a long conference table, eight men sat around the table as the cameraman gave out cigars. We were acting as though we had John Means, a local California politician, "in our hip pockets." I had no idea who John Means was. He could have been a communist for all I knew.

"Smoke 'em, gentlemen," the cameraman said.

One participant protested. "I don't smoke," he said.

"You need to for this set," the cameraman rebuked.

The protester acquiesced, as did the rest of us who didn't smoke.

"Smoke up the room," the cameraman said.

We smoked up for the room for possibly five minutes.

"Gentlemen, some of you were smiling. This is not a humorous piece. Now smoke 'em up again."

There must have been a half dozen takes, each one requiring us to smoke up the room again. At the point where the cameraman was satisfied with one of the takes, we were free to go.

When I had walked the five or six blocks to get to the set, the sun was shining. I had yet to learn that the weather in Oregon changes at the drop of a hat. On the way home, it started pouring rain.

My $350 Christian Dior suit rippled. I took it to a launderer the next day.

"Ruined," the owner said. He explained that American suit makers put cheesecloth inside the lining to make the suit seem substantial. Once that cheesecloth got wet, there was nothing he could do for it.

I received thirty-five dollars for the commercial, and I had to call the agency several times to get that.

★★★

Eugene reminded me of Friendly View. Each village was left to suffer its own decline. I learned a very valuable lesson. I called it village mentality. Most communities believe what is going on in their community is going on in the rest of the world. What folks saw on television was no substitute for having been there.

The Eugene Mission provided meals to tens, if not hundreds, of out-of-work people every meal. I gave them as much money as I possibly could since I had sold my three properties prior to going to Eugene. One comment that seemed to come up several times, especially from those who were down on their luck, was "You people from the East are high on yourselves."

I met a man named Lionel who had been a chef at the Eugene Country Club until he became angry and walked out of the facility one night when he was responsible for cooking meals for over 150 guests.

He was now unemployable in Eugene. His unemployment checks would soon run out.

"Why don't you go to the DC area? With your skills, you could land a job instantaneously," I said.

"Because, I'm from Eugene," he said simply.

I found that attitude prevailed there. I had dinner with a couple one evening who had been married for thirty-five years. When I asked a friend of theirs where they had been, she simply said, "They're getting a divorce. The financial strains are just too much for them."

★★★

Joyce Thompson led the MFA program that year. She had written screenplays for Dustin Hoffman and published several novels, a couple of which had become movies. I called two people to whom I had provided chapters of my book and asked them to send them back to me, if they still had them. They were not continuous chapters. I felt uneasy reading two chapters that were disconnected. So I only read one chapter.

After I read a chapter of *The Little Bit Berserk Blues* in class, Thompson said, "You don't need to be here. Go home and spend the time you would have been here rewriting your novel, and I'll take a look at it when you're finished."

After her words of encouragement, I received a phone call from my friend Homer. "You need to come home," he said.

In DC I rented a room in a group house and spent my days rewriting *The Little Bit Berserk Blues,* as Joyce had suggested. In just eight months, I rewrote a work that had originally taken me ten years and numerous rewrites to complete.

After sending it to Joyce Thompson, I received a letter from her: *I was surprised to find your novel in the mail today. I am writing a screenplay for Dustin Hoffman, am pregnant, and getting ready to move. I won't have time to give you a line by line, but I'll get back to you as best I can.*

I never heard back from her. I surmised the rewrite was not as well written as the original chapters that got me into Oregon's MFA workshop. When it came to my fiction, I had always been conflicted between the lukewarm critique I had received from Ms. Curtler and the compliments I received from Dr. Duke, who had compared my writing to Tom Wolfe.

Arturo Vivante and Dr. Duke had given me references that helped me get accepted at the University of Oregon, one of the top fiction MFA programs in the country. Even then, I questioned whether my writing got me into Oregon's program or if it was a result of the two strong references. I questioned my abilities. I gave up fiction writing. Life had seemed like fiction enough. Fortunately, my manic days were behind me, but not the depression.

The remainder of the year was spent breaking up, getting back together, and breaking up a final time with a woman I had seen on and off since divorcing Rene. I had met her in AA in 1975. She was in an unhappy marriage and often showed up at my door unannounced. I had few friends in AA. So over the years, I had been at home writing at night, working for Jack Smith in Lansing, or attending the University of Oregon's MFA program. I broke it off with her a number of times, but it never seemed to matter; she always pursued getting back together.

At one point when I was no longer seeing her, she put a copy of Barbra Streisand's *The Way We Were* in my mailbox. It worked for weeks just before I headed out to Oregon.

After coming back from Oregon, I wanted to make a clean break with her. Fortunately, as it turned out, my time in Oregon had given her enough time to find another relationship with another AA man.

I had given away nearly all the cash I had prior to going to Eugene. Still, I sent money to Lionel and the Eugene Mission. There were moments I cried for Lionel. There were moments I cried for Eugene in general, for what seemed to be *their* Great Depression of 1982, when interest rates had sucked out what was left of individuals' bank accounts and emotions. If there were happy moments after returning to the DC area, they were few and far between.

I was about to make a significant life change.

My brother, age sixteen, and me after I returned
from Oregon. I was thirty-four.

Approximately a year after I returned to the DC, after I'd taken time to rewrite my novel, I started once again working in the moving business as a salesman. In one instance, I performed an estimate for the wife of a CBS executive. She must have thought I was insane when I started crying and said, "Please have your husband report on what is going on in Eugene, Oregon. The people are going hungry there."

My words seemed to fall on deaf ears. Without having seen it, without being in a community where hunger was such an issue, Eugene seemed to them just another town three thousand miles away.

1983: John Elliott Pitts Becomes Jonathan Ian Elliott

After I had spent ten years on my novel with no recognition or publication and had begun to feel like a failure as a result, my depression soon returned without any of the previous theatrics, with one major exception: I had not completely given up the idea of suicide. I contacted the Arlington County, Virginia, counseling service. Rates for therapy were based on an individual's income. I had no income.

My sister had recently come back from a visit with my father. He had gone to Lookout Mountain in Georgia, where he found new financial success. He had built a seven-store shopping center, mainly by himself. He owned one store, a hardware store, and leased out the other six stores. He filled a warehouse with woodstoves, risking whether or not he could move the inventory. He needed to buy in bulk, he said, to compete with the larger retailers. He sold them all.

The parking lot was typically full. Still sober, he had the golden touch when it came to making money. He also owned a four-hundred-acre farm where he raised cattle. Hang gliders came from miles around to jump off a nearby cliff and land in his pasture.

He built three custom homes and took back the mortgages at usury rates for members of his church who couldn't get a mortgage otherwise. He was a deacon and later became a lay minister of the church.

"Do you know what he had the *nerve* to tell me?" my sister asked when she got back from her visit. "He said he wished he had never had children!"

I had been working on asking for forgiveness from the people I had harmed—the fourth and fifth steps of AA. I had even written down several instances where I felt it was important to ask my father for forgiveness for avoiding him for years. This was necessary for "cleaning up my *moral and ethical inventory.*"

After hearing what my father told my sister, however, that changed. Remembering the many trips to West Virginia where I had felt so alone, the memories of my father's mental and physical abuse toward me and my mother—it all came back to me.

I went to a lawyer's office. "What will it cost me, and how long will it take to change my name?"

The attendant at the desk, a paralegal, said, "Two hundred and fifty dollars and about six weeks."

I had been running low on cash since coming back from Oregon. A therapist once told me that what I did for other people, I wished they would do for me. I gave away most of the cash I had in Oregon to people who needed it. Now I needed it.

I left the lawyer's office and went to the Fairfax County Courthouse. At the desk, I asked the same question of the person on the desk. He turned out to be the county clerk of the court.

"You don't need a lawyer," he said. He pulled out a form. "This is the form most lawyers' offices use. Just type out what you see, fill in the blanks where it asks for it, and give a brief synopsis why you're doing it. It will go to the judge, and you'll have your name change in ten days."

"How much?"

"Once you fill out the form, bring it back to me, and you'll pay the court ten dollars. I would recommend getting the white legal paper the lawyers use. Just makes it look more official." He winked.

Within ten days, I was no longer John Elliott Pitts. My name was Jonathan Ian Elliott, with the sound of a novel writer or poet. The sense of freedom for naming myself whatever I wanted to be—it was the most important step of my newly found therapy.

Nineteen years later, just after my father passed, Uncle Chester took my cousin Shirley—Turman's daughter—and me to a country church graveyard in Sparta, Virginia, about twenty-five miles outside Richmond.

"I want the two of you to know where this gravesite is. It's where many of your relatives are buried."

We walked from one gravesite to another of the Pitts clan who had lived in Sparta since the late 1700s. Only a few branches of Pittses had gone to Oklahoma and North Carolina.

The church historian came out to the graveyard as we were going through it.

"Can I help you?"

Chester explained to her that many of these sites were of our kin.

She looked at Shirley. "You are the spitting image of a woman who was surely related to you. She owned a large farm nearby and just recently passed away."

Chester took me to my grandfather's gravesite.

"I bought him a new headstone. I wanted to do that before I passed."

After taking photos of many of the gravesites of relatives, we walked back to Chester's car.

"I have something for you," he said to me, opening the trunk of his car. "Why don't you pick that up for me." It was my grandfather's old headstone. "I want you to have it."

I still have it in my attic. At times, I think of getting rid of it. But when he gave me the headstone, Uncle Chester had recently nearly died of a quintuple bypass operation and had finally come out of a coma after several weeks. So even the thought of getting rid of it feels like I'm about to commit family heresy.

The conflict between John Elliott Pitts and Jonathan Ian Elliott remains today and has been the source of hours of therapy and self-reflection.

Chapter 21

1983-1985: GUARDIAN ANGELS
COME IN STRANGE WAYS

The reasons for going through therapy again were mounting. Arlington County, Virginia's social services assigned me to a child social worker named Fran, who also saw adults. When I walked into her office, I immediately smiled when I saw all the toys on the floor. *This is where I belong*, I thought. At that moment, if someone had asked me what I liked best about my childhood, I may have asked, "What childhood?"

Well into our sessions, maybe four weeks or more, I said simply, "Sometimes I contemplate suicide."

Maybe it was because I caught her off guard, maybe she thought I wasn't serious because of the matter-of-fact way I said it, but the social worker smirked and asked, "How would you do it?"

I recall thinking that was an odd response, maybe even unprofessional. She wrote down a few notes. I explained in detail how I had attempted, or nearly attempted, suicide, as recently as in the VA hospital. As the session ended and I was nearly out the door, she called out, "Please don't do it!" which I thought at that moment was equally unprofessional ... and compassionate.

I had never undergone therapy longer than a year or so before with any one therapist, except for Dr. Burbach, who had prescribed lithium for nearly five years. That relationship had quickly turned into one of regular six-month visits to check my mental state while on lithium.

Fran was different. The relationship was certainly a patient-therapist relationship. But I came to trust her, to the degree that I discussed with her my experience of sexual abuse that occurred when I was ten from a relative-in-law who knew we had no place else to go. Fran sensed my pain and never brought up the subject again. With the exception of this memoir, neither have I.

After over three years of therapy with Fran, I told her I thought it was time for me to go.

"Before you go," she said, "I have something I want you to remember. I deal with distressed children daily, and many of them have come out of institutions or will go into institutions. You have gone through every bit as much as those children have gone through. You are a *very* strong person! I think you're going to do fine. But if you ever need me, just call. I'll be here."

Months later, I called on Fran again. She had her own practice by then. I smiled and said, "Fran, I need a tune-up." What I was really saying was that those suicidal thoughts were coming back, although not as strong and maybe not as often as before. But they were a recognizable enemy. I needed my therapist-warrior, one who guided me through my last thoughts of suicide.

1983: "I've Never Seen You Look at a Woman That Way Before"

Since coming back from Oregon, I had lived in a group house of professionals—four of us sharing expenses in a four-bedroom rental. I was the only nonprofessional, since I was out of work. But I was obviously well educated and only wanted a room to complete the remake of *The Little Bit Berserk Blues*. I sold myself to the group based on the fact that the only noise they would ever hear me make was the sound of my IBM Selectric typewriter keys.

In the evenings, when they had friends over, I took off for Al's AA Social Club. I had also been doing some volunteer work mentoring a young man, Jeremiah, who had been released on my recognizance from the Fairfax County jail and would remain out only if I reported back that he had been attending meetings with me. He had pulled a knife on someone in an undesirable neighborhood when he had been drinking. Otherwise, he had no previous record.

He attended nearly every meeting I attended.

One evening, a member of the group house, Andrew, said that they were having a party in a few days and wanted to know if I'd like to stay for it. Missing a meeting was something I rarely did, and I had the added responsibility of mentoring the young man.

But I accepted the invitation to attend.

That night, I brought Jeremiah with me to the get-together. I thought it was going to be a casual get-together with a few intimate friends. Instead, the house was packed.

Andrew, who had invited me, whispered in my ear, "Why did you bring him?" He pointed to Jeremiah. Immediately, I realized this was not the venue for either of us. Nearly everyone had a glass of wine.

People in the group house knew I didn't drink. So I said to Andrew, "I don't think I can stay long anyway."

I had confided to Andrew recently that I didn't want to date for a while. I was living mainly off a credit card and a few thousand dollars cash I had come back with from Oregon.

I told him the story about asking a woman to go to a French restaurant with me the week before. She accepted, and when I picked her up at her door, she asked if it was okay to bring her twelve-year-old son. At the restaurant, they had hors d'oeuvres, surf and turf, and dessert. Over $150.

No, I had no interest in dating anyone for a while.

Yet that night I stared at a tall blonde-haired woman who had been talking to a guy in a motorcycle jacket. She was beautiful but seemed engaged in conversation with the guy.

"I've never seen you look at a woman like that before," Jeremiah said.

I was silent, then walked over to Andrew.

"Who is that, Andrew?" I asked, trying to be discreet in looking at the woman out of the corner of my eye.

"I don't know. She came with a friend of ours."

Soon, she broke away from her conversation with the guy in the motorcycle jacket. And for one of those moments, as I had done with Carrie at fifteen years old, I felt I had nothing to lose.

"Hi, I'm Jonathan," I said as I approached her.

"Kate," she said. I would soon learn she was a bit of a stoic, a woman of few words.

"This may sound forward—and I don't mean to be—but I recently came back from Oregon after dropping out of an MFA program ... and I gave away nearly all of my money while I was out there to help people who were really struggling—"

"It's okay," she said, "you don't need to go into your financial history," she said, laughing.

"I guess what I was building up to is, I need to take this young man home, but I was wondering if you would wait for me, and maybe we could go out for a cup of coffee?"

She smiled, "Yeah, I like coffee."

I chanced driving over the speed limits and running through just about every stop sign. All I could think about was that I would return and she would be gone with the guy in the motorcycle jacket.

But when I returned, she was standing near the door, alone.

We went to a fast-food place called Roy Rogers and drank coffee for the better part of three hours.

Mainly I talked, excitedly, attempting to be as humorous and as engaging as I could. For the most part, she just listened. I walked her up to her doorstep. On her steps, I felt confused. She had been so stoic.

Again, as I had with Pat, I felt I had nothing to lose and said, "You know, Kate, I can't tell whether you like me or not." Spending three hours with me drinking coffee should have been a clue. She turned away and then finally stared at me.

"Well, I'll tell you something about you," she said laughing, "you really like your own material."

Three months later, we moved in together in her townhouse.

Several weeks after that, Kate wanted to take me to meet her parents.

"I don't know if they'll like me," I said.

"You have a full set of teeth. They'll like you," she said.

Kate was nearly thirty-four, and her parents were beginning to wonder if she would marry again. She had walked out on a marriage when her former husband said she couldn't have her own credit card. It was a last straw in a deteriorating relationship that had started when they were fifteen. Married at twenty-one, she divorced at twenty-four.

We lived together for nearly thirteen months. One day I came home from work a bit earlier than usual. When she came in, we usually started our salutations with "How was your day today?" or, "I'm really glad you're home."

As I sat on the sofa, she looked down at me. "You're either going to marry me, or you can get your ass out of here!"

Maybe it was just the proposal I needed. My depression in recent years had been a significant barrier to forming relationships. Now I felt like life was just beginning to go my way, but as with most of my life, everything seemed tenuous.

Later I read a copy of the notes from my Arlington County child social worker: ... *has a problem maintaining relationships.*

"Do you think we can really make it?" I asked.

"I don't think in those terms! My parents have been married for nearly fifty years!"

I began to feel something fill me. It was a very strange feeling: hope. I had been sober for seven years. Why wouldn't a marriage work out as well?

What I failed to realize when Kate and I first moved in together was that, for the first time in my life, I was going to be part of a stable family. Her father, Floyd Boring, had been in the Secret Service from the ending days of FDR's tenure through the first months of the Johnson administration. He had started an organization for retired Secret Service agents.

Kate and I have now been married for thirty-seven years, all because a purported drifter, the Eugene police presumed, stole my

Little Bit Berserk Blues manuscript, thinking the heavy box they took and ran with had some value. Drifter-thief turned guardian angel: thank you.

I wish I'd been there when you opened the box.

Our wedding vows, married January 1, 1985. "Why didn't you get married a day earlier? You would have received a tax break," some folks asked over the years. The answer was simple: "I wanted to start life over again." New year, new life.

Chapter 22

1985-2008: KATE'S DAD AND HIS MENTORSHIP

"You should work for the government," Kate's dad told me. "Get yourself a pension." Kate's father and mother would become stabilizing influences in my life, and I would become the son they never had.

But our relationship was tenuous in the beginning. I had started taking one graduate course a semester immediately after Kate and I were married, until she said, "You need to spend your time taking a full load for your MBA and get it over with. We have enough to live off of with my working." I agreed and did some substitute teaching to supplement our income.

My first assignment was in a poor neighborhood where many teachers called in sick. The morale was extremely low among permanent teachers, so substitute teachers took up much of the workload and were often blamed for the poor showing of their students.

In one class, I taught earth science, which was designed, among other simple tasks, to teach students, mostly high school juniors, to read a road map. Many were illiterate and had been pushed through the system so they would hold a high school diploma.

One challenged student who was serious about learning called out to me, "Sir, will you help me?" He was staring at a road map.

"Can you please show me where Winchester is?" His finger was very near Winchester on the map. I pointed to it.

He looked up and said, "Thank you, sir." Then almost in a moment of glee, he noticed the label on my suit coat. "Hey, man, Oscar de la Renta!" He was right.

In one session, a tall, heavyset kid was beating up on a smaller student. I got between them and called to the class to get the principal or one of the guards, who were paid to proctor the hallways. No one moved, obviously intimidated by the larger kid.

After the class, the teacher in charge of substitute teachers nearly ran into the room.

"I heard you got between two students who were fighting!" he said.

"I did. I'm a former Marine. I didn't think they would hurt a teacher."

"Maybe you want to talk with two of our teachers who are on permanent disability!"

Shortly after that day, I received a call. The school was meeting with all the substitute teachers in the gymnasium. The vice principal addressed us in a tone that wavered between a pep talk and accusations. The substitute teachers were going to have to do a better job of encouraging students, he said.

One young substitute teacher interrupted him.

"I have a question for you. Why didn't you let me know that a student who attacked me with a knife had mental problems?"

"We're not allowed to divulge that information," the vice principal answered.

"You're concerned about the well-being of a student with severe mental disabilities, but you're not concerned about my well-being?"

Shortly thereafter, the vice principal adjourned the session. The school had so many altercations during night football games that the county only allowed them to play games on Saturdays during daylight.

I took more than a month off to study for final exams at Marymount University during December. When I returned, more than a third of the students in the earth science class had been redlined in the student roll book. They had dropped out permanently.

When Kate came home in the afternoon after I returned home from teaching, she simply said, nearly every time, "You look pale. Almost gray."

"These are not the schools we grew up in," I told her.

In another instance, I taught basic math to an eighth-grade class at a junior high school. There was a knock on the door. The principal and a policeman asked me to come into the hallway.

"I want you to call out [name] into the hallway. Her brother is in a gang and has hurt another gang member. That gang has threatened to kill this young lady. This officer is here to make sure she arrives home safely."

I had been frustrated about attempting to teach among the many antics and disruptions in the classroom. Suddenly, my attitude changed. What heroes some of these kids were, just to leave home and come to school!

★★★

Kate's father didn't take it well that I wasn't working full time.

"Some people would call you a gigolo," he said.

But shortly after taking several stock portfolio analysis courses, I said to him, "Floyd, why do you keep all of your money in Treasury bills making less than three percent? You're not even covering inflation."

"It's safe," he said.

"Would you like to take a small amount and put it in the stock market? I think you could do well," I suggested.

Surprisingly, he set up an account and in the first year made over 50 percent in one mutual fund called Brandywine, run by a guy named Foster Friess, who was known for having a pet pig.

"I really love that pig!" he would say, chuckling.

I went on to convince him to put some cash into relatively new companies, Microsoft and Intel among others, that performed well.

His only complaint was at the end of the year when Brandywine posted considerable capital gains. I took care of Floyd's taxes for him, and when I handed him his tax returns for that year, he said, "Are you sure you know what you're doing? I've never paid this much in taxes before!"

For several years, he increased the amount of money in mutual funds and stocks. And I had become very welcome most every weekend at their home. But the tax burden still irked him. While our relationship remained strong, he hired a former White House employee to do his taxes.

Based on Floyd's advice, after completing an MBA at Marymount University, I applied for government jobs. No offers came in for the first six months. Then within a few days, I received two interviews and eventual offers—one from the Federal Aviation Administration (FAA) and the other from the Defense Fuel Supply Center in Alexandria, Virginia.

At Defense Fuel, the human resources manager, after looking over my application, asked, "Can this be true? You lived in more than thirty residences by the time you were eighteen?"

I smiled and wanted so much to say, "Ma'am, you don't know the half of it." Instead, I said, "I'm not sure I remember all of them."

Taking Kate's dad's advice, I accepted the position of contract specialist, GS-7, with Defense Fuel, by taking a pay cut of half my last salary in the trucking business.

When I took the job at Defense Fuel Supply Center in 1989, Floyd gave me counsel regarding how to survive federal government employees who were jealous or who saw me as being a threat when promotions came. I hardly ever ignored his advice. Though I was slow to rise in the beginning, the US Mint hired me as a cost-price analyst, and I became a GS-12 in 1993. I had no idea I would rise to a GS-15 prior to my retirement. In just over twelve years, I was making more than seven times what I made initially.

In 2001, I was hired by the Treasury Department on a temporary basis as a GS-15 financial advisor and senior consultant to the Office of Finance, which mainly included advising the deputy chief financial officer (DCFO) who later became the CFO of Treasury. As a result of some work I had performed at the Mint as a troubleshooter on their new PeopleSoft system, my new boss wanted me to take over as a co-project manager for its implementation of a new Oracle system.

A week after I was hired, 9/11 occurred. Treasury lost a great deal of its workforce to Homeland Security. I had hired interns at the Mint to help get me through some understaffing issues I had there. Eventually, my boss at Treasury allowed me to hire interns to help implement the new Oracle system as well as other sorely needed work.

I hired forty interns in the four years I served there. Many of them came from either single-parent or blue-collar homes. Their families' social statuses never came up in interviews. I typically interviewed them twice by phone and never met them until they showed up for work. I found it astounding how many of them had grown up in such a comparable environment to my own.

I chose interns from resumes sent to me by the Washington Center. On the interns' first day, I'd congratulate them. "It's more difficult to be chosen as one of my interns than it is to get into Harvard." I had set a high bar.

When the time came for clearances that required delving into my background, I mentioned that my father-in-law was Floyd Boring. As one investigator put it, "Then this clearance is going to be a slam dunk." Floyd's name, at least on that one occasion, saved me from an investigator going deeper into my past, even though I gave him the names of my past therapists and psychiatrists.

Later, I was offered interviews for presidential appointments and even went on two interviews. But knowing those positions required higher-level scrutiny eventually, in both cases I asked to have my name removed from consideration. Maybe I could have excelled in both positions, maybe not, but the price of possible rejection for my previous mental illness, or even if selected regardless of my past, the humiliation of having my superiors know was more than I could bear. My mother's voice rang in my head. *Don't let them know what goes on in our house.*

Likely, Floyd knew of my past, although the subject never came up. He was still connected to the Secret Service. He had founded the Association for Former Agents of the Secret Service. Many of the older agents would want to join the retired-agents group. It would have made sense that he had me checked out. I may have been paranoid, but there seemed to be just too many instances where men in sunglasses and dark suits came into restaurants and sat within hearing distance of where I was sitting.

But his daughter had found someone she loved. That was enough for him.

The Oracle implementation at the Treasury Department—where we took thirty-two systems that only interfaced with each other and turned them into a system where most of those systems became integrated—came in under budget, due significantly to the work of my interns over a several-year period.

As a thanks, the Treasury Assistant Secretary for Management held a picnic for our organization. I had some work to do at the office and showed up late. The secretary had arranged for a temporary stage and a large tent set up to shield us from the sun. There were possibly a hundred chairs set up for members of our organization.

I stood at the back of the tent. At one point, I heard "award ... excellent ..." but couldn't hear the rest. I recently learned from an audiologist that I lost almost all my hearing in my left ear and only have about 75 percent hearing in my right ear, likely as a result of training exercises in the Marine Corps with 3.5-inch rocket launchers.

Several of my interns stood up and screamed, "Jonathan, he's calling for you!" Others screamed, "Jonathan, get up there!"

The assistant secretary shook my hand and told me how important my work had been to completing the Oracle projects with my interns over several years. I received new interns every semester, but they were quick to catch on to what needed to be done. I gladly accepted the award that included a misspelling of my name.

"Where Are My Interns?"

In retirement, Floyd loved nothing better than to tell stories of his life in the Secret Service to each new batch of interns. The interns typically sat around his chair while he told the stories time and time again about his experiences with FDR. He was outside FDR's door when he died, and Floyd was a Secret Service agent involved in protecting President Truman in the Blair House shootout against two militant pro-independence Puerto Rican activists. He was also a supervisor in the White House when Kennedy was assassinated but was not in Dallas that day.

Every day, he had received notes from Jackie Kennedy from under her door to let him know her intended activities for the day. When he retired, he threw away the notes, thinking no one would ever be interested in them. He served under President Johnson for a short while prior to Johnson moving Kennedy's Secret Service protection to other assignments.

When he had told the same story to me several times, my mother-in-law, Ruth, would place two fingers in the form of a *V* on the side of her cheek so he could go on to another story.

She gave me maternal support I had never had before. She had indeed become my mother figure—stable, funny, and always interested in what I had to say. One day when I answered several questions on *Jeopardy!*, she said, "Jonathan, you ought to go on that show." When I mentioned to her that Kate typically answered more questions than I did, she quickly dropped the subject. I knew something Ruth chose not to acknowledge: Kate is exceptionally bright.

"The girls don't like me," she once said. "They only like their father." Yes, Floyd was the showman, but he depended on Ruth's caretaking. Kate and I often said that was why he outlived her. She was worn out. I loved her dearly. She helped me grow into someone who felt he mattered, someone who felt loved. She was eighty-five when she died. Floyd would live to be ninety-two, passing five years later.

*Ruth Boring, my mother-in-law, who used to pinch me on the
ass after a visit, then giggle. She had the greatest giggle.
She was the great stabilizer of the family. She was one of the
greatest stabilizers of my life, along with my wife Kate.*

When Floyd's health appeared to be failing near the end of his life,
he noticed that I hadn't brought any interns to him that semester.

"Where are my interns?" he asked. He loved them as an audience.
They loved him for his stories.

I took my interns hiking on weekends, to lunch, to various
gatherings. Feroza, the woman who ran the intern program for the
Washington Center, said to me one day, "I make them keep a journal.
And each semester, I read their journals about their experiences in
Washington. Without a doubt, they always say their best experience
was meeting your father-in-law." And therein lies the makings of
humility, so easy to have asked, "What about me?"

Below are seven interns, circa 2005.

Floyd Boring, my father-in-law, with my interns.
He was ninety-one when this photo was taken.

"You Need to Be More Self-confident"

In 2004, one of my interns, Rachel, came in at the end of her semester. Her stay at the Treasury Department was also coming to an end, but two years later she would earn her CPA and come back to Treasury, ultimately as a manager.

"I have something for you," she said. "You have always been there for us. You've gone out of your way to make our stay meaningful here. And I'll always remember how you mentored us. So I want you to have this." It was a small piece of notepaper. On it, she had written three notes she wanted me to take to heart.

"You always supported us and want us to have confidence in ourselves." With that, I took the notepaper.

I carried around the notepaper in my wallet for years. I don't recall two of the three things she suggested. The one I do recall was "You need to be more self-confident." As an ex-drunk, manic-depressive, suicidal person who had been found nearly frozen in a dirty alleyway, I took it to heart.

My Greatest Depression Fighter

It was no secret that Dad and I lived in different universes. Yet some of our stories were so similar. We both immersed ourselves in helping others later in life. Not a small part of it was to make up for significant bad behavior we had engaged in earlier in our lives.

In my case, I focused my attention on helping others. I mentored a Little Brother in the Big Brothers Big Sisters program and went out of my way with several interns to make sure their stay in the DC area was productive and that they found some enjoyment in being there. A number of them had never been away from home. And in the instances when people asked me why I did what I did for them, my answerer was always the same.

"I'm not doing this for you. I'm doing this for me." And it was true; the most selfish thing you can do in life is help others. While my response seemed confusing to them, even nebulous, I felt I owed them that, even if I was unwilling to go into my past.

Over the years, I've felt quite sure Dad had similar reasons for his generosity to strangers.

The next year, the Washington Center, which seemed irritated with me for sending back numerous resumes only to request that they send me more, awarded me as their Federal Government Supervisor of the Year at the National Press Club.

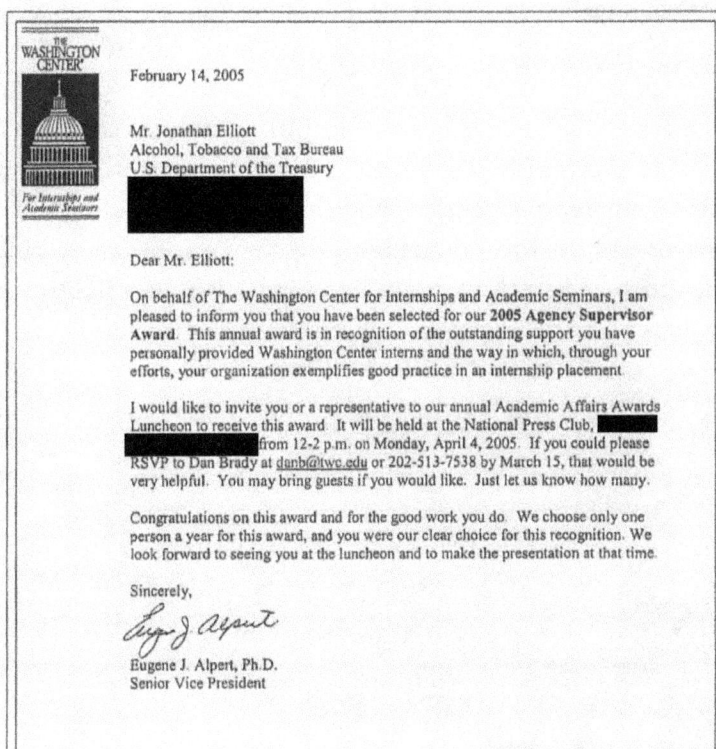

One government supervisor, during a Q&A session after I gave a brief and somewhat self-effacing speech, asked, "How did you pick your interns?"

Many of them had been athletes and showed an eagerness to work. Each semester they wanted to do more than the previous semester's interns. They set the bar higher for themselves than I ever could have. I mentioned those qualities and also said, "Some of it was intuition, and some of it was pure luck. Some of them are here today. I want them to stand up because they are the reason I'm getting this award today."

More than a half dozen former interns had shown up for my award, mostly those I had helped find government jobs. When their potential bosses had called me for references, I always started by saying, "If you hire him/her, it will be a win-win situation for your organization and for them." Many of those interns stay in touch with me, even today. Several years later, one of my interns, who had said I was more like a father than a mentor, wrote to me. His father had left his mother and him at age twelve, the same age I was when my father left us. I shared my story of abandonment with him.

That intern, who later became an FBI agent and had to change his name to protect himself and his family, had gone on to become a great baseball player in college. When his father read about him in the newspaper and tried to contact him, the young man ignored him. I would like to believe that at some point in his life, he will forgive his father. Forgiveness is important for self-peace and serenity.

Date: Wednesday, October 15, 2008 1:46:19 AM   [View Source]

Jonathan,

Hope everything is going well. I wanted to keep you informed that I received a call from Northeastern's Graduate Program last week (actually the day after I applied) and they wanted to speak to me in person for a short interview as part of their enrollment process. I actually have the interview next Monday. I've never been turned down after an interview, but I guess there can always be a first! I haven't heard from Jim since your last email reached me, but I know it was only a couple weeks ago and you did state that he was traveling for a short period of time. I'm sure everything will work out for the best regardless.

The main reason why I'm writing to you at 1:20 a.m., as I should be in bed already, is that I just got done reading a book called The Last Lecture. It's about a Carnegie Mellon professor (Randy) who has pancreatic cancer and only has a few months to live. With this said, he decided to give a "Last Lecture" to reflect on his life achievements and say thanks to the people who has helped him become the person he his today. He specifically mentions his old professor as being a huge mentor who gave him great advice and opportunities to further his career. As I kept reading, I couldn't help but to think of you as Randy's old professor because I share the same appreciation as Randy when it comes to your guidance and efforts that have helped me along the way. I know I've said this before, but I feel there's is no harm to repeat my gratitude for you looking out for me. Growing up with a single parent, I never try take anyone for granted who has offered the help and that especially includes you. So I just want to say, no matter what happens in the future, thank you.

Man I'm going to be tired tomorrow, ha.

An email from my intern turned FBI agent

Shortly after retirement, I volunteered to read essays for foster kids who were applying for scholarships. It was a different experience than I'd had with my interns. I would never meet these young people— only know them by their stories or, in a few cases, mentor them in their studies over the telephone.

How much would I learn from foster kids? What would I learn from a young girl whose father sexually abused her from the time she was ten until child services pulled her out of that "relationship"? She would go through a number of foster parents, attend three high schools, and become the valedictorian of her last high school.

How much would I learn from a girl who lived in a box behind a Walmart for two years, who had loyal friends who brought her food daily until she was picked up pilfering health and life-supporting items from Walmart, only to be sent to child services. I read her essays and asked the Foster Care for Success foundation to provide her with a college scholarship. More so than Joe or me, I wonder what kind of support it would take for her to go on to make something of herself or just to get through college.

I learned that there were others who had had it so much tougher than what I went through, and everyone I've ever met when volunteering has a story that needs to be told. It wasn't difficult to feel a chill go up my spine reading their stories or even shed a tear that I was unaware I could even shed.

One time, the foster care program made me their Hero of the Month. When the foster care program director asked me to provide a brief summary of what made me want to help those kids, I gave Mom a great deal of the credit: "a woman who worked for fifty cents an hour on the assembly line in Chicago to help get us by." They pasted my response on their website.

Many of our students and alumni would not be where they are – in colleges and training programs, making careers, and raising families – were it not for the support of a special person or organization. Foster parents, caseworkers, CASAs (Court Appointed Special Advocates), educators, mentors, coaches and more all make a difference in the lives of America's foster youth. Every month we celebrate one such Foster Care Hero. Check out this month's hero below!

Check out our Foster Care Heroes

September 2012 Hero

This month's hero is Jonathan Elliott.

I'm wearing a cap that Kate's father gave me that had been special to him.

When I showed Mom the response, she sent me a long letter. She wrote, *You are no longer my son! How can you say I only made fifty cents an hour? I made a dollar an hour!* Two weeks later, she wrote again and asked for forgiveness. While it had become a familiar scene from time to time, these outbreaks always sent me from often moderate to more severe depression.

***

It had become a pattern for me to give more than I really had the energy to give. When I entered my doctoral program, my altruism had taken another form. From 1986 when I first entered Marymount University until I completed my Education Specialist degree at George Washington University (GWU), I spent thirteen years attending classes at night and on weekends.

In 2007, the acting director of the GWU program had an earnest discussion with our cohort of twenty-five students. She had just taken over the program while the director of the program took a year's sabbatical. She told us that the powers that be at GWU were dissatisfied with the program's success rate in terms of number of students who completed the program. Now that she was the acting director, she felt responsible to ensure that students stayed with the program.

I understood her concern, but I was exhausted, partly from having helped a couple of the struggling students while performing my own doctoral work and working forty to fifty hours a week at the Treasury. I made it known that upon passing my written and oral exams, I would likely drop out of the program. I didn't feel I could physically continue.

Several of us in the program, including a family therapist who was working on her doctorate, spent weekends helping the two students who were struggling. Ironically, those two students were the first to have their doctorates conferred after I quit.

As I was walking into the room to take my written exams, the acting director of the program met me at the door.

"I know what you've done, and I know the sacrifices you've been making," she said.

I passed both the oral and written exams and, as I had promised, dropped out of the program after having only completed the first three chapters of my dissertation.

The acting director sent me an email just before I left.

Elliott, Jonathan

From:
Sent:
To:

------- Forwarded Message: -----------

Subject: Re: Thank you
Date: Thu, 31 May 2007 13:22:35 +0000

Jonathan - as I've mentioned to you on various occassions, you're one of
those souls that inspires me! I feel honored to have you enter into my
life. Your positive energy, thirst for learning, and compassion for
others will have an enduring impact on me. If there is
every...anything...anything at all...that I can do for you - please
don't hestitate to call.

Respectfully and with the warmest regards

It's because I was exhausted that now I think back on the therapist's suggestion that I was doing something for others that I wanted someone to do for me. In the end, my helping others seemed to lead to self-destruction on a number of levels.

One intern later said that I had sacrificed too much of myself for the interns. All the therapy I had taken over the years still didn't seem to help me protect myself—my physical health, my mental well-being—or provide me with time off to be with Kate.

After I had left the GWU program and was near retirement, a dear friend of mine, who had become an executive at the IRS, said, "I was so worried about you. You looked like death warmed over."

While I may not have been feeling the direct effects of bipolar disorder, many of my actions were similar. I didn't know when to stop pushing myself. The end result was I would go to a neurologist to try to learn how to sleep again. I was operating off three to four hours' sleep a night. My photo online for my retirement announcement said it all.

I spent my last few working years at a new Treasury bureau helping them get their strategic planning group off the ground. And as usual, I mentored a number of interns while there.

TTBweb
an online community for the staff
of the Tax & Trade Bureau

Main Navigation

Retirement Announcement for Jonathan Elliott

After 20 years of Federal service, Jonathan Elliott, TTB's Director of Strategic Planning, will be retiring on May 31, 2008. Jonathan began his Federal career as a procurement analyst at the Department of Defense. In 1992, after four years with DOD, Jonathan accepted a position at the Department of the Treasury's United States Mint. Jonathan's ten year tenure at the U.S. Mint provided him with an opportunity to serve in a variety of challenging positions including cost accounting manager, staff member for the Deputy Chief Financial Officer, and staff member/cost analyst for the Associate Director of Procurement.

Prior to coming to TTB, Jonathan served as the Financial Advisor/ Senior Consultant to the Acting Chief Financial Officer at the Department of Treasury where he provided cost management expertise for the Treasury Franchise Fund and co-led the functional implementation of Oracle Financial Systems for Departmental Offices. During his time at TTB, Jonathan was instrumental in the Bureau obtaining an effective rating on its Collect the Revenue PART (Program Assessment Rating Tool) and he drafted TTB's Master Strategic Plan. Throughout his career, Jonathan has served as a mentor to more than forty Federal interns.

A reception in Jonathan's honor will be held in the Administrator's Conference Room on Thursday, May 22, 2008, at 2 p.m. See the invite.

TTB ©2005 All Rights Reserved. Valid XHTML, CSS, 508, Contact TTB Webmaster.

Elliott, Jonathan

From: [redacted]
Sent: Thursday, January 03, 2008 1:33 PM
To: Elliott, Jonathan
Subject: Re: Upcoming Retirement

Jonathan!

My goodness it's so good to hear from you! Many times I've wondered how you're progressing (or have already progressed) through your PhD program. Lately, especially, I've considered emailing you but wasn't sure if you were still with ttb. I didn't want to write a long heartfelt email and then have it get lost in cyberspace somewhere. I should just pick up the phone right now and call you...though I'm sure you're hard at work so I'll save that for an evening chat sometime in the near future. I'm too excited!! I want to write now!! Haha.

First, congratulations on your retirement. If I still have you "pinned" correctly, I'm sure retirement isn't something you're entirely up for. You're too much of a busy-body John! Never do I remember you putting your feet up. You were always out to do anything and everything for somebody else. And now's the time to do something for yourself, right?! Vacations w/ Kate, reading, hiking...heck, you could even write a book! The title: *A Life Dedicated To Others; A memoir depicting Jonathan Elliot's patience, sacrifice and devout stewardship.* Haha- see, I've taken care of the hard part for you! :-)

Gosh- it was so long ago but the memories are so vivid. What would I have done if you didn't take a chance on me? The list of "Thank you's" are endless. If nothing else, I hope I brought some smiles to you and TTB. Being away from home for the first time was a bit difficult to handle every now and again but you were always there to talk to and somehow make it all manageable.

So what are your plans if you don't mind me asking? I'm curious to know. Everyone (and their sister) knows you won't be able to stay away from maintaining some sort of mentor position. If you think you can get away from that you're crazy. You won't last a month!! haha. I'm almost certain you don't want to see that happen either. You have a very unique talent of bringing out the best in your students. I'm certainly lucky to be one of the 40 interns who have become a product of that.

Again John, it was great to hear from you! I'm sure you need to get back to work. I don't want to keep you. I should get back to studying anyhow. This CPA exam is taking the life out of me!! Five more months...five months and it'll all be over. I'll have a life back. And please, I'd love to hear back from you. Anything to take my eyes away from this Financial Accounting workbook.

Take care,
[redacted]

p.s. Think I could have an updated address of your whereabouts? I'll understand if you don't want that disclosed however.

One of my interns even recommended that I write a memoir. Well, kiddo, here it is.

Chapter 23

MY FATHER'S RISE FROM THE ASHES

In 1986, when Kate and I had been married for nearly two years, she said, "You speak about your mother quite often, but I never hear you talk about your father."

"There isn't much to say," I said. "We haven't really talked in years. My sister told me he actually said he wished he never had children."

Kate could tell how the name change, what my father had told my sister, and my father's words were all weighing on me and sending me into a reminiscence of the past. One day she said, "If you don't make that relationship right, you're going to pay a dear price for it after he dies. I suggest you call him and at least talk."

I sat by the phone for a while. *What do you say to a man who wished you'd never been born?* I called. Even as the phone was ringing, there was a part of me that hoped that he wouldn't pick up, that I could say, "I tried, but *what the hell*, it just wasn't meant to be."

He answered.

"This is Jon," I said meekly.

"I've been thinking about you a lot," he said. He told me that he had spent the greatest part of his life preaching and taking care of his three hardware stores. He also had a couple hundred acres of land where he raised Charolais cattle. The surprise came when he said, "I'd like to come up and see you. Would that be all right?"

"Sure," I said. There seemed little more to say but to give him the address and phone number.

He came to see us within a couple of days.

He took us to dinner the first night. He had rented a room in a Hampton Inn nearby before we could invite him to stay with us. I think he was as leery of how the get-together might go as I was.

At dinner that night, tears flowed down his cheek. If I had ever seen him cry before, I didn't recall it, beyond the time he told us about his red wagon. Based on what my sister had said, I thought he had tried to block out his past. At dinner that night, I learned nothing could have been further from the truth.

"I'm so sorry for what I did to you when you were a child. I don't sleep some nights thinking about it." He had joined AA years before but had stopped going to meetings. Every indication was that he had stopped drinking and was much respected in his community. I welled up inside, and I still well up sometimes thinking about that dinner.

"You don't need to lose sleep over me," I said. "Look at me ... I have a great career; I have a great wife. I've put those days to rest. I really hope you will too."

I left out how it had taken ten years with four therapists, a gutter experience, and a psychotic break to begin healing. The depression still invaded me from time to time, but this was not the time or place to share that with him.

This was a man who was truly sorry. I could see it, feel it, and it felt nice—not that he was in pain but that I felt, maybe for the first time, that I had a caring father.

After meeting my father for the first time, Kate said, "You walk like him, you talk like him, and at times, you act like him."

Prior to my father and I reuniting, I felt that I had done just about everything I could do to be the *opposite* of him. But over the years, genetics and behavioral learning provided me with a road map to emulate my father in so many ways.

Later in life, and not just because my father had asked for forgiveness but also because a revelation came to me, I forgave him. His bad behavior, his not being there, even his violence hadn't been about Mom and me; those things were more about him—all that he had to work through, considering his childhood and the war.

We both had a lot to work through prior to our meeting.

I finally had a father I could be proud of. He wasn't the perfect father for me. What father is? He would never have been the father who would play catch with me. He never complimented me but nearly always criticized me for every decision I made—though much less so in the last years of his life. But he was a decent man, one who in his own way cared for people as best he could.

He had fought his demons. By the time he passed away, it appeared he had conquered most of them, but not all ... not by a long shot. The ones that remained were the biggest and toughest to overcome. He was still haunted by that little boy who ached for and needed constant approval, never getting enough of it, always raising the bar throughout his life, giving in, time and again, to that inferiority complex with a superiority façade. ... Yes, exactly what I had done much of my life.

Dad would have given anything to reach that level of love from others that he couldn't achieve for himself, that level of love from others too high for anyone to achieve. I see this in my own desire to have people like me for my knowledge and intelligence, even when I feel I know so little and have felt lacking so many times. As I grow older, it dawns on me how much we were alike. Yet the friction between us, even the competitiveness, at times existed to varying degrees right up to his death.

I suffered through that same inferiority complex, only becoming aware of it during those last three years of therapy. Still, the priorities of finding peace through self-love and strengthening my bond with those I love have always waxed and waned.

In 2002, when Dad's wife called to let Kate and me know Dad had lung cancer and was dying, we immediately went to see him on Lookout Mountain, Georgia, ten hours away. He had gone there, he said once, to get away from the rat race.

His breath challenged, it took him longer to say what would have taken him less than half the time previously. At one point, after a period of an hour or so, he had walked toward the bathroom, and I became concerned about him after some time had passed by. I walked back to his bedroom, where I saw him asleep in bed with one leg hanging over onto the carpet.

I tucked his leg under the covers and rubbed the sweat off his forehead. I realized then it was the first time I had ever touched my father's face. I didn't want him to awaken, not then. I didn't want him to see the tears flowing down my cheeks.

We made the trip four of the next six weekends he was alive, in spite of the fact that I was working nearly fifty hours a week at Treasury. The cancer had gone to his brain. The last time I saw him, he stood, legs shaking, at the door to see us off. It became evident. This was the last time I would see him alive.

He looked at Kate and said, "You made a man out of him." *Okay, maybe one last shot*, I thought. But I would also take it as the best compliment he had ever given me.

As Kate and I walked to the car, and I slid into the driver's side, this man, this father, stood frail; it must have taken everything he had just to make those few steps onto the porch outside his living room to wish us goodbye.

He waved meekly. I wailed. Blurry-eyed, I ran from the car up the few steps of his porch and hugged him, probably too tightly.

"I love you, Dad. I love you!"

"I love you too, son."

Maybe it's not the best father-son story ever told. But I can still become teary-eyed thinking back on that moment. Kate had to drive home. There was no stopping the tears, no stopping the missed opportunities to try, just for a while, to live in his world.

He had invited me to go to Russia with him, where he had started several missions. He wanted me to see him in his world. I declined. For that, Kate's words came back to me. *I would be sorry* for that missed chance. I was, and even now, still am.

My father at a convention in Russia. The woman next to him and likely carrying his Bible is his interpreter. He kept a count of "saving souls" in his later life like he kept count of his wealth after he stopped drinking. "I gave the Russians in Volgograd a million dollars," he once told Kate and me. When he died, he left my sister and me $3,000 each. His last will had been changed just before he died at the request of his wife, who had worked beside him for years in one of his three hardware stores. Posthumously, he was named in a local Volgograd paper.

Dad would never have told me this story, but when one of his Russian interpreters visited the US with him, she told me, "Your father is a very generous man. There is a woman in our village who has bent over nearly all her life. Your father paid sixty thousand dollars to bring her back to the States to Houston, Texas, to have surgery to straighten out her back." I would discover from his wife and interpreters that there were many stories just like that one.

Dad's wife had worked closely with him in their three hardware stores. She was *not* happy that, in her words, "Your father is giving away *our* money!" Dad did admit once that he had spent nearly a million dollars on the Russians and on the three missions he sponsored there.

Chapter 24

THE PASSING OF THOSE I LOVED

Dad passed away on September 3, 2002, at eighty years old. Mom outlived Dad by seventeen years. In her assisted living room, she once said to Debbie, "Did you see that man outside? He's messing around with some hussy!" We could only surmise she meant Dad. She very rarely talked about him the last fifty years of her life.

She had led a rather tranquil life the years after Bucky got sober until his death. Shortly thereafter, she showed signs of dementia and at one point ran out of her house screaming that her house was going to flood. There was a gentle rain that day, and she lived on a hill. Neighbors brought her into their home until they could reach my half-brother, Keith.

In assisted living in Richmond, Virginia, Mom suffered from Sundowner syndrome. Her peaceful mood during the day turned to agitation, cursing others (which she rarely did all during her life), and in several cases, turning abusive both to other residents and to staff.

I received a call from Debbie just months before Mom's death.

"I got a call from the Crossings [the progressive care unit in Richmond where Mom had been admitted to one of their assisted living units]. Mom attacked one of their residents today. Mom thought the woman was in her room. It was the woman's room. The director said Mom will have to go to memory care."

In memory care, Mom fell from her bed and broke her pelvis and dislocated her hip. It was the second of such falls that year. During one of her more lucid moments, she said, "No one should have to live like this. Not even an animal." She remained in hospice care for approximately six months before she passed.

She died November 3, 2019. Her temperament between being a most loving, caring person to one that quickly turned to aggression remained with her until the end.

Bucky had passed two years previously of pancreatic cancer. My half-brother, Keith, slept in a chair beside him for much of Bucky's hospital stay prior to his passing.

★★★

Cousin Joe passed away in September 2019, two months before Mom died. Like me, he had had a drinking problem for much of his early adult life. But when he quit, he became quite the family man.

At one point during a recession, CVS Pharmacy offered Joe 2 million dollars for his adjacent property where his car lot was located.

"Why won't you take it?" I asked him.

"Johnny, my boys are going to need that dealership as they get older." By the time he passed, he had two dealerships, and my half-brother Keith was the service manager in his mechanical shop.

Joe and I stayed close throughout our lives. Our lives in Friendly View had bonded us more as brothers than cousins. While his birth name was Joe Harris and mine was John Pitts, everyone in Friendly View referred to us as "the Tucker boys."

It always astounded me when Joe called me for financial advice, especially as it related to the stock market.

Several times during our lives, Joe said, "Johnny, you're the smartest person I know."

And every time he said it, it made me feel less intelligent. I had attended thirteen colleges and universities and had accumulated seven diplomas. One of the diplomas was an MBA degree in finance and economics with an emphasis in portfolio analysis. But during my adult life, when I thought of someone successful, I thought of Joe: someone who came out of a great period of abandonment to develop a keen business sense, something I only marginally possessed. Maybe my on-again, off-again stays in Friendly View over the first seven years of my life and Joe's nine years of abandonment contributed to our unique abilities to problem solve in different ways—a more intellectual approach for me, a very practical approach for Joe.

Joe and I had a mutual respect for each other. Like my father, Joe had turned just about every venture he had undertaken into financial success.

Joe had become one of the wealthiest men in Manassas, Virginia, at the time of his death. He had sold seven acres of land that were adjacent to Potomac Mills, a large shopping mall. He owned more than a dozen rental properties and two car dealerships. He was generous with local charities in Manassas, especially those that supported boys' clubs, like the local little league teams. I told my wife as we stood in line with the hundreds, if not over a thousand people, who came to Joe's viewing when he passed, "I would settle for enough folks as pallbearers at my funeral."

It would be the end of our relationship on earth: two abandoned boys from Friendly View. My cousin, my brotherly cousin.

Joe's wife, Gloria, passed away from complications of breast cancer some years before he passed. Afterwards, when I asked him if he was going to sell his house, approximately four thousand square feet, he said, "I thought about it. But then I thought, 'the grandkids love this pool.'" He often had family gatherings where the children played most of their time in the swimming pool. Often, Joe just watched them play while he smoked cigars, which he smoked often.

It became clear to me while writing this memoir that Joe wanted for his children and grandchildren what he had never had during those years of abandonment—stability, knowing that he was going to be there for them as long as he lived.

Even in adulthood, he always saw me as his younger brother, one who in some instances still needed protecting. And just like my mother had, he chided me for forgiving Dad.

In one such instance, Joe asked, "Don't you remember what Tommy did to you as a kid?" Again, it was his way of trying to protect me, especially when it came to my mental health. He had often been my go-to person, along with Homer, when I broke down mentally.

While he may have fought me on occasion as a boy, he always protected me against other kids. I was one of the physically weakest kids in Friendly View. But everyone knew if they bothered me, they were going to have to take on Joe.

I am still depressed over his passing, the loss of his friendship. My world became so much smaller that day, only to have my mother pass away two months later, and then my best friend from college, Alan Smith, three months after my mother's death.

Joe was nearly seventy-three when he died.

★★★

My best friend, Alan, was seventy-one when he passed. Alan had always been destined to become a doctor. In our college days, he confided in me often that he had wanted to become a doctor even as a young boy—and he did. He also knew he would marry the girl in his third-grade classroom who had become his best friend. They married in their early twenties.

While my future as a writer had always been in doubt, Alan made it clear to me over the years: medicine wasn't a reasonable pathway for me either. He never told me why; I never asked.

Chapter 25

CURRENT REFLECTIONS

It was a long and winding road through the educational maze, often dropping out, likely due to my mental and/or physical illnesses, yet nearly achieving the equivalent (converting quarter hours) of 350 semester hours of completed coursework:

Elon College	1965
Washington Bible College/ Capitol Seminary	1968
Carson-Newman University	1969-1971
University of Richmond	1971
Virginia Commonwealth U.	1971-1972 BA, English, Honors
Purdue University	1972-1973
Northern VA Community College	
(Nonconsecutive Attendance)	1975-1987
	AA, General Studies
	AS, Science
University of Oregon	1982
Marymount University	1986-1988 MBA, Finance/
	Economics
Florida Institute of Technology	1989-1991 BS, Contract
	Management
Marymount University	1994-1996
	BS, Internal Auditing
George Washington University	2004–5, 2006–7
	Education Specialist

For all the times Dad criticized me over the years for nearly every decision I made and every time I felt inadequate in any area of my life, I went back to school. I—unrealistically—wanted to become a Renaissance man, only to set myself up for feelings of failure, even when others sometimes saw me as successful. It validated my intern Rachel's note that I lacked a certain confidence and, to a large extent, still do.

That lack of confidence had never been more evident than when, during my doctoral program, George Washington University hired a leadership management specialist from Minnesota. Based on the result of a number of interviews and our backgrounds and education, he assessed the potential for each of us as leaders. The title of the dissertation program was Executive Leadership.

Although there were a number of small business owners and corporate executives in the program of twenty-five students, I had scored first or second among my peers in each of twelve categories with one exception: self-confidence. Rachel's notepaper immediately took on even more validation. I was ranked in the lower middle of the pack in that category.

I asked the consultant, "How can that be? How can I score well in almost all the other categories and score so poorly in that one?"

"It happens a lot," he said. "You feel like you have something to prove, more so than those around you. You may do a good job managing people, and they may like you, but I can only imagine the stress you feel when you go home at night."

He was spot on. That also gave credence to all the coursework I had taken over the years; I always felt inadequate that I didn't know enough to carry on in my work or even just maintain basic knowledge.

Love, Health, Security

One of my greatest takeaways from the GWU doctoral program occurred on a university-sponsored trip to Chile around the time of my government retirement. The program was designed for us to study psychology, sociology, anthropology, education, and business.

The Chilean trip was designated as an opportunity to understand how women and those who had lifted themselves from poverty in Chile became successful business people.

Between conference visits, I shared my experience with our interpreter—as a boy who came from a coal camp to end up advising a president and other high-level executives. When I mentioned that my experience wasn't all that different from the Chilean executives who shared their experiences with us around a long conference table, the interpreter said, "We all want the same thing. We want to be loved, we want to be healthy, and we want to be secure."

I've often thought about the wisdom of his words. I would add that, for those of us who have come from the ashes to survive and even prosper, we also desire peace and serenity. Like my father, I still require the love of others to feel loved. Self-love is a very ephemeral thing that seems to come and go with me, as it did for my father.

Dad suffered three heart attacks but each time came out of it to help others. I never heard him complain about his heart condition. In 2013, I was shocked to find that I needed to have an arterial aneurysm repaired as well as the replacement of a heart valve. I called it my tune-up. With that have come certain limitations. What it has done, along with the AA teachings, is to help me live for the day. And when I do that, as I do more times than not nowadays, peace and serenity become my *default* position. And as with the AA teachings, responding to others' needs gives me greater mental, and even more physical, strength.

★★★

While Kate and I rarely went on vacations during our work years, we saved and put aside funds for retirement. However, life has a way of teaching us that security is more a function of our mental outlook than acquiring financial success. It's then I turn to my poetry and find a sweetness in life. And that young man who wanted to become an English professor and write his poetry? Well, he achieved half of it.

Since August 2014 when Kate and I moved to Cornelius, North Carolina, an area known for its arts and artistry, I have written several thousand poems. Some of the peaceful, natural settings and the kindness of others here remind me of the best of Friendly View— the river, the good folks like Aunt Betty, and the Daltons, who always looked after me. Recently, after my first ride in an ambulance with what appeared to be a slight stroke, many neighbors, even some who have never known me (I'm still a bit of a loner), asked Kate, "What can I do?" So many have looked after me along the way. Even Mom Tucker, who taught me what it meant to survive.

When I write about these caring folks, I recall the familial nature of Ruth and Floyd, and I stare at Kate at night, even as she sleeps, and say to myself, "I am a very lucky man."

Acknowledgments

It took a village to write this memoir. In addition to Tony's encouragement, Barbara Henn, my former next-door neighbor and a former English teacher, has reviewed and provided assessments on over a thousand poems I wrote over a seven-year period. After reading a number of my memoir poems, along with Tony, Barbara gave me a great deal of encouragement to write this memoir. She has also provided me with valuable feedback after reading drafts.

One very important contributor to my memoir is my cousin Shirley Houck. As the keeper of so many important family records, the ones that gave a great deal of detail and credence to this memoir were the near daily journal entries she kept from our paternal grandmother. Shirley sent me copies of those entries dating from 1945–1952. This memoir would have been considerably more generic without them.

Maybe an equally great contributor is my wife, Kate, who often asked, "Aren't you going to write today?" It was her way of saying the time it took me away from our time together was okay. And those hours expanded over time.

The title poem for this memoir, *Crimson Roses and Purple Irises*, was written during a poetry workshop that Nancy Lingle, the Librarian at Charlotte Mecklenburg Library, Davidson North Carolina hosted. Nancy also provided several venues for Tony Abbott's *old poets* to honor him after his death. It was Tony's kindness and poetic expertise that made all of us who were guided by him better poets and better people.

Lastly, I want to show my thanks for Amy Ashby, the vice president and editor-in-chief of Warren Publishing. Without her outstanding editing, this memoir would have suffered from lesser detail and clarity. I mentioned to Amy that when I worked on my doctorate, I had hired an editor. My comment to Amy was, "That editor couldn't light a candle to your editing and expertise."

And so the village has done its work, as have I.